The Private Provision
of Public Services
in Developing Countries

EDI Series in Economic Development

The Private Provision
of Public Services
in Developing Countries

Gabriel Roth

Published for the World Bank
OXFORD UNIVERSITY PRESS

Oxford University Press

NEW YORK OXFORD LONDON GLASGOW
TORONTO MELBOURNE WELLINGTON HONG KONG
TOKYO KUALA LUMPUR SINGAPORE JAKARTA
DELHI BOMBAY CALCUTTA MADRAS KARACHI
NAIROBI DAR ES SALAAM CAPE TOWN

Library of Congress Cataloging-in-Publication Data

*Roth, Gabriel Joseph, 1926–
The private provision of public services in developing countries*

*"Published for the World Bank."
Bibliography: p.
Includes index.
1. Privatization—Developing countries. I. Economic Development
   Institute (Washington, D.C.) II. Title
HD4420.8.R68 1987   338.91'09172'4   86-23880
ISBN 0-19-520544-8*

多少事從來急天地轉光陰迫
一萬年太久只爭朝夕

So many deeds cry out to be done,
And always urgently;
The world rolls on,
Time presses.
Ten thousand years are too long,
Seize the day, seize the hour!

MAO TSE-TUNG

Foreword

ECONOMIC DEVELOPMENT is a complex process that depends for its success on effective contributions from both the public and private sectors of the developing countries. In general, public sector activities are undertaken to meet community objectives, whereas private sector activities are more narrowly focused on the prospects of profit. The appropriate mix of public and private sector activities varies from society to society. Some facilities (such as public parks) are almost invariably provided by public agencies, whereas others (such as retail stores) are often provided privately.

Services such as education, health, electricity, telecommunications, transport, and water supply are generally considered to be appropriate only for the public sector. Under some circumstances, however, they, too, can be privately provided, at competitive standards and prices; public sector managers are then able to concentrate on activities that only governments can provide.

This volume presents examples of the private provision of "public" services in developing countries. In publishing these cases, neither the Economic Development Institute nor the World Bank wishes to suggest that they should be replicated in other countries, or even that they could be. The purpose of this book is to widen the options available to governments by showing how public services are in fact being privately provided in some developing countries. Any views or policies referred to in this book should not be taken to represent the views or policies of the Institute or of the World Bank. Rather, the points raised are offered as a modest contribution to the ongoing debate on how best to manage scarce resources to achieve the maximum impact on economic development.

CHRISTOPHER R. WILLOUGHBY
Director
Economic Development Institute
The World Bank

Contents

Preface

THE STARTING POINT of this book is the observation by A. W. Clausen, former president of the World Bank, that "the presence and value of an indigenous private sector in developing countries need enhanced recognition"; that "not nearly enough is known of what the private sector can or cannot do"; and that "the role of the private sector in development is probably the least discussed of all major development issues" (Clausen, 1985, pp. 3–4). My objective is to shed some light on this neglected area by presenting several examples of how the private sector in developing countries is participating in the provision of "public" services, specifically, education, electricity supply, health, telecommunications, urban transport, and water supply and sewerage.

I open the discussion by explaining my use of the terms "public services," "private provision," and "developing countries" and briefly examine how the public and private sectors differ in their supply of services. I also review the circumstances—as commonly described in the economic literature—in which "market failure" precludes reliance on economic markets for the efficient supply of needed services.

The discussion then turns to the examples themselves. Some might ask why they should be described at all. Does it matter that private buses in Calcutta operate today without subsidy or that a private indigenous company provided an electricity supply system for Caracas in 1897? The information is offered to decisionmakers in developing countries to inform them, through concrete examples, that there are different ways of providing public services, and that, in certain situations, private suppliers can be called in when publicly supplied services are considered to be inadequate.

In preparing these examples, I did not intend to suggest that private provision is invariably, or even occasionally, more desirable than public sector provision; or that every service in every country should be, or could be, privately provided; or that privately provided services are necessarily less costly or more beneficial than

publicly provided ones. Comparisons of that kind risk being con-
jectural, for who can tell what would have happened in a particular
situation in the absence of private supply? It might be possible, by
comparing different periods and numerous countries, to come up
with some general conclusions about the applicability of private
(or public) enterprise to this sector or to that. But such comparisons are beyond the resources available for the preparation of
this volume. Moreover, each situation has to be examined on its
merits and dealt with in the light of the traditions of the society
concerned and the available resources, both private and public.

When a private organization is given a monopoly—for example, to provide electricity or telephone service—regulation by the
government is generally necessary to prevent abuse. Typically, this
regulation covers the prices that may be charged and the standards
of service that have to be met. Regulation is also necessary when
services (such as road maintenance) are contracted out; here, detailed specifications must be prepared and a thorough system of
inspection must be in place to ensure that the works are completed
in accordance with the specifications. Thus, regulating and supervising private suppliers can give rise to substantial administrative
problems, but the book does not attempt to deal with them in
depth.

What, then, is the purpose of the book? Its main purpose is to
refute the conventional wisdom that only the public sector can
supply public services in developing countries. I hope that at least
a few of the private sector alternatives described in the following
chapters will encourage hard-pressed governments to try out new
service arrangements that might reduce deficits and at the same
time enhance the quality of services, particularly for low-income
people. The book emphasizes services that directly benefit low-
income people, not because World Bank staff are encouraged to
"wear their hearts on their sleeves," but because the well-to-do are
routinely provided with such services in most societies. Indeed, it
is a paradox that, in many countries, the rich are supplied by the
public sector, whereas the poor have to rely on the private sector
for their necessities. In Karachi, for example, many poor people
have to obtain their water from private vendors, and they spend
more on this item than do those whose houses are connected to the
public piped water supply, and whose consumption is much
higher. Similarly, in East Africa the children of the better-off can
pass the examinations that allow them to enter state schools, while
the children of the poor often have to choose between private
education or no education.

The Director of the Economic Development Institute (EDI), Christopher R. Willoughby, encouraged me to spend a year on this project in the new Studies Unit that the EDI established in 1984, under the leadership of F. Leslie Helmers. The function of the Studies Unit is to produce innovative, high-level training material for the guidance of EDI's clientele—officials in developing countries. Dr. Helmers therefore assembled experienced writers from both inside and outside the World Bank and protected them from much of the bureaucratic routine that is an inevitable part of the Bank's operational work so that they could explore their subjects in a collegiate atmosphere. The work that follows is one of the first full-length volumes produced in the Studies Unit, and my special thanks are due to Leslie Helmers for his leadership and valuable comments; to Sotero Arizu and Richard Carroll for assistance in research; to the Bank's reference librarians (in both the Joint Bank/Fund Library and the World Bank Sectoral Library) for successfully pursuing even the most obscure references; and to the untiring support staff, led by Sonia Hoehlein, for typing numerous drafts. The text was meticulously edited by Venka Macintyre.

In seeking material for this book, I received assistance from numerous individuals and organizations, especially from World Bank colleagues and from staff in the U.S. Agency for International Development, the Department of Transportation, the Department of Energy, the American Public Health Association, the United Nations Development Programme, and the National Rural Electric Cooperative Association.

1

Introduction

The important thing for government is not to do things which individuals are doing already and to do them a little better or a little worse: but to do those things which are not done at all.

—J. M. KEYNES, "THE END OF LAISSEZ-FAIRE"

THE APPROPRIATE POINT at which to begin discussing the role of the private sector in providing public services in developing countries is to define some basic terms. The reader must understand what is meant by "public service," "private provision," and "developing countries" before the discussion can go forward.

Public Services

Public services are defined here as any services available to the public, whether provided publicly (as is a museum) or privately (as is a restaurant meal). For the purposes of this discussion, I concentrate on some of the services that are generally considered the responsibility of government, whether central, regional, or local. These services are education, electricity supply, health, telecommunications, urban transport, and water and sewerage. However, many of these "public" services are already provided privately. For example, rickshaws and taxicabs, which are generally private, provide a public transport service in the sense that they are available for hire to all members of the public.

Among the most important services not considered here are those that make up the transport infrastructure: roads, ports, and airports. They deserve a volume in themselves.

Private Provision

Private provision is taken to mean the production or provision or delivery of services by the private sector in one or more ways.

1

Where there are many buyers and many sellers, for example, conventional markets can be organized to enable customers to seek the best values from competing suppliers, while suppliers attempt to make the best possible deals with competing customers. Private suppliers can, however, provide goods or services in at least five other ways:

> Contracts from public agencies
> Monopoly franchises
> Management contracts
> Vouchers
> Consumer cooperatives.

Contracts from Public Agencies

Even where one government agency is responsible for a whole sector—such as roads—some activities of this sector can be contracted out to private firms. In Brazil, Costa Rica, India, and Zaire, for example, road maintenance is carried out by private contractors; and in Lima, Peru, much of the civil engineering work for the laying of telephone lines is contracted out to private firms. These contractors are selected after a bidding process, on the basis of work specifications prepared by the road authorities. Thus contracting out can be defined as public financing of private production.

Monopoly Franchises

Wherever a "natural monopoly" or economies of scale[1] require that an area be supplied by a single organization, a private company can be appointed by a public authority to provide those services on a monopoly basis, at specified standards and tariffs. In many areas of France, for example, private companies have been appointed to supply water to different cities. The companies compete among themselves for this right. Because the equipment used has a long life, such contracts are usually given for a period of twenty to thirty years. The company involved will make the necessary investment. Water is also supplied in this way in the Côte d'Ivoire and other West African countries. Monopoly fran-

---

1. Economies of scale are said to exist when a given increase in all inputs in a production process gives a greater proportionate increase in output. Given constant prices for inputs, this implies that the average cost of producing individual units of output declines as the level of output rises.

chises for the supply of electricity were common in many countries in the past, but now few remain outside the United States. (Franchising need not necessarily be monopolistic; for example, a number of competing taxi firms may be franchised in the same area.)

Management Contracts

In the case of monopoly franchises, it is customary for the company awarded the franchise to make the required investments. Alternatively, the public agency can retain responsibility for the service but arrange for private management, as in the case of the Botswana telephone service, which is managed by Cable and Wireless PLC. In the United States, many urban bus companies are municipally owned but managed by private management firms.

Vouchers

Vouchers, a device that may appear in a variety of forms, enable consumers to obtain goods or services free or at reduced cost while retaining the power to choose between competing suppliers. Vouchers are best known in the United States, where they are used (in the form of food stamps) by poor people to obtain subsidized food without the authorities having to open special low-priced food shops. At the end of World War II, vouchers were also used successfully in the United States to give former servicemen access to a higher education. In this case, they took the form of cash grants that could be applied at any approved educational establishment of the recipient's choice. Another type of voucher is currently used in Chile (see chapter 2) to provide children with government-funded education at primary schools chosen by their parents.

Consumer Cooperatives

Consumer cooperatives—which may range in size from a few dozen members to hundreds of thousands—are self-governing, voluntary organizations. Unlike shareholders' companies, which distribute surpluses to their members in proportion to the shares they own, consumer cooperatives distribute surpluses in proportion to the members' purchases. Designed to serve the interests of their members, consumer cooperatives are particularly acceptable in monopoly situations (for example, in the supply of village electricity) in which consumers cannot benefit from competition among suppliers.

Although this section has focused on the options for the private provision of services, the examples illustrate that the government as well as the private sector can act as a buyer or seller of public services, or both. (For a graphic presentation of this concept, see the appendix to this chapter.)

Developing Countries

The term "developing countries" is loosely used to denote those countries in Africa, Asia, and Latin America that are at a relatively early stage of their economic development and that receive financial and other assistance from external sources. The term is misleading, however, in that it implies that any country outside the group is no longer developing. Moreover, it implies that economic development proceeds in a different way in these countries, in comparison with others. This is not the place to settle these questions, but to state that, wherever possible, the examples in this book are taken from poor countries at low levels of economic development, because readers in, say, Nigeria might feel more at home with examples from, say, Kenya than from, say, Canada. However, when suitable examples are not available from the countries generally referred to as "developing," they are taken from economically advanced countries and pertain either to an earlier stage of their development (for example, water provision in Paris during the eighteenth century) or, where relevant, to the present (for example, recent energy legislation in the United States).

Economic Markets versus Politically Determined Rules

Economic development is characterized by the cheap and efficient production of the goods and services that people want. This production can be organized in two ways:

- Through economic markets, in which a variety of enterprises work for private profit
- Under government administration—at the central, state, or local level—whereby the goods or services are produced in accordance with politically determined rules and procedures.

In general, the supply of goods and services in economic markets is motivated by the prospect of private gain, whereas under government administration the supply is conditioned by what the government regards as the social good. Virtually all societies rely on both of these methods, but the mix varies greatly from one society to another. So-called free enterprise or capitalistic societies (typified by the United States) rely more on private sector activities, whereas so-called command economies (typified by the U.S.S.R.) depend more on governmental decisions. But even in the United States, some services (such as defense, justice, or roads) are provided by public agencies working for what is perceived to be the public good, while in the U.S.S.R. some services (such as taxicabs) are provided by the private sector working for profit.

As the examples in this book illustrate, the role of the government is not limited to direct production. Governments are also engaged in financing and regulating production by the private sector. Subcontracting and franchising are widespread. Even where private markets are predominantly competitive, governments may need to restrain monopoly, protect competition, establish and enforce property rights, and so on. Thus, the crucial question is not *whether* governments should participate in the provision of services, but *what form* such activity should take. Private provision does not mean *no* role for government. Rather, government should put in place the "ground rules establishing a framework in which private enterprise can operate effectively and in a manner responsive to the needs of society" (Clausen 1985, p. 6).

It is not the purpose of this book to argue whether goods and services should be provided by private enterprise or by governments. All societies will continue to depend on a mix of services, and it is up to the people in each to decide where to draw the line. However, the administrative capabilities of all governments, not least those in developing countries, are severely strained by the weight of their numerous activities. The question I wish to pose is whether economic development could be accelerated by moving to the private sector those responsibilities that could be handled more efficiently there. Such an arrangement would allow hard-pressed administrative systems to concentrate on activities that they are best equipped to provide. Even in situations where government administrators could provide better services than the private sector, it may still be beneficial to transfer activities to the private sector if such action would enable the administrators to concentrate more fruitfully on activities that *only* government can provide.

In any society, decisions concerning the allocation of government resources and manpower must constantly be reviewed. Economic, technical, social, and political considerations are forever changing in the light of experience. What was appropriate yesterday is not necessarily so today. Adaptation to change is an essential part of the development process.

Consider some of the changes that have taken place during the past decade:

- New technologies have emerged that have changed the nature of competition and led to the restructuring of some industries (notably telecommunications and electricity generation).

- Economic analysis of ownership, transaction costs, the nature of regulation, uncertainty, and the dynamics of competition has not only shed new light on how governments and markets work, but has also challenged the conventional view of the appropriate role of each.

- Practical experience with regulation, deregulation, nationalization, privatization, socialism, and the mixed economy has changed political attitudes quickly in countries as diverse as Brazil and Yugoslavia, and China and the United States.

Officials in developing countries are well aware of these changes and are beginning to consider how to respond to them. It is hoped that this book will make their task easier.

Choosing between Public and Private Provision

Economists have conventionally analyzed the choice between the public and private provision of goods and services on the basis of the potential "market failure." Broadly speaking, private markets are said to function effectively if they provide the pattern of goods and services that consumers most prefer, given their levels of income. Production is also considered efficient if there is no slack in the economy by which more or better goods could be produced to make everyone better off. If these desirable properties do not hold, markets are said not to function effectively. At times, governments step in to improve matters. Depending on the nature of the "market failure," the appropriate "remedy" may be regulation, taxation, or subsidized production by private contractors at public expense, or even production by government employees, as is the case in most post offices.

In the past decade or so, however, economists have become aware of important qualifications to this analysis. It cannot be taken for granted that governments in the real world will be willing or able to put things right. The information available to them may not necessarily be better than that available to private markets—it may be worse. Furthermore, public agencies may be more responsive to political pressures than to consumer preferences. Regulation may protect the regulated industry or some other vocal pressure group rather than the customer.

In sum, the possibility of "government failure" as well as "market failure" must be considered. The private market may be faulty, but the government "remedy" may be worse. The need is therefore to choose, not between alternative hypothetical ideal cases, but between alternative institutional arrangements as they would actually work in practice.

The concept of potential market failures is nonetheless helpful in identifying situations that may generate problems and that may call for serious consideration of the appropriate role of government. If market failure is not indicated, competitive private provision may well be the most efficient form of organization, within a general framework of rules established and enforced by government.

The economic literature describes five situations in which private markets cannot necessarily be relied upon to provide the most efficient and appropriate pattern of services:

Where natural monopolies exist
Where increased production is associated with decreasing costs
Where substantial externalities exist and are not reflected in the accounts of private suppliers
Where it is difficult to charge for a service or to exclude those who do not pay
Where merit goods are involved.

Natural Monopolies

When a factor of production cannot be duplicated, a natural monopoly is said to exist. For example, a city may be able to obtain its water supply from just one source. In these circumstances a private owner of the water source would not be subject to direct competition and would therefore be in a position to exploit those who depend on the service by charging prices considerably in excess of the costs of extraction and distribution. In such a situation, there would be advantages if the service was provided by a public agency that is politically responsible to the beneficiaries. However, there would also be disadvantages if public provision led to higher costs of production and a reduced rate of innovation. The question then would be which is the lesser of two evils (or failures)? Those are not the only options, however. Other policy alternatives such as regulation or franchising may also deserve consideration.

Decreasing Costs

The efficiency of a productive enterprise, measured as the ratio of output to costs of input, can often be increased by enlarging the scale of production. This increase in efficiency can happen for a number of reasons. On a larger scale it becomes possible to use specialized equipment (such as a machine tool) that cannot be used on a small scale, workers can specialize on a narrower range of activities and thus become more proficient, and inputs can be bought more cheaply in large quantities. If economies of scale are so great that the industry can support only a few firms or only a single firm, there is a danger of monopoly power. Here, again, government regulation or ownership may have to be considered, but the disadvantages as well as advantages of the alternatives must be kept in mind.

The early history of urban transport provides an example of decreasing costs by expanding production. When transport was provided by electrically powered vehicles (trams or streetcars), it was found that one large generating system could power many vehicles and additional vehicles could be accommodated at a comparatively small increase in power costs. This provided a strong case for establishing large, single enterprises to provide urban transport. This tradition of organizing urban transport services into large, centrally directed fleets has continued in many cities even though the electrically powered systems have been replaced by individually powered, diesel-engine buses that are not necessarily cheaper to operate in large numbers.

Other important examples of decreasing costs in public services are the distribution networks for water, electricity, or telephone services. The economies of scale in providing water, electricity, or telephone connections through one local network are so pronounced that these are generally regarded as natural monopolies. As shown in later chapters, however, there are cases in which competitive duplicate electricity distribution systems are associated with low costs, and the question of whether economies of scale extend to telecommunications is even more debatable and subject to continuing changes in technology.

Externalities

At times buyers and sellers who exchange goods and services create externalities, that is, costs and benefits for people not directly involved in the exchange. For example, factories and automobiles may pollute the air people breathe (negative externalities) while beautiful gardens are a source of pleasure (positive externalities) to passersby. Economists used to argue that, in the absence of government action, goods or services involving negative externalities would be overproduced and those involving positive externalities underproduced. Various remedies, such as taxes, were suggested to discourage negative externalities, while subsidies were recommended to encourage positive ones.

This view is now increasingly considered to be too simplistic. Externalities, it has been pointed out, arise only when it is too costly for those affected by the actions in question to negotiate with those responsible for the actions. If a factory could be sued for causing pollution, it would be fully accountable for any damage its method of production caused; there would be no externality. Even if the factory had the right to emit pollutants without legal liability for damages, a group of affected households could offer to pay the factory not to pollute; in this case, the factory might be better off using a nonpolluting method of production and, once again, there would be no externality (Coase 1960). Of course, even if there is no externality, the distribution of benefits—whether the factory has to pay the household or the households the factory—will depend on who has the property right.

In practice, transactions costs are often significant and sometimes insuperable. It may not be practicable for all the inhabitants of a town to get together to sue a factory for pollution or an airline for noise—although local authorities can act on behalf of their citizens, and in some countries class actions by a representative citizen are feasible. In any event, modern analysis leads us to categorize potential externality problems into "small-number" situations, in which the problem is likely to be resolved by private negotiations, and "large-number" situations, in which transactions costs are likely to make such negotiations impracticable. In either case, governments can play an important role in establishing and enforcing property rights, so as to reduce transactions costs; in the large-number situation, however, additional measures may be needed along the lines indicated earlier (that is, regulations, taxes, or subsidies).

Activities relating to education and public health are often associated with positive externalities, insofar as people benefit when their fellow citizens are better educated and healthier. It is therefore often suggested that these services should be financed or subsidized by governments, or even provided by public agencies, and not left to the private marketplace. Education and health are also considered merit goods, which will be discussed below.

Inability to Charge Users or to Exclude Nonpayers

Some goods and services have to be provided to a group as a whole and cannot be subdivided for the benefit of particular individuals. Typical examples are national defense, street lighting, and radio broadcasting. Economists have named goods and services of this kind "pure public goods." Whatever level of service is provided is available to everybody, regardless of the extent to which each individual chooses to avail himself of the service. Furthermore, there is no way in which individual users can be charged or in which nonusers can be excluded from payment. For example, a radio broadcast can be picked up by any radio in the area. Because of the impossibility of charging or of excluding nonpayers, the private market would not find it profitable to supply "pure public goods." Hence their provision is regarded as a responsibility of government.

The government has several options here. One is to provide the service itself and to finance it through taxation, as in the case of defense, or through a more specific tax on all users, as in the case of a television license in the United Kingdom. Another possibility is for the government to authorize a private organization to impose and collect the charges necessary to run the service. Systems of this kind have long been used to operate lighthouses in the United Kingdom and air traffic control in Switzerland. Still another option is to tie the public good to a private good that the market is prepared to pay for (such as advertising between radio and TV programs) and to use this revenue to finance supply. With public goods, as with other "market failures," the advantages of public provision have to be weighed against the disadvantages and compared with the alternatives. In the case of radio and TV, for example, a tax may cost little to collect and be less of a nuisance to the consumer than advertising; however, a tax does not take into account the amount of usage, nor does it reflect which programs consumers watch. As a result, the broadcasting authority is left to select programs without knowing what consumers prefer.

Merit Goods

Economists apply the term "merit goods" to those goods and services that society considers to have special merit but that might be produced in insufficient quantity if left to private markets. Health, education, and housing are often thought of as merit goods—at least up to a certain minimum level. Other examples are school lunches and water fluoridation programs. Merit goods may be associated with positive externalities, but this need not always be the case inasmuch as their distinguishing feature is not that third parties benefit from the provision of such goods, but that the recipients themselves benefit to a greater extent than they themselves believe. Because people would not voluntarily buy enough merit goods, the government can either provide them free or finance or subsidize provision by the private market.

These, then, are the situations most commonly cited in the economic literature as the ones in which private markets alone may not provide goods and services satisfactorily. The list is not comprehensive; indeed, some argue that all goods and services should be provided by public agencies, while others say that none should be. Most would agree, however, that when private markets cannot by themselves provide the range, quality, or quantity of services considered desirable, governments must consider alternative methods. As already noted, one alternative might be to place production directly in the hands of government employees, such as policemen, mail carriers, and public health experts. But there are other methods: consumer cooperatives might be appropriate in some situations, regulated franchises in others, or service contracts with private firms in still others. The evaluation of alternative methods of provision is not easy in any situation and may even create controversy, as will be seen later in this volume.

The Treatment of Charitable Organizations

Many public services, especially education and health, are provided by charitable organizations. The Roman Catholic Church, the Seventh Day Adventists, and Oxfam, for example, finance numerous activities, in both developed and developing countries. India's Tata Foundations provide a host of educational, medical, and other activities on a charitable basis; most, but not all, are in India. The Aga Khan Foundation finances education and health services in Asia and Africa. Should these activities be included in a discussion of the role of the private sector in providing public services?

At first the answer might seem to be no, as the activities provided by these charities are not motivated primarily by the desire to earn profits. Yet they *are* provided by the private sector, and many of them would not be provided at all in the absence of a private sector. Therefore I propose to include in this book charitable activities (such as those of the Lutheran Shipping Company in Papua New Guinea) that are financially viable (or are intended to be). Activities that rely on charity for their continued operation are excluded.

Private Provision, Not Cost Recovery

The emphasis in this book is on private provision, not cost recovery. Its purpose is to give examples from developing countries of the private provision of services that are generally regarded as being more (or only) suitable for provision by public agencies. The discussion is not primarily concerned with whether a public agency ought to charge for its services and, if so, whether the charges ought to recover the full costs of services provided, as indeed is often the case in Romania, Yugoslavia, and many other countries.

My intent is not to tell policymakers or researchers what should be done, but to provide examples of what is being done already, so that officials in developing countries will know what additional options may be available to them in their efforts to make the best use of their countries' resources for the benefit of their peoples.

Appendix: Private and Public Sectors as Buyers or Producers of Services

The concept that the government as well as the private sector can act as a buyer or producer of public services, or as both, may be illustrated by a matrix (see figure 1-1). The top quadrants represent the private sector as buyer, and the bottom quadrants represent the public sector as buyer. The quadrants to the right represent the private sector as producer, and the quadrants to the left represent the government sector as producer. Most goods and services can be placed in one or more of the quadrants, depending on the country concerned. Furthermore, activities can move from one quadrant to another as, for example, services are taken over by the public sector or released to the private sector.

**Figure 1–1. Government and Private Sector as Buyer
and Producer of Public Services**

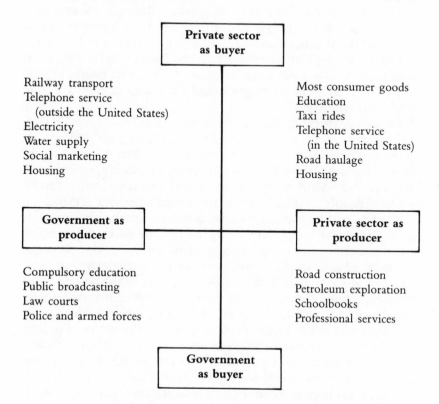

The top right-hand quadrant represents cases in which both buying and producing are done privately. These typical private sector activities also include public services that are privately produced in most countries, such as taxis, bottled water, and many medicines.

The top left-hand quadrant represents activities in which governments act as producers and private individuals as buyers. These include nationalized industries, public corporations, and, in the U.S.S.R., almost all goods and services. Another activity fitting into this quadrant would be "social marketing," whereby health agencies (for example, those in Cameroon) sell medicines; the buyers are individuals, whose purchases are determined by their own needs and preferences.

The bottom left quadrant covers sectors in which public agencies act as both buyers and producers of services. A typical example is free and compulsory primary education, where a public agency employs the teachers and also decides what and whom they should teach. Decisions are reached through political processes in which the people concerned may have important roles, but once the decisions are made individuals cannot influence the results except by further political action. For example, if the decision is made that a particular language will not be taught at state schools, parents cannot shop around for a state school that does teach that language.

Other activities in this quadrant are the armed forces, police, and the law courts—the government employs the judges and decides which cases they are to work on. Arbitrators, who perform very similar work but are employed privately, would be in the top right-hand quadrant, as would private security forces, private schools, and (in the United States) telephone services.

Finally, in the lower right-hand quadrant are the activities that are produced by the private sector but that are bought by government. Contracting out and management contracts come into this category. One example is road construction or maintenance: government decides where the roads are to be built, and to what standards, but employs private firms to build or maintain them. Self-employed doctors, working under a national health scheme, would also be in this quadrant: they work as self-employed professional people, but their remuneration comes out of public funds.

A shift from public to private provision would involve a shift from the left-hand side to the right-hand of this matrix. However, this does not invariably mean a shift to the top right-hand quadrant (that is, to the normal private market). As the examples in this book will show, a move to the bottom right-hand quadrant may have its advantages. The government would still be involved in the provision of services, but in a different role—as buyer instead of producer.

References

Clausen, A.W. 1985. "Promoting the Private Sector in Developing Countries: A Multilateral Approach." Address to the Institute of Directors, London, England. Washington, D.C.: World Bank.

Coase, Ronald H. 1960. "The Problem of Social Cost." *Journal of Law and Economics*. 3:1–44.

2

Education

Those parts of education, it is to be observed, for the teaching of which there are no public institutions, are generally the best taught. When a young man goes to a fencing or a dancing school, he does not indeed always learn to fence or to dance very well; but he seldom fails of learning to fence or to dance.

—ADAM SMITH, "THE WEALTH OF NATIONS"

THE ORIGINS OF EDUCATION are obscured in prehistory. When people lived in groups as hunters or food gatherers, education was no doubt primarily vocational; children were taught the arts of survival, and the teachers were presumably parents and other members of the family group. It may be assumed that in those days efficiency in education was a matter of life and death, as those unable to learn the arts of survival did not, in fact, survive.

Historical Background

In the earliest periods of recorded history, religion appears to have played a leading role in education, as must surely be admitted by even the most hardened agnostics. In most known societies, priesthoods had special roles not only in preserving and transmitting religious beliefs, but also in developing the mathematical sciences for astronomical applications. Furthermore, there is evidence that writing was developed to record religious texts. The power of transmitting texts without writing should not be underestimated, however. The Bible and the Hindu Vedas and Upanishads were transmitted orally for many centuries before being written down, as was Greek classical literature.

For help in the preparation of this chapter special thanks are due to Stephen Heyneman, Robert Myers, George Psacharopoulos, Nwanganga Shields, and Jee-Peng Tan, the World Bank; Mark Blaug, the Institute of Education; and Frank Sutton, the Ford Foundation.

In more modern times, religion has had profound effects on education in developing countries. Koran schools have been influential for a millenium over an area extending from Indonesia to West Africa. and the Christian church has played a leading role in educational activities in many countries, both developed and developing. Indian education owes much to the Hindu gurus who taught the Sanskrit scriptures, and the Buddhist *Wats* of Thailand were, until the twentieth century, the main source of education for the common people there.

The question of interest here is whether education provided under religious auspices should be considered a publicly or privately provided service. To the extent that it is not compulsory, that it has to be paid for by users, and that it is not provided by salaried state teachers, it has some of the main characteristics of private education. Religious organizations everywhere seem to be perennially short of money, with many claims on their scarce resources, so that education provided by Confucian, Christian, Jewish, or Moslem authorities has at least one thing in common: it requires at least some payment from users and, not being compulsory, it has to provide curricula and standards that appeal to users. The ideal of "free compulsory" education seems to be of more interest to political fraternities than to religious ones.

The concept of free compulsory education, for which the state should be responsible, originated in Europe and North America but was not widely promoted until the nineteenth century. It is thus of comparatively recent origin. Private education has a much longer history, as may be seen from the following sketches.

China

Scholarship in China has traditionally been accorded great respect. For example, the Chinese invented competitive scholastic examinations, and the winners received the top jobs in government. For many years, education in China was mainly private. Confucius is reported to have declared that he would teach anybody who brought him a meal, implying that he did not mind how much he was paid, as long as the principle of payment was accepted. Boys born into middle-class and wealthy families in the Ch'ing period (1644–1911) began learning to read and write at home, where a boy might learn to recognize as many as 2,000 characters. Boys from poorer families could be sent to schools run by teachers in their own homes or in nearby temples. A visitor to China in the nineteenth century noted that "there are numerous primary schools in China supported by the people of a neighborhood who choose to send their children. There are no school-houses, schools being commonly held in a spare hall or room belonging to a private family, or in part of the village temple. There is no village tax nor any aid from government received for the support of schools. Each parent must pay the teacher for the instruction of his children" (Rawski 1979, p. 25). An early nineteenth century estimate from Kwantung suggested that in rural districts 50 percent of the men could read, and that an estimated 80–90 percent within the city of Canton could do so. Furthermore, most people knew enough arithmetic to carry on business.

A common practice among villagers in China during the Ch'ing period was to invite a teacher to set up classes, as is evident from contract forms found in popular almanacs. The expenses of operating a school were not very great since the desks of students were often supplied by their parents. Although teachers' salaries had to be paid, they were generally quite low. Because government officials were selected from the ranks of scholars and could bring honor and wealth to their villages, it was in the interest of every community to encourage the education of its talented members. In some areas (as in the early American colonies), parents who refused to pay school fees for bright boys when they could afford to do so were punished. And when the parents could not afford the fees, scholarships were available.

In the absence of direct government funding, schools in China were established by local officials, local elite families, or by guilds or groups of villagers. The most vital task in establishing a school was to secure the funds needed to keep it open year after year. Many schools were endowed with money, land, or buildings, but land was particularly important as a permanent source of income for schools in China throughout this period. School lands differed from privately owned plots in that they could not be sold freely. Donations of land came from private citizens and officials, who transferred confiscated plots, untaxed lands, or temple holdings to schools. The lands were then rented out to tenants who paid rent either in cash or in kind, and the funds thus obtained were used to defray salaries and other educational expenses. A similar method of funding is used today in Africa: when the private Kamuzu Academy was recently established in Malawi, 250 acres of tobacco land were donated to it as a permanent source of income.

India

In India, the concept of universal education, of providing a minimum standard of education to every boy and girl, is as old as the beginning of civilization in the subcontinent. Around 1500 B.C. the Vedic Aryans prescribed a fairly long period of education for all children, not on the basis of any state legislation—the concept of the state itself did not then exist—but through religious practice. The education of boys and girls began in about the eighth year, when they were introduced into the home of their guru, where they studied for eight to sixteen years. The curriculum included not only religious texts, but all branches of knowledge as they were then known. That this system—which amounted to at least eight years of compulsory schooling for every child—was universal among the Aryans is certain; but to what extent this or a similar system prevailed among non-Aryan peoples is not known. Unfortunately, this system of education later disappeared almost completely owing to social changes that took place in later years. Women lost their social status, and the right to education was denied to them. As the caste system became more and more rigid, educational opportunities became restricted even among men, the majority of whom belonged to lower castes (Mathur 1973).

Toward the end of this ancient period, the Hindu system of education developed two main types of schools: the Tol and the Pathshalas. The Tol was the Hindu school of higher learning. Instruction was in Sanskrit, and the curriculum covered all sectors of traditional classical learning. The teachers were Brahmins, and the pupils received free education and lived on stipends or scholarships given by the king or rich persons. For boys of upper castes who did not attend the Tols, there were large networks of less demanding schools, or Pathshalas, which provided instruction in the three R's. The teachers were persons of humble origins and were rewarded for their teaching with gifts of cash or payment in kind by the parents of the children who attended the schools.

With the advent of the Muslim period in the ninth century, other systems of education were imported into the subcontinent. The Maktab, which corresponded to the Hindu elementary school, was generally attached to the mosques and was designed to teach boys and girls to read and write; emphasis was placed on reading the Koran. The Madrasha, which corresponded to the Hindu institutions for higher education, prepared a highly selected group of men to be priests, judges, doctors, or members of other professions.

The British authorities were the first to involve the government as a major factor in education in the subcontinent. They directed their attention to reviving Indian learning and founded the Calcutta Madrasha in 1781, at the request of a Muslim deputation. In 1792 they established a Sanskrit college at Benares. An act passed in 1813 enabled the government to devote no less than 100,000 rupees each year to education. However, bitter arguments arose over the language of education in the subcontinent—whether it should be English, the classical Indian languages, or the vernacular languages spoken by the common people. The struggle between the Orientalists and the Anglicists was won by the latter, and a system of English education was adopted and encouraged by the government. Meanwhile, the Christian missionary movement, whose goal was to reach as many people as possible, began printing books in the vernacular and teaching in local languages.

The government, following proposals made in 1854, attempted to create in India a comprehensive system of education from the primary school to the university. It set up departments of education in each of the Indian presidencies, instituted universities in the presidency towns, gave more attention to vernacular schools for both secondary and primary education, recommended a comprehensive system of scholarships, and introduced a system of grants-in-aid. These grants were awarded subject to inspection and other conditions that were unacceptable to some of the Indian schools. The problem they faced was that, if they wanted to be free of government controls, they had to depend solely on fees; yet the dependence on fees meant that the poor could not be taught. Many schools nevertheless preferred to do without the grants and were able to do so because they obtained some support from nongovernment sources and their teachers accepted smaller salaries. The government complained that these schools were spreading political propaganda against British rule. In 1904 the viceroy, Lord Curzon, ordained that every school, whether it received grant aid or not, had to be recognized if it was to be allowed to exist. And seeking recognition meant submitting to controls (Naik 1967).

This brief sketch of the development of education in the subcontinent not only shows the historical role of the private sector there, but also indicates a major reason for government involvement in education: a desire to control the curriculum for political reasons.

Since 1947, when India gained its independence, both the private and the public sectors have played important roles in education. In Bombay, for example, about 1,300 of the 2,040 schools there (with 73 percent of primary and secondary pupils combined) are financed and managed by the municipality of Bombay. Two of the nonmunicipal schools are run by the central government, but all the others are owned and operated privately by religious and caste organizations, missionary societies, charitable trusts, private educational foundations, industrial houses, and the like. Of the 765 secondary schools in Bombay, 714 are run by private bodies, and only 51 by the municipality. However, some of the private schools, both primary and secondary, are aided with state funds. Municipal schools charge no tuition fees at the primary level and a nominal fee at the secondary level. In contrast, except for the few private schools that have been established as charities, the private schools charge tuition fees ranging from 4–5 rupees a month to upward of 200 rupees a month (Chitnis and Suvannathat 1984).

The high fees paid to the better schools not only ensure "exclusiveness," but also high-quality physical surroundings and academic facilities (including teaching aids, laboratories, and libraries), a smaller student-teacher ratio, more variation in courses, and better-organized extracurricular activities. Parents who can afford to do so send their children to private schools that offer them a greater chance of higher education. These schools thus gain students from home backgrounds supportive of schooling. In contrast, the free municipal schools and the private charity schools are used by the mass of children from working-class backgrounds, many from educationally disadvantaged homes. The educational facilities available to poor children are clearly unsatisfactory, but there is no easy way to improve them. At the same time, the associations of teachers are demanding that the private schools be nationalized. Their case is very clear because "to be a teacher in a government school is to ensure a good salary, a good pension and no responsibility to do any work" (Naik 1967). However, private schools in India have the constitutional right to exist and cannot be abolished. It is beyond the scope of this volume to discuss whether the education of poor children in India could be improved by privatizing the state schools; this is something that can be found out only by trial and error.

Sub-Saharan Africa

It is difficult to generalize about education in Sub-Saharan Africa because of the variety of conditions prevailing there. Indigenous education was almost entirely an oral tradition since only the Vai of Liberia and the Mum of Cameroon had invented systems of writing. Nevertheless, it must not be assumed that Africa's non-literate societies did not value education, nor that all young people learned the same skills in any particular society. The Yoruba society, for example, had marked specialization in occupations, as well as distinct social hierarchies. The various societies had certain educational practices in common, however, such as training in relevant practical skills, the development of desirable characteristics (courage, tact, loyalty, and so on), and the inculcation of community traditions. Responsibility for education was shared by the family and the group, and to that extent it contained elements

from both the private and the public sector. (These and the following observations are based on Yates 1984.)

Islamic education was established in tropical Africa about a
thousand years ago. Its impact on Africa was profound. In East
Africa it arrived with the coastal traders, and in West Africa it
spread overland from the north. According to traditional belief, in
1085 a Muslim dynasty began to rule the kingdom of Bornu. By
the sixteenth century, many individual Muslim scholars had pene-
trated West African towns and cities and established centers of
Islamic literacy in the midst of what was generally a pre-literate
culture. In the seventeenth century, Islamic Madrashas, or schools
of higher Islamic learning, were established in Katsina and Kano,
and by the end of that century their influence reached as far south
as what is now Western Nigeria. The Muslim scholars who taught
there possessed a knowledge of Islamic law, theology, philosophy,
and classical Arabic literature. Islamic education was in general a
private sector activity, in the sense that the teaching was not
supported by the state, but by fees and the voluntary contributions
of the believers.

Western-type education was introduced to Sub-Saharan Africa
by Christian missionaries, both foreign and local. Schools for
children and Sunday evening classes for adults developed as a
natural accompaniment to the founding of churches. Although no
school fees were charged in the initial period, they were gradually
introduced to make the schools self-financing. Teachers' salaries
were paid from church funds. During the early decades of the
twentieth century, the demand for this type of education increased,
mainly because these schools were considered stepping stones to
wage-paid jobs with commercial firms and the government. Because of the appeal of Westernized education, the Islamic authorities opened schools at which Muslim children could gain this
type of education without the parents being concerned about
Christian proselytizing. Some that met government standards received grants-in-aid, but even without this assistance, many mission and "private venture" schools emerged throughout Africa to
meet the gathering enthusiasm for formal education. Parents were
willing to pay fees, which were often high in relation to their total
incomes, in order to see their children get ahead. After the interior
of Zaire was exposed to Western goods and literate people who
were role models, the enrollment of Zairians in Western-style
schools increased, from zero in 1877 to 9,000 in 1898, and 21,000
in 1903 (Yates 1984).

Thus, before the Sub-Saharan countries achieved their independence they had a large variety of schools at all levels, some pro-

vided by the government and some by private institutions. After independence, most of the newly formed governments established comprehensive state education systems, but the private sector continued to play a major role, as was observed in Uganda by Castle (1966, p. 133):

> There are in Uganda a large number of unaided private secondary schools run for private profit which absorb thousands of children unable to enter the aided system. No accurate figures are available, but in 1963 there were over 4,000 pupils in these schools paying anything from 300s [shillings] to 900s per annum in fees, and there are indications that these numbers are steadily increasing. This is a phenomenon almost wholly confined to Uganda. One surprising aspect of this situation is that in some of these schools over 90 percent of the pupils come from Tanzania and even Central Africa, where restrictions on private schools are much more severe. The teaching and living conditions, with few exceptions, are thoroughly bad. In addition to paying fees, students are usually expected to buy books and consumable materials; they are crowded onto benches often without the table section to write on; there are practically no visual aids except here and there an ancient map, and the teachers' libraries are, as one inspector has remarked, "at the maximum, meagre." Some owners make good profits, but most of them declare that, after paying teachers' salaries, little money is left to pay for equipment.

The proposition that students from neighboring countries would pay large fees to attend "thoroughly bad" schools is puzzling; presumably there were no better alternatives open to these students, who were unable to enter the schools supported by public funds. Outside observers of the educational scene in Africa cannot but admire the tenacity with which so many of its people seek an education. And some have wondered whether the situation could not be improved by giving more encouragement to the private sector.

Latin America

Not enough is known about indigenous education in Latin America to specify the role of the private sector there. The schools and universities established by the European colonizers were generally private, and many were associated with religious organizations. Latin America contains the oldest universities in America, several dating from the early sixteenth century; most are private foundations.

One example of church involvement in education is the campaign by Francisco Marroquin for the education of all races. By the end of the sixteenth century, Guatemala had a variety of schools, chiefly conducted by Franciscans and Dominicans. By the beginning of the seventeenth century, the Jesuit Colegio de San Lucas, a secondary school, had a library of more than 5,000 volumes. These educational activities reflected important writings by Indians and records of pre-Columbian culture. In 1676 the University of San Carlos was founded in Guatemala; one of its first five professorships was in a major Indian language, Cakchiquel. Even after Guatemala gained its independence from Spain, education remained chiefly in the hands of the church until the middle of the nineteenth century. A presidential decree in Honduras in 1847 required that students be examined every four months before the local authorities and priests (Waggoner and Ashton 1971). In Peru also, the church controlled education in the colonial period. In 1551 it founded the University of San Marcos in Lima, and shortly afterward institutions of higher education in Chuquisaca, Huamanga, and Cuzco.

Private Education Today

Data on private education in developing countries are difficult to come by. Official statistics often ignore private schools, as do many educational planners employed by international lending agencies. Unesco stopped publishing private school enrollment data in the early 1960s and financial statistics for private schools in 1973. The reasons for the lack of data are many: the size and complexity of the sector; statistical variations across countries; lack of uniform definitions (a school receiving a state grant might be classified as "private" in one country or period and "public" in another); and even a reluctance on the part of some governments to admit that private education has a role to play in their countries. In the People's Republic of the Congo, for example, private education is illegal, and in the Republic of Korea it is illegal for parents to pay tutors to help prepare children for the state examinations.

The available data on enrollment in the primary and secondary schools in developing countries were assembled by Jee-Peng Tan (1985). Table 2-1 shows that the percentage of private enrollment has been declining since the 1960s. A percentage decline does not necessarily reflect an absolute decline. The percentage might drop

Table 2-1. Percentage of Total Enrollment in Private Schools by Country and Level, 1965–79

Region and country	First level				Second level			
	1965	1970	1975	1979	1965	1970	1975	1979
Asia (mean)	14	n.a.	13	n.a.	44	n.a.	29	n.a.
Bangladesh	n.a.	n.a.	8	n.a.	n.a.	n.a.	9	n.a.
Indonesia	12	n.a.	13	12ᶜ	n.a.	n.a.	60	47ᶜ
Korea, Rep. of	1	n.a.	1	n.a.	48	n.a.	45	n.a.
Philippines	4	n.a.	5	n.a.	66	n.a.	38	n.a.
Singapore	40	n.a.	35	n.a.	3	n.a.	1	n.a.
Sri Lanka	n.a.	n.a.	6	n.a.	9	n.a.	n.a.	n.a.
Thailand	13	n.a.	11	n.a.	50	n.a.	32	n.a.
East Africa (mean)	53	43	43	42	36	51	45	48
Botswana	4	5	5	2	10	59	30	27
Burundi	96	94	92	100	30	36	22	n.a.
Ethiopia	25	28	25	18	15	n.a.	n.a.	n.a.
Djibouti	n.a.	23	13	9	n.a.	n.a.	n.a.	n.a.
Kenya	4	n.a.	1	n.a.	29	42	49	60
Lesotho	96	100	100	100	100	89	89	90
Madagascar	27	20	23	n.a.	66	70	49	n.a.
Malawi	77	11	10	10	5	13	13	13
Seychelles	n.a.	91	8	3	n.a.	18	4	4
Sudan	2	4	2	n.a.	45	n.a.	13	3
Swaziland	80	76	80	80	4	n.a.	n.a.	n.a.
Tanzania	7	2	4	0.4	n.a.	24	29	41

Rwanda	n.a.	n.a.	n.a.	n.a.	n.a.	n.a.	21	n.a.
Zaire	91	n.a.	n.a.	n.a.	57	n.a.	n.a.	n.a.
Zambia	n.a.	27	24	n.a.	4	n.a.	2	n.a.
Zimbabwe	n.a.	n.a.	n.a.	83	n.a.	n.a.	n.a.	66
West Africa (mean)	26	23	18	16	41	38	30	28
Benin	40	33	5	4	54	56	18	4
Burkina Faso	34	n.a.	7	n.a.	38	36	43	54
Cameroon	61	54	43	36	73	66	57	48
Central African Rep.	n.a.	n.a.	n.a.	n.a.	2	n.a.	2	n.a.
Chad	12	8	10	5	7	7	6	n.a.
Côte d'Ivoire	28	22	19	16	n.a.	25	28	30
Equatorial Guinea	n.a.	n.a.	24	n.a.	n.a.	3	3	n.a.
Gabon	53	n.a.	45	n.a.	43	39	32	44
Gambia	n.a.	31	16	16	54	46	46	34
Liberia	25	34	35	36	48	38	43	44
Mali	8	6	4	4	10	11	11	n.a.
Mauritania	34	29	28	25	77	n.a.	6	n.a.
Niger	6	6	5	5	2	22	14	16
Nigeria	76	38	26	n.a.	n.a.	n.a.	41	n.a.
Senegal	13	12	12	12	22	n.a.	25	33
Sierra Leone	n.a.	n.a.	78	n.a.	n.a.	n.a.	87	n.a.
Togo	40	34	29	25	55	39	16	10

(Table continues on the following page.)

25

Table 2–1 (continued)

Region and country	First level				Second level			
	1965	1970	1975	1979	1965	1970	1975	1979
Europe, Middle East, and North Africa (mean)	8	n.a.	6	n.a.	18	n.a.	8	n.a.
Algeria	2	2	1	0.2	7	0.5	1	1
Cyprus	1	n.a.	n.a.	n.a.	11	n.a.	13	n.a.
Egypt	13	n.a.	5	5	41	22	22	14
Iran, Islamic Rep. of	8	n.a.	8	n.a.	26	n.a.	17	n.a.
Iraq	2	n.a.	1	n.a.	24	n.a.	n.a.	n.a.
Jordan	28	n.a.	30	8[c]	13	n.a.	7	5[c]
Libya	3	0.5	2	n.a.	7	0.4	0	0.6
Morocco	6	5	5	3	14	10	8	6
Saudi Arabia	6	n.a.	3	n.a.	4	n.a.	2	n.a.
Syria	10	n.a.	5	n.a.	37	n.a.	6	n.a.
Turkey	1	n.a.	n.a.	n.a.	n.a.	n.a.	2	n.a.
Yemen Arab Rep.	n.a.	n.a.	1	n.a.	n.a.	n.a.	3	n.a.
Latin America and the Caribbean (mean)	14	n.a.	13	n.a.	39	n.a.	33	n.a.
Argentina	14	n.a.	17	n.a.	41	n.a.	45	n.a.
Barbados	n.a.	n.a.	9	n.a.	26	n.a.	21	n.a.
Bolivia	26	n.a.	9	n.a.	26	n.a.	24	n.a.
Brazil	11	n.a.	13	n.a.	49	n.a.	25	n.a.

Country							
Chile	27	n.a.	18	n.a.	38	n.a.	23	n.a.
Colombia	14	n.a.	15	n.a.	58	n.a.	38	n.a.
Costa Rica	4	n.a.	4	n.a.	24	n.a.	6	n.a.
Dominican Rep.	7	n.a.	12	n.a.	n.a.	n.a.	n.a.	n.a.
Ecuador	18	n.a.	17	n.a.	38	n.a.	30	n.a.
El Salvador	4	n.a.	6	n.a.	47	n.a.	47	n.a.
Guatemala	19	n.a.	14	n.a.	54	n.a.	43	n.a.
Haiti	26	n.a.	42	n.a.	43	n.a.	76	n.a.
Honduras	7	n.a.	5	n.a.	53	n.a.	51	n.a.
Jamaica	n.a.	n.a.	5	n.a.	n.a.	n.a.	76	n.a.
Mexico	9	n.a.	6	n.a.	29	n.a.	25	n.a.
Nicaragua	16	n.a.	15	n.a.	44	n.a.	n.a.	n.a.
Panama	5	n.a.	5	n.a.	17	n.a.	14	n.a.
Paraguay	10	n.a.	13	n.a.	24	n.a.	37	n.a.
Peru	14	n.a.	13	n.a.	24	n.a.	17	n.a.
Suriname	n.a.	n.a.	65	n.a.	57	n.a.	52	n.a.
Trinidad and Tobago	n.a.	n.a.	—	n.a.	41	n.a.	—	n.a.
Uruguay	10	n.a.	17	n.a.	17	n.a.	—	n.a.
Venezuela	13	n.a.	11	n.a.	23	n.a.	18	n.a.

n.a. Not available.
Source: Tan (1985).

if the private sector expands more slowly than the public sector or if the private schools are incorporated into the public sector.

Although the general trend is for the proportion of pupils receiving private education to decline, there are some exceptions, as shown in table 2-2. Tan suggests two reasons for an increase in private education in these cases.

- Private schools provide a better education than do public schools, and this difference in quality outweighs the cost difference. This was the case in Malta in 1973, when there was a large influx of children into private schools following politically mandated changes in the public schools. (The government attempted to phase out private education by freezing fees at 1972 levels and, in 1984, abolishing fees by legislation.)
- The public sector is strapped for funds and cannot meet the demand for secondary or even primary education. This has

Table 2–2. Percentage Share of Private School Enrollment in Countries Showing an Increase, 1965–79

Level and Country	1965	1970	1975	1979
First level				
Liberia	25	34	35	36
Argentina	14	n.a.	17	n.a.
Brazil	11	n.a.	13	n.a.
Colombia	14	n.a.	15	n.a.
Dominican Republic	7	n.a.	12	n.a.
El Salvador	4	n.a.	6	n.a.
Haiti	26	n.a.	42	n.a.
Paraguay	10	n.a.	13	n.a.
Second level				
Botswana	10	59	30	27
Burkina Faso	38	36	43	54
Côte d'Ivoire	n.a.	25	28	30
Kenya	29	42	49	60
Malawi	5	13	13	13
Tanzania	n.a.	24	29	41
Gabon	43	39	32	44
Niger	2	22	14	16
Senegal	22	n.a.	25	33
Argentina	41	n.a.	45	n.a.
Haiti	43	n.a.	76	n.a.

n.a. Not available.
Source: Tan (1985).

been happening in a number of African countries, for example, Kenya, Nigeria, and Uganda. The supply constraint tends to be more of a problem at higher levels of education than at lower levels, where education is accorded higher priority and is generally considered to be easier to provide, in that the teachers at that level need little specialized training.

The overall picture then is that in developing countries in recent years more and more lower-level, general education has become the responsibility of public authorities, while the private sector has been concerned more with specialized education such as higher-level and vocational education. To what extent is this tendency desirable? Why does this happen? One way to answer these questions is to apply to education the criteria set out in chapter 1 for judging the appropriateness of the public or private provision of services.

Criteria for Public and Private Provision

Few of the traditional criteria used to determine whether public provision is appropriate apply to education. There are economies of scale in teaching, but not of the kind that justify public involvement. There are also externalities to elementary education: for example, ignoring health and hygiene practices can have deadly consequences; further, society finds it easier to deal with people who can read and sign their names. But these externalities also apply in the case of the production of books and newspapers, and it would be difficult to make a convincing case for public provision of them. Moreover, there is no technical difficulty in charging for education or in excluding from classes those who do not pay. Neither is education invariably a merit good, although it can be said that children benefit from education more than they think they do.

However, two aspects of education lead some to believe that it should be a public sector activity. First, many of the beneficiaries—the children—are considered to be too young to make choices for themselves. Second, it is said government should make the choice for them and should provide the service because parents may not recognize their children's educational needs or have the means to pay for meeting them.

This argument is weak for two reasons. First, it relates not specifically to education, but to all services provided for people who are not able to look after their own affairs. These include not only the very young and the very old, but also those incapacitated by disease. The fact that some people, such as the very young, are unable to look after themselves implies that society has a responsibility to ensure that their interests are not neglected. But it by no means implies that education should be provided by a public agency. Society requires that young children be looked after. It quite rightly punishes parents who neglect their children and in some cases removes neglected children from parental care. But the duty of the state to ensure that children are not neglected does not imply, for example, that children have to be fed in state institutions. Similarly, the proposition that society has an interest in ensuring that children obtain an education does not imply that the education has to be provided by a public agency.

Second, there is no obvious indication that state provision is the best solution for poor families who cannot afford to pay for their children's education. The needs of these families can be met by systems of student loans, or by scholarships (grants). As noted in chapter 1, public authorities can provide money for a service without providing the service itself. And there are strong arguments for having private institutions serve these people: private institutions are more likely to tailor their curricula to the needs of their clients; they are more likely to be economical in the use of their teachers and of other scarce resources and have greater incentives than government agencies to avoid waste; and private schools are better adapted than state institutions to change their methods to meet new requirements.

Furthermore, "free education" is not necessarily the best way of advancing the interests of the poor. Many developing countries, for example, lack the resources to provide all children with more than some years of elementary education. In order to advance to higher levels, children have to pass examinations or show other evidence of academic progress. In this selection process, children from poor families are at a substantial disadvantage because the children of better-off parents have better health and learning conditions and a more favorable cultural environment. As a result, the children of the better-off are able to capture most of the free places available at the higher levels. Places may be found for poor children who are brilliant enough to succeed under the most adverse circumstances but, in general, poor children either drop out of the educational system or, if their parents are able to find the fees, go to a fee-paying school. Considerations of these kinds suggest that the best way to help the children of the poor (such as those in Bombay, mentioned earlier) might be not to provide free education to all children, but to introduce special programs to help underprivileged families. In this connection, it is possible that the most cost-effective form of assistance to young children would be prenatal and postnatal care for their mothers.

Another reason frequently given for the public provision of education is that it is necessary for national unity or defense. This reasoning lies behind the indigenous education of young men in Africa and the provision of free public education in frontier areas of seventeenth-century China. One can find more modern examples in societies that absorb people from different origins; for example, the U.S. public school is regarded as the "melting pot," which takes in children as immigrants and discharges them as cultural Americans. Similarly it is claimed that in Israel compulsory army service promotes cultural cohesion. The other side of this coin is the reluctance of minority communities to lose their cultural inheritance; for example, the Chinese in San Francisco insist on running their own schools. The desire of governments to influence the education of their citizens and the conflicts that can arise thereby between cultural groups raise issues of acute political sensitivity that cannot be pursued here. If governments are impelled by reasons of state to provide education in their territories, there is little that outsiders can say on the subject. However, the costs of this approach can be considerable, as may be seen from the results in Uganda.

In 1962 Uganda gained its independence, and in the following decade the government obtained a monopoly over the training of teachers, school inspections, the appointment of school management committees, the contracting and the purchasing of school furnishings and supplies, and the handling of all school funds. Significant losses in efficiency ensued. Before independence, most primary schools were associated with religious institutions (Catholic, Protestant, or Muslim), and each school had a large degree of financial and administrative independence. Schools were run by committees that had the power to allocate the funds available for the school and to appoint the headmaster, who was responsible for day-to-day management, including the appointment of other teachers and the purchase of supplies. Schools were subject to inspection by the Catholic, Protestant, or Muslim agencies, which had a strong interest in maintaining school standards because of interreligious rivalry.

Following the postindependence reforms, individual schools lost the power to govern their own affairs. The government combined schools into groups of three or four and put a management committee in charge of each group. School fees were made uniform throughout the country, and thus serious burdens were imposed on poor families and poor districts. All teachers were placed on the same salary scale and were appointed and placed by the Ministry of Education, and the local schools had no say about their selection. Furniture was no longer made to order for individual schools, but was standardized and had to be obtained from designated suppliers at double the cost of furniture available locally. Moreover, under the old system, local schools could order their own supplies out of funds for which the school's management committee was responsible. Under the new system, school fees were collected by the headmasters, but remitted to district education offices. These funds were to have been held for the credit of the schools and used to pay the Uganda School Supply Ltd. (a state monopoly) for supplies, but some of these funds were inexplicably diverted so that the schools did not receive their supplies. Researchers noticed that school supplies tended to go to the schools closest to the supply depots (particularly in urban areas), presumably because headmasters of these schools could readily visit the depots and collect all the supplies needed, whereas rural schools without private transportation had to depend on delivery through "normal channels" and tended to receive less than their quota (Heyneman 1983).

The example from Uganda illustrates that even though the centralization of schools may have its advantages—in this case, weakening of the religious and ethnic connections can be considered an advantage by some—the costs can be substantial.

Private Education in Developing Countries

The preceding sections have provided some of the reasons that might be advanced for and against privately provided education. But is it practicable, in this day and age, to provide education privately in developing countries? The following sections deal with this question by looking at examples of

> Privately provided education
> (primary, secondary, university, and vocational)
> Education loan plans
> Scholarship plans.

Private Primary and Secondary Education

Chinese Education in Southeast Asia. The schools set up in the first half of this century by Chinese immigrant communities in Southeast Asia—that is, in Indonesia, Malaysia, the Philippines, Singapore, and Thailand—demonstrate the viability of providing private education for children of all age groups and income classes (some very poor). Private tutorial groups providing a classical education for a small number of children have been common in many expatriate Chinese societies. In the twentieth century, the concept was expanded and new schools were established to provide a modern, Chinese-style education to all Chinese youth, both boys and girls. In some areas, such as Singapore, these Chinese schools received governmental help. Elsewhere, as in the Philippines, the Chinese schools were privately financed, as are most secondary schools and universities in that country today. These schools provided a much more demanding education than did other schools in the Philippines because they were allowed to operate only on the condition that they followed the standard Filipino curriculum in addition to the Chinese curriculum. To meet this requirement, many Chinese schools offered the Filipino curriculum in the morning and the Chinese curriculum in the afternoon. The double primary curriculum was covered in the normal six years but at the secondary level it took another six years to complete, whereas the normal Filipino secondary curriculum takes only four years. The quality of this education may be gauged by the fact that those who completed it were eligible to enter universities in Taiwan. Students could also continue their university education in Chinese colleges in the Philippines, where teachers were trained to teach in the local Chinese schools.

The number of children being educated in Chinese schools in the Philippines increased rapidly after World War II, rising from 20,000 students in 1948, to 56,000 in 1956, 64,000 in 1963, and 75,000 in 1971. Despite a certain amount of local hostility to the Chinese schools, they were allowed to operate by virtue of the 1947 Treaty of Amit between the governments of Taiwan and the Philippines. In 1975, the Philippine government ended diplomatic relations with Taiwan and removed the main diplomatic reason for allowing the Chinese schools to continue. By 1976, there were only 138 Chinese schools operating in the Philippines, down from the 1971 total of 152 schools. In April 1976, the government announced that all Chinese schools were to be banned from offering Chinese subjects other than the Chinese language, and that the Chinese classes were to be limited to two periods a day. The schools were also to be opened to Filipino students, and knowledge of Chinese was no longer to be a requirement for admission.

Although the future of the Chinese schools in the Philippines has become uncertain as a result of these restrictions, these schools have shown that private education at both the primary and secondary level can be financially and academically viable even when free public education is widely available. In this example, it was available at the primary level. At the secondary level, however, most Filipino schools, whether private or public, charged fees. The figures on enrollments suggest that the proportion of students proceeding to Chinese secondary education was comparable to the percentage proceeding to non-Chinese schools. This might indicate that, at the secondary level, some parents transferred their children to non-Chinese schools, perhaps because of the possibility that their children might choose to go to a non-Chinese university (Orr 1977).

Pakistan. When Pakistan became independent in 1947, education was not widely available, and both the government and the private sector made a strenuous effort to improve the situation. The establishment and management of private schools in the Punjab has been documented by Ahmed and Mirza (1975), who visited and described eleven privately managed schools there. One of these, known as school "N" in Lahore, provides an interesting example of the private provision of education in Pakistan.

The school was founded in 1951 by four people, three of whom were journalists. Their objective was to establish an Islamic system of education in Pakistan. The school was to provide a pure educational environment in which to design a model system of education and training; create a generation of Pakistanis who are true Muslims in their hearts, minds, thoughts, and actions; and develop the mental and physical potentialities of the pupils so as to make them useful and enlightened citizens of Pakistan. The school attracted many children and flourished. In 1955, it added a middle school, and in 1958 a high school. The high school was separated from the first-level school in the late 1950s. The enrollment in the high school increased from 225 in 1961 to 325 in 1966 and 459 in 1971 (more than double the figure for 1961). The enrollment could have been higher but the school could not accommodate all those seeking admission.

In the early years the school faced many financial problems. As a result, the teachers often had to go without pay for months at a time or were given just enough money to purchase meals and pay their rent. However, the teachers were imbued with the same spirit that had prompted the opening of the school, and they suffered the inconvenience with fortitude. Despite the growing financial problems, the founders were determined to keep the school going and thus asked the parents of pupils to pay a subscription in addition to the government-approved fees.

At that point, about 86 percent of the income of the school was derived from private sources. Government support, which had increased in the mid-1960s to about 20 percent, dropped to less than 10 percent in the late 1960s. In 1971 the government grant, which was already shrinking, was further reduced to one-half of the previous allocation. This was an unexpected cut, but the school was able to absorb the shock because donations had been growing with the increasing requirements. In fact, in the words of the headmaster, "The donors have never failed the school; they have always come forward to help whenever we have gone to them, only we are shy of asking as we do not want to get money from someone who could interfere with the policies of the school." The school, however, accepted donations only from individuals who were either members of the management committee or were otherwise committed to the objectives of the school. Inevitably, their number was not large; in 1971, only eighteen people made contributions to the school funds.

The quality of education provided by the school was high, dropout rates were negligible, and the pupils did well in the public examinations.

Self-Help in Kenya. The self-help effort in Kenya can be traced back to the traditional pattern of communal work and cooperative effort characteristic of African societies. This tradition, along with the European form of school education introduced into Kenya by the missionaries, helped to shape Kenya's educational system, although the European schools were not accepted at first. The missionaries had built a few model schools on their stations, but initially attracted only such people as famine victims, outcasts, and the very poor. Gradually, however, Africans began to realize the potential of schools as a means of improving their material way of life and their relative status in colonial society. Thus partnerships developed in which local communities provided land, built classrooms, and eventually provided support for teachers, while the missionaries developed teaching materials and trained the teachers.

Following independence in 1963, the *Harambee* movement emphasized self-help at all social levels. Once the movement got under way, there was an immediate general demand for secondary education, particularly in areas that already had high primary school enrollments. In those areas, many had discovered on leaving primary school that they could not find employment without some secondary education. Furthermore, African families who had observed the success of elite schools in Nairobi either sent their children to those schools when they could or used all means available to improve local education. The more progressive districts—where wealth, organizing experience, and talent were more readily available—led the way in the self-help education movement. Although some attention was given to expanding and improving first-level education, priority was given to the new task of extending this stage of education, both at the preschool level for the three- to six-year-olds, and at the secondary level, where schools were needed to cater to the rapidly increasing numbers coming out of the first-level schools.

The self-help groups were able to channel a number of important resources into new schools: local materials and voluntary labor, cash, professional advice, and professional assistance. All of these were tapped, in various degrees, by local communities. However, three factors in particular affected the establishment of Harambee schools. First, competition between different areas played an important role. News of the establishment of schools in one area led communities in other areas to hold public meetings and gather support for new schools there. Second, the Harambee movement developed a partnership with the church-missionary bodies. Legally, no school could be established without an "approved manager," and in the early days after independence only two such categories were recognized: the government itself and the various church-missionary bodies. Because of the bureaucratic difficulties of obtaining "approved manager" status, most new groups were unable to establish schools. Many schools found a way out of this predicament by becoming associated with an approved missionary society and registering under its name. In some cases, the relationship was purely nominal, but the interests of the Harambee committees in the church caught the imagination of several missionary societies, with the result that some church-missionary schools became more African and less Western than they had been earlier. Third, on the principle of "no taxation without representation," self-help is invariably associated with a committee of local people, who provide a focus for the activities of those working to start a school and subsequently play a major role in its management. School committees in Kenya have proved to be so useful that they have been given official status and have even been established for schools that are government financed.

The idea of the school committee arose when formal schools were first established in Kenya and communities had to come together to provide land and buildings. At that time, schools were closely tied in with mission churches, and committees tended to be composed of church elders. In due course, however, democratic procedures developed. Although church nominees still sit on many committees, these are now largely composed of members elected by the locality.

The actual process of election varies, but committees are usually elected at open meetings by the parents from the school catchment area. Ideally, respected and responsible people are chosen, and the committee becomes the focal point for educational interest in the area. It is the official body that negotiates with the educational authorities and others on all matters concerning the school. Together with the headmaster, the committee also determines the type of support that parents will be asked to give the school: this may consist of such tasks as constructing or repairing buildings or digging latrines. In cases where parents fail to turn up, the committee usually imposes a "fine"—that is, it requires financial contributions in lieu of labor. The committee may arrange money collections among parents to provide for building materials, and it has to account for the funds raised and used. Further, it has to keep the parents informed about school affairs, arrange for parents' visiting days and parent-teacher meetings, and also keep the headmaster and teachers informed of the parents' views concerning the way the school is being run. It is likely to press for good examination results and to become critical of teachers if these are not obtained.

The Unesco publication *Organization and Financing of Self-Help Education in Kenya* (Anderson 1973) describes some schools that have been financed, built, and managed by local self-help groups. Some of these operations are discussed in the following subsections.

Thogoto Unaided Day-Care Center. The Thogoto nursery school is located eighteen miles from Nairobi. When it was built, it served an area that was poor and practically illiterate. It was developed in the 1950s by Red Cross and community workers in the area, who joined together to bring groups of children, many of whom were fatherless and suffering from malnutrition, to centers to be fed and cared for. The Red Cross eventually relinquished its responsibility, but the community development assistant for the area fostered the school and encouraged it to be self-supporting.

The school was controlled by a committee that consisted of a chairman, secretary, treasurer, community development assistant, and ten other members. There were few "formal" committee meetings and no minutes were kept of proceedings. Nevertheless, the committee exercised firm control. For example, if parents were unable to pay fees, the chairman was authorized to rent them some of the school land for a limited period in order that they might work it and thus raise the necessary fees. This arrangement worked surprisingly well. The committee organized communal work and required parents to pay 5 Kenya shillings (KSh) per day if they failed to participate. It also appointed staff and negotiated their salaries.

The committee chairman was a well-respected leader in the area who was a firm believer in self-help. A man of about sixty with first-level teaching qualifications, he had taught for many years and had been headmaster of one of the nearby first-level schools for three years. He was involved in other projects in the area besides the day-care center. The treasurer was a local business woman of about forty who was literate and influential. The secretary was a thirty-year-old housewife, with first-level schooling but no further education. The rest of the committee consisted of seven men and three women, all middle-aged and respected members of the community.

The salaried staff consisted of two. One, mentioned above, had worked at the center since its inception. She had had about four years of education herself and could speak a little English. Her role was primarily to supervise the children at playtime and contribute to the singing activities. She received a salary of KSh72 a month. The second teacher was much younger and had had eight years of education. She was responsible for the actual teaching at the school.

The school had no fixed timetable. Children started arriving about 8 A.M. and many would still be arriving an hour later. Most of the time was occupied by storytelling and playing outside. The children also enjoyed singing. In the middle of the morning, the children had a long break during which they helped to clean the school under the supervision of the teachers. Afterward, the younger teacher taught reading and writing. The methods were crude because teachers were not well trained, but some of the older children (those aged seven) could do a little reading and writing. The youngest children, those three to four years old, had a compulsory rest after 11 A.M. The rest room was equipped with hard benches, sacks, and one or two blankets. School ended at about noon.

The school was built of offcut timber and had a tin roof. There was little in the way of equipment—one small blackboard and a few books. "Writing" was usually done with sticks in the sand outside. Most of the money for the original building came from personal donations, and there were plans to construct an additional classroom and provide more desks. The labor required for this project was to come from the parents on a community work basis.

The school had a bank account on which checks could be drawn when authorized by three of the four signatories: the chairman, treasurer, secretary, and community development assistant. Most of the expenses consisted of salaries, and income was obtained from school fees, which were KSh10 per term. Fees totaled about

KSh500 per term as there were approximately 50 children at the nursery. Salaries amounted to KSh474 per term, so there was virtually no money left to buy equipment after a few defaulted or children withdrew during the term, as often happened. However, there was no backlog of debt and the center was financially self-supporting.

Kahuhu Unaided First-Level School. The Kahuhu school was established in 1967 through the joint effort of the local Roman Catholic church and the local community, notably the twelve people who formed the school committee. They provided ideas and drive, but did not know how to start such a venture, particularly how to finance the school. However, with the assistance of the local Roman Catholic priest, the project got under way. He was instrumental in formalizing the committee, which became strongly influenced by him. He established himself as a consultant to the committee, and his advice was sought by the four most important committee members. He also acted as treasurer for the committee, even though there was an appointed committee treasurer.

The role of the Catholic church in the venture was of special interest, for the area was predominantly Protestant, and there was a tradition of rivalry around Kahuhu between the Catholic church (the Consolata Catholic Mission) and the Protestant church (the Presbyterian Church of East Africa). The Catholic church made an initial contribution consisting of half of the corrugated iron sheeting required for the first two classrooms together with a substantial loan. The committee also relied on the church for assistance with the school's legal constitution and its accounts. School fees (KSh20 per child per term) were paid directly to the headmaster, who then sent the money to the bishop's office in Nyeri, where an official arranged to have it banked. These fees were used to pay the salaries of the two teachers (KSh172 per month) and the headmaster (KSh205 a month) and to buy books and stationery. Thus, the money for school fees was normally not handled by the local committee. The committee kept a record of parents, however, and checked whether they appeared for community work on appointed days. A fine of KSh5 was imposed on those who failed to show up. Otherwise, the committee handled finance only when money had to be raised for specific projects. Such projects had been kept to a minimum for in 1967, after a decision to levy KSh40 per parent to pay off the debt for the school roof, eleven parents withdrew their children. Withdrawal had to be resisted at all costs, as the school had to be run to full capacity to be financially viable. From time to time emergencies arose with regard to finance: for example, in August 1968 and December 1969, both school holidays, money could not be found to pay teachers' salaries.

This case shows why some of the independent schools had difficulty in maintaining a proper accounting system. The committee did not draw in the money and then run the school. Instead, the school just seemed to continue, although many parents were in debt, teachers were occasionally unpaid, and the committee members were forced to provide money from their own pockets. If accounts were to be audited, especially if they showed a deficit, parents might become disillusioned and might then withdraw their children and jeopardize the school still further. Clearly, the Kahuhu school was not financially viable, but it kept going.

An Unaided Second-Level School. Kenyatta High School, in the Mahiga, an isolated part of the Nyeri district, was built in 1965–66 by voluntary self-help. The organizing committee developed around a nucleus of old Kikuyu independent school leaders who, soon after independence, began to urge the people to start a self-help second-level school in the area to replace one closed down by the colonial authorities during the emergency. A committee was formed and began to organize a massive self-help effort to construct a school. Initially, an adult population of about 7,000 people was called upon to support the school, but as plans for other second-level schools developed in the locality, the actual supporting force dropped to about 4,000 adults.

At first, this committee was under the sponsorship of the African Independent Pentecostal Church, which had been responsible for many independent African self-help schools in colonial times. The elders who came to the first meeting had considerable experience, both in organizing self-help work and in running schools. Therefore, despite setbacks due to the death and illness of one or two members and some serious disagreements between various local and religious factions, an effective and well-led school committee emerged, able to unite the 4,000 residents of the southern part of Mahiga location in support of the school. Capital development received some help from Nyeri County Council, the Community Development Department, and other donors (for example tradesmen in Nyeri), but the total cost of this help was only about KSh14,000. Thus, well over 90 percent of the money for this capital development was found by the local community.

Construction of the school started in September 1965. Collections were made in cash and materials, cement, stone, and so on, and self-help labor, provided mainly through women's cooperative working groups, was used for the heavy work, such as digging and providing ballast for the foundations and sand and shingle for concrete mixing. Such materials were obtained without cost from local river valleys, but the building stones had to be transported by a contractor from a quarry seven miles away. Small-scale local contractors provided the building skills, and an old Ministry of Works plan was the basis for the classroom design.

The main school block was divided into eight classrooms and an office. Three teachers' houses were built, and a hydraulic pump was installed to provide piped water. Nearly all the furniture for the school and the teachers' houses was built on the site by local workmen using only hand tools.

Total costs are difficult to assess. The cost of all the building materials, provision of water, and leveling and draining of land has been estimated at approximately KSh180,000, but if the heavy labor and managerial expenses are taken into account, the cost is considerably higher. If a contractor from Nyeri had taken on the task, he would have charged at least KSh300,000. The cost of a government classroom of similar dimensions would have been at least twice as high as the actual cost to the Mahiga community.

Initially, the main problem was the provision of education rather than capital development. No suitably trained local headmaster was available to advise the committee on educational matters, and most of the staff obtained in the early years were second-level graduates with poor grades who were looking for temporary posts until they could find more permanent work in some other sphere. The teaching was erratic and for the most part of poor quality; too few textbooks were available and, in general, they were badly chosen. Even so, the results of its first Kenya Junior Secondary Examination (form 2) were only just below the national average for unaided schools.

In 1967, the management committee obtained the services of two volunteers, one a university graduate and one with a higher-level certificate, who provided support for the school staff and an untrained local headmaster with a secondary school certificate. Since then, the teaching and textbook situation has improved considerably with the help of a series of volunteers, and the school has progressed to the form-4 level. The first school certificate examination was taken in December 1969.

As an institution, Kenyatta High School now runs remarkably smoothly. It is organized along the traditional lines of second-level schools in a former British colony, with a house-prefect system. All pupils buy school uniforms, attend lessons regularly, and contribute to school maintenance by cleaning classrooms and looking after the school yard. The school offers a full range of certificate subjects, including general science. Extracurricular activities are well organized and include games, a debating club, a dramatic society, and a young farmers' club, which is strongly supported by the pupils and has its own pigs, poultry, and vegetable plots.

Recurrent expenses are handled by the secretary and treasurer of the committee, who bank the fees and approve any disbursements.

Table 2–3. Kenyatta High School, Accounts for 1969

Income	Kenya shillings	Expenses	Kenya shillings
Fees		*Teachers' salaries*	
Form 1: 30 pupils at KSh650 a year (KSh450, fees + KSh200 building)	19,500	2 graduate volunteers at 700 per month	16,800
Form 2: 40 pupils at KSh600 a year	24,000	2 higher school certified volunteers at 600 a month	14,400
Form 3: 35 pupils at KSh700 a year	24,500	1 higher school certified teacher, local, at 650 a month	7,800
Form 4: 24 pupils at KSh700 a year	17,500	1 school certified teacher, local, at 500 a month	6,000
Total income	85,500	Subtotal	45,000
		Administrative staff	
		2 maintenance staff at 300 a month	7,200
		2 office staff at 180 a month	4,320
		1 typist at 150 a month	1,800
		2 watchmen at 75 a month	1,800
		Subtotal	15,120
		Total salaries	60,120
		Miscellaneous (estimated)	
		Cost of stationery and equipment	8,500
		Cost of maintenance and building materials	7,000
		Committee, transport, and office expenses	6,000
		Balance	3,880
		Total expenses	85,500

Source: APICE (1979).

The headmaster advises on expenses but does not handle any money. Table 2-3 sets out the accounts for 1969 and shows that the school now runs almost entirely on fees, which are supplemented by considerable donations for equipment. The British Council provided tools, chemistry equipment, and other materials. Books have come from the U.S. Agency for International Development (USAID) and several individuals and commercial enterprises, which have also provided science equipment, including a microscope. In addition, the volunteer teachers have sometimes used portions of their salary to buy teaching materials. The accounts of the school suggest that thus far the Mahiga community has managed to meet the expenses of a four-year, second-level school leading to the East African school certificate examination. However, the considerable work put in by the committee secretary and treasurer may not be adequately accounted for.

Kenyatta High School is a tribute to local community energy and sacrifice. It reveals the capacity of a relatively poor peasant community to meet its education costs. The situation at Mahiga is not typical of most Harambee schools, however. Although conditions vary greatly, few schools handle their finances as effectively as this one. Many are like Kahuhu first-level school and have accumulated debts. Kenyatta High School has shown that with a sufficiently able and dedicated committee, a small second-level school can run on an annual per capita cost per annum of about KSh30–KSh35, as it did in 1969. But it must be stressed that the basis on which the school operated was very fragile. Thus, Anderson (1973) questions whether Harambee education is viable and appropriate in the long run. In any case, it clearly demonstrates the enthusiasm of African communities for modern education and their ability to obtain it under the most difficult circumstances.

Private Universities

A description, or even a listing, of private universities in developing countries, is beyond the scope of this volume. Most are in Latin America. As an example of the number and variety of these institutions, table 2-4 lists twenty-one private universities in Argentina, together with numbers of faculty members, teachers, and students.

Technical Universities

Many private institutions for higher technical education exist in developing countries. They range from the Asian Institute of

Technology (AIT) in Bangkok to the El Zamorano agricultural school in Honduras.

Asian Institute of Technology. Founded by the Central and East Asia Treaty Organization (CEATO), the AIT has since become independent and offers postgraduate courses in a variety of fields, including agriculture, energy, and transportation. The AIT has developed a unique method of fund-raising: it appeals to governments, charitable foundations, and businesses for scholarships for its students and has been successful enough to attract a high-caliber faculty, which in turn draws high-caliber students.

Table 2–4. Private Universities in Argentina

University and year of data	Number of			Student-teacher ratio	Loan schemes (L) and scholarships (S)
	Schools	Students	Teachers		
Pontificia Universidad Católica Argentina (1959)	13	10,777	2,449	4.4:1	(L), (S)
Universidad del Salvador (1959)	14	6,871	1,652	4.2:1	—
Instituto Tecnológico de Buenos Aires (1960)	1	647	280	2.3:1	—
Universidad del Museo Social Argentino (1961)	6	1,711	381	4.5:1	—
Universidad de Belgrano (1968)	6	6,871	878	8.1:1	—
Universidad Argentina de la Empresa (1968)	6	6,648	577	11.5:1	—
Universidad de Moron (1968)	10	11,681	1,410	8.3:1	—
Universidad Católica de La Plata (1968)	6	3,652	552	6.6:1	(L), (S)
Universidad Católica de Cordoba (1959)	9	4,591	828	5.5:1	(L), (S)
Universidad "Juan Agustin Maza" (1963)	6	1,386	239	5.8:1	(L)
Universidad del Aconcagua (1968)	4	838	160	5.2:1	—
Universidad Católica de Cuyo (1963)	7	1,882	431	4.3:1	(L), (S)
Universidad Católica de Santa Fe (1960)	10	2,126	440	4.8:1	(L), (S)

Table 2–4   (continued)

University and year of data	Number of			Student-teacher ratio	Loan schemes (L) and scholarships (S)
	Schools	Students	Teachers		
Universidad Católica de Santiago del Estero (1965)	4	2,061	173	11.9:1	(L), (S)
Universidad del Norte (1968)	10	2,572	419	6.1:1	—
Centro de Altos Estudios en Ciencias Exactas (1968)	1	3,515	168	20.9:1	—
Universidad Argentina John F. Kennedy (1968)	14	6,075	246	24.7:1	—
Universidad de la Marina Mercante	2	701	79	8.9:1	—
Universidad Notarial Argentina (1968)	16	1,473	62	23.8:1	—
Universidad de Concepción del Uruguay	2	398	79	5:1	—
Universidad Católica de Salta (1967)	7	2,223	302	7.4:1	(L), (S)

—Information unknown.
Source: World Bank.

Escuela Agrícola Panamericana (Pan American School of Agriculture). This agricultural school, also known as El Zamorano, is a high-level training institution founded in 1981 by an American, Wilson Popenoe, a pioneer in tropical horticulture. It is located in Honduras, about twenty-five miles from the capital Tegucigalpa. Its property includes 2,600 hectares of arable land and pine tree forest. The school has more than a hundred buildings, which contain classrooms, dormitories, dining rooms, dental and medical clinics, a library, a botanic garden, and sports and recreation facilities. This small college is completely independent of the government and has established an international reputation as one of the finest education centers in its class.

The school has twenty-five full-time teachers who reside on the premises. It has 250 students from fourteen Latin American countries who take an intensive three-year study program that includes both theoretical and practical work. In 1984 the school had 1,585 technical graduates, many of whom became teachers, while some became agronomists with governments or the private sector.

The annual budget of the school is equivalent to US$1.5 million. It offers scholarships that cover living expenses as well as tuition. Students not receiving scholarships pay the equivalent of US$600 a year for tuition. This amount represents 10 percent of the education costs. The other main source of finance is a fund set up by the United Fruit Company in 1941. The school also relies on donations from individuals, companies, and foundations.

Management Schools

The private sector in developing countries has also been active in financing and managing management schools. It has been assisted in this effort by charitable organizations such as the Ford and Rockefeller foundations. These schools depend for finance partly on fees from students (often paid by their employers) and partly on gifts from industrial and commercial firms. The Asian Institute of Management (AIM) is one example of these schools (see Thompson, Fogel, and Danner 1976).

Asian Institute of Management. AIM is a private nonprofit educational organization in Manila established under the laws of the Republic of the Philippines. It is a graduate school of business administration modeled on the Harvard Business School. AIM is an outgrowth of a cooperative effort of three leading graduate schools of business—the colleges of Business Administration of the University of the Philippines (U.P.), De La Salle College, and the Ateneo de Manila. In 1963, the Ford Foundation provided these institutions with a grant of US$250,000 that was to be used to strengthen business education. The grant was also expected to stimulate research, which would lead to the preparation of case studies for classroom use.

Although this effort was successful, the three institutions recognized the need for one strong graduate school with full-time faculty and students. A proposal was developed for a joint endeavor, but U.P. College of Business Administration dropped out, leaving De La Salle and Ateneo to pursue the project. The rectors of Ateneo and De La Salle solicited financial and other support for the project. USAID was enlisted in the effort. The Ford Foundation, which had provided the original grant for upgrading the business schools, was an important catalyst. In September 1968, AIM was incorporated as an affiliate of the Ateneo de Manila University and De La Salle College for the purpose of offering high-quality, full-time management education designed to meet Asian needs.

The package brought together to form AIM consisted of a donation by the Ayala Corporation of 13,000 square meters of prime real estate, then worth about 6.5 million pesos (US$1.6 million), in the prestigious Makati commercial district; a donation by the Eugenio Lopez Foundation of 6.5 million pesos (US$1.6 million) for the building; a grant by the Ford Foundation of US$244,000 for faculty development (including visiting professors during the initial period); a grant by USAID of 1.3 million pesos (US$341,000) for library facilities and equipment; and a loan of 3 million pesos (US$769,000) from the social security system (a government financial institution) to finance student loans. In addition, twenty of the most prominent Philippine and foreign business firms and individual businessmen gave an average of 250,000 pesos (US$64,100) each to endow faculty chairs. In November 1968, the AIM Scientific Research Foundation was incorporated as a private nonprofit organization to accept and manage funds from donations and endowments. Besides the five leading "social investors" and the donors of the twenty faculty chairs, eighteen charter members of the foundation contributed large, though varying, amounts. It was an impressive mobilization of private funds for an educational project.

Initially AIM offered a two-year full-time master of business management program, but now other major programs are available. In addition, AIM offers several short management programs, usually in cooperation with industry associations. For example, it has developed a special two-week course for airline executives from all over Asia. The program is considered to be highly useful to the airlines; therefore, AIM is able to charge full costs plus a small profit, which can be used to subsidize its regular programs. As the institute grew in regional importance, it received increasing regional support. For example, Sony Corporation of Japan endowed a faculty chair, and a group of Malaysian financial institutions have contributed to a faculty chair to be filled by a Malaysian.

AIM has some income from endowments, but not enough to cover all its expenses. The gap is filled by tuition fees, by varying the program mix so that more fee-producing, short training programs can be offered to meet specific needs of the business sector, and by pricing these programs high enough to leave some surplus for the basic academic programs. The institute also solicits grants (for example, from USAID for the Asian scholarship program) and accepts research commitments (for example from International Business Machines [IBM] in the Philippines for work on the development of information systems).

Local and overseas scholarships are available. For Filipino candidates, there is a loan fund of 3 million pesos, made possible by the social security system. Students may borrow the necessary funds for the program at relatively low rates of interest.

Vocational Training

Private sector vocational training is particularly important in developing countries. Those who provide it can succeed only by teaching subjects for which there is immediate demand, and by teaching them well. The situation in Ibadan, Nigeria, in the 1960s provides a case in point:

> In Ibadan there are no less than 327 typing institutions, some with only two or three typewriters, some with as many as twenty. Because so many of the unemployed school leavers attend these "schools," a 10 percent sample design was worked out and 32 proprietors interviewed. The typing schools have been started in recent years by civil servants, clerks to big firms, a few school teachers, a few enterprising school leavers who themselves have had training in the same system. These schools draw not only those without jobs, but also those with some kind of work who want to improve their prospects. Some take clients only in the afternoons and evenings, when the proprietor himself is present to give the coaching. Many operate all day with typewriters clattering from early morning to late at night and echelons of pupils coming and going at the end of each hour. A senior pupil may supervise the trainees during the owner's absence during the day; in return he will have his fees waived and perhaps other compensation as well.
>
> Other skills can also be learned part-time from qualified tutors: for instance draughtsmanship, radio and television engineering, and sign-writing. Fees are well established; for example, "radio and T.V. engineering" for 2 to 2½ hours each weekday costs £1 5s.0d. [1 pound, 5 shillings] a month. Most artisan skills can be learned part-time from a master or journeyman by special arrangement, with fees set by a competitive market. (Lloyd, Mabogunje, and Awe 1967, p. 204.)

Numerous formal training schemes in developing countries are provided by the private sector. Two examples from Africa are given to illustrate the variety available.

Nigerian Drivers and Maintenance School, Lagos. In the early 1960s, the Nigerian Motor Drivers and Allied Transport Workers Union became concerned about the increasing demand for motor drivers and about the horrific number of road accidents in the country, so it decided to establish a motor driving school. In 1963 the first apprentices were admitted to the school, which offered one course: driving and vehicle maintenance in theory and practice. The course lasted three months, and the school ran three sessions each year. Between sessions students took their initial driving tests or repeated tests if they failed. Different motor engines were used to teach the apprentices the rudimentary workings of a vehicle engine.

The school opened with one building on five acres of land on the outskirts of Lagos. The building included a workshop, a classroom and attached storeroom, kitchen, toilet facilities, and a gasoline-filling station owned by the school. There was also a 1,700-foot tarred driving range and a separate track for reversing. The school started with two secondhand Land Rovers but later acquired more than a dozen training vehicles. The director was also the general secretary of the Nigerian Motor Drivers and Allied Transport Workers Union. The school's four driving instructors held driver mechanic certificates, grade 1.

The school's annual cost was estimated to be US$25,000, which did not include the purchase cost of land, buildings, and vehicles. Fees were paid by students but did not cover the costs of the school. Most of the funds were provided by the Nigerian Motor Drivers and Allied Transport Workers Union and international labor bodies such as the Austrian Federation of Labor, the International Transport Workers Federation, the American Federation of Labor and Congress of Industrial Organizations (AFL-CIO), and the African-American Labor Center. The school received no financial assistance from the Nigerian federal or state government (see Sheffield and Diejomash 1972).

Pilots' Training Center and Aviation Maintenance School, Addis Ababa. In the mid-1960s the management of Ethiopian Airlines established two schools to promote the participation of Ethiopian nationals in the company. The first was designed to train pilots, the second to train aviation maintenance technicians. The official goal of the program was to ensure a continuous flow of qualified personnel to meet the operational needs of the airline and train as many Ethiopian personnel as possible within the shortest practicable time. Although the school was started for the benefit of Ethiopian personnel and Ethiopian Airlines, it later developed as a training center for pilots and technicians from other African countries.

Both schools were located at the Addis Ababa Airport. The maintenance school was probably the best equipped of its kind in Africa. It employed highly qualified veteran instructors, many of them Ethiopians, and its curriculum met both U.S. and U.K. standards of repair instruction.

The maintenance school offered three-year courses in which the first eighteen months were devoted to basic training, and the last eighteen months to specialized training. Classes typically contained twenty to forty technicians. To gain entrance, candidates had to meet physical fitness criteria and hold a high school diploma or equivalent. The full costs of training are not known, but the fees charged to trainees from other countries were equivalent to US$100 per month for room and board and the same for tuition. Thus, for each non-Ethiopian, the total cost of training came to US$7,200.

The pilots' school had a fifteen-month curriculum that was divided into three phases: preflight (three months), primary phase (five months), and advanced phase (seven months). Graduates were qualified to serve as second officers on jets or as first officers on DC-3's. Fees for non-Ethiopians were equivalent to US$105,000 for the fifteen-month course.

Both schools were divisions of Ethiopian Airlines and depended for their financing on long-term government loans that were routed through the airline. Although the faculty was mainly Ethiopian, many of the teachers at the beginning were supplied by Trans World Airlines (TWA) under contract (see Sheffield and Diejomash 1972).

Apprenticeship Schemes

Apprenticeship is a long-term arrangement (whether by written contract or not) in which the trainee surrenders his or her labor for an agreed length of time and receives in return instruction in a trade or profession. Often the apprentice pays an annual fee to the master and at some point may receive wages or food and shelter from the master. The system can be found throughout the world and has been in use for many centuries, but it has been particularly important for private sector activities in Africa: Calaway (1973) has shown that 75 percent of Nigeria's small business proprietors have been trained through this system, which imparts working skills to men and women denied formal education. Among the African industries in which apprenticeship plays an important role are textiles, tailoring, carpentry, and automobile and bicycle repair.

The local systems in Africa have no organized labor markets for apprentices. They commonly find work with the help of a parent, who approaches the proprietor, or the proprietor may discuss his needs with neighbors, parents, or relatives. Once recruited, an apprentice is not regarded as a worker with definite hours for work. Rather, he is seen as part of the establishment and is even expected to perform activities that are unrelated to his training schedule.

Entry into apprenticeship has no age limit or restrictions based on educational attainment. A youth just out of primary school may be apprenticed directly, or an elderly farmer from a land-scarce community may migrate to an urban area to learn a trade. Married unemployed women may do the same. In general, however, parents apprentice their children at a relatively young age, often between twelve and fourteen years of age. Because most apprentices are young, the decision to seek training is usually made by parents or by relatives who can finance the cost of training. When apprentices are old enough to make their own decisions concerning their careers, they essentially consider the same factors that their parents would. Important among these are the rates of return likely from training in different industries, which often depend on the demand and supply of skilled labor in a locality, and the relative success of people who have learned similar skills in the area.

When workers are free to change their jobs, apprenticeship schemes can generate inequities, in that firms that provide good training may find themselves losing trained staff to their competitors. One way to handle this problem is to ask trainees to pay for the training, either in cash or in an agreed period of employment at less than market rates. Another approach is to legislate for industry-wide training levies, which can be used to reimburse the firms that provide the training and also to finance industrial training centers. Such schemes are to be found throughout the developing world, for example, in Benin, Brazil, Kenya, Korea, Liberia, Malaysia, and Mexico.

Education Loan Plans

When education, especially professional education, becomes associated with increased earnings, the private sector might be expected to provide loans to promising students. For example, middle-aged market women in Ghana have been known to offer scholarships to promising young men so that they can study medicine or law in the United Kingdom, the only condition being that, on their return, they must marry the women and thus provide security for their old age. The young men are expected to fulfill their obligations; it is socially unacceptable to ignore one's obligations to a patron (see du Sautoy 1968).

However, comparatively few people finance their education by promising marriage. The more usual arrangement is to repay the loan in cash. But the riskiness of lending to students who lack collateral has inhibited financial institutions from making such loans. Furthermore, the combination of inflation and subsidized government credit has made private lending particularly difficult to obtain in many developing countries. Nevertheless, in recent years, a number of countries have established student loan schemes, most of which have involved the government as guarantor. Maureen Woodhall (1983) examined the international experience of student loans as a means of financing higher education and some of her findings are discussed in the following paragraphs.

Latin America

Most student loan schemes in the developing world can be found in Latin America. The first national scheme was the Instituto Colombiano de Crédito Educativo y Estudios Técnicos en el Exterior (ICETEX), which was established in 1950 by Gabriel Bettancour Mejia. Bettancour became interested in the subject as a result of his own experience in borrowing to finance his postgraduate education. By 1978, there were national loan institutions in at least eighteen countries in Latin America and the Caribbean, as well as a Pan-American fund administered by the Organization of American States (OAS) and a student loan scheme established by the Caribbean Development Bank for eleven small Caribbean countries. Table 2-5 lists twenty-four such institutions (some of them private) in sixteen Latin American countries.

The Latin American institutions cooperate internationally through the Pan-American Association of Educational Credit Associations (APICE), whose aims are "to foster the development of national and international systems for the financing of higher education using the student loan model, with the participation of the public and private sectors of the economy, in order to provide equality of opportunities to students, so that they can contribute to the cultural, economic and social transformations of their respective countries" (Woodhall 1983, p. 31). In addition to providing technical assistance to student loan institutions, APICE holds a Pan-American Congress on Educational Credit every two years,

Table 2–5. Summary of Educational Credit Institutions in Latin America

Country and institution	Year established	Sources of finance[a]
Argentina		
Instituto Nacional de Crédito Educativo (INCE)	1969	50 percent Treasury and Ministry of Social Welfare, 50 percent commercial banks
Bolivia		
Centro Impulsor de Educación Profesional CIDEP)	n.a.	
Brazil		
Fondo Nacional de Desarrollo de la Educación (FNDE)	1968	Tax incentives, federal lottery, bank deposits
Caixa Economica Federál	1976	Federal sport lottery, Bank of Brazil, Petrobras (state-owned oil company)
Associagas dos Profissionais Liberais Universitarios de Brasil (APLUB, a nonprofit trade union institution)	1971	Fees to institutions for services, donations from APLUB
Colombia		
Instituto Colombiano de Crédito Educativo y Estudios Técnicos en el Exterior (ICETEX)	1950	Government funds, administration of funds of enterprises, bank loans, Central Bank, IDB
Costa Rica		
Comisión Nacional de Préstamos para Educación (CONAPE)	1965	Central Bank, government funds, IDB
Chile		
Junta Nacional de Auxilio Escolar y Becas (JNAEB)	1964	Social security contributions, government funds
Catholic University of Chile	n.a.	
Ecuador		
Instituto Ecuatoriano de Crédito Educativo y Becas (IECE)	1971	Government funds, oil revenues, payroll tax
El Salvador		
Fondo de Garantia para el Crédito Educativo		Government funds
Fondo de Desarrollo Económico (FDE)		Central Bank
Honduras		
Educrédito	1968	Government funds, IDB, USAID

(Table continues on the following page.)

Table 2–5 (continued)

Country and institution	Year established	Sources of finance[a]
Jamaica		
Students' Loan Bureau	1971	Government funds, Bank of Jamaica, IDB
Mexico		
Consejo Nacional de Fomento Educativo	1971	n.a.
Banco de México Oficina de Crédito Educativo	1965	Federal government, Banco de México
Nicaragua		
Instituto Nicaraguense	1963	Private donations, USAID
Panama		
Instituto para la Formación y Aprovechamiento de los Recursos Humanos (IFARHU)	1965	Government funds, payroll tax (education insurance), IDB
Peru		
Instituto Peruano de Fomento Educativo (IPFE)	1962	Donations, bank loans, USAID
Instituto Nacional de Becas y Crédito Educativo (INABEC)	1973	Government funds
Dominican Republic		
Fundación de Crédito Educativo (FCE)	1964	Government funds, USAID, donations
Venezuela		
Educrédito	1965	Government funds, donations
Sociedad Administradora de Crédito Educativo para la Universidad de Oriente (SACEUDO)	1969	Government and regional funds

n.a. Not available in the original source.
a. Excluding loan repayments.
Source: Woodhall (1983).

offers technical seminars to help with the training of institution staff, and organizes the exchange of information on educational credit. APICE publishes an information bulletin, a journal, and a bibliography, all in Spanish.

Educational credit is provided both for tuition costs (including fees where they are charged) and maintenance costs. Loans are given both for study within a country or study abroad. In some countries, educational credit institutions are solely concerned with student loans, whereas in other cases their functions include administration of other financial aid programs such as scholarship schemes.

The programs vary considerably in size, from a few hundred loans a year to many thousands. Table 2-6 shows the numbers of loans awarded between 1976 and 1978 by the main educational credit institutions in Brazil, Colombia, Ecuador, Panama, and Venezuela, together with the number of students in 1978. Both in terms of the number of loans and the proportion of students assisted, the programs in Brazil and Colombia are far bigger than the other three. It has been estimated that, between 1969 and 1974, about 10 percent of all students in Colombia were able to finance their studies by means of loans. This figure is higher than the proportion aided by Educrédito in Venezuela or the 2 percent who receive loans in Honduras. In contrast, 26 percent of the university population in Jamaica reportedly obtain loans.

There is no general pattern of administration. Some of the student loan institutions, such as ICETEX in Colombia, the Instituto Nacional de Crédito Educativo (INCE) in Argentina, and the Fondo Nacional de Desarrollo de la Educación (FNDE) in Brazil are public institutions, established as autonomous agencies. Educrédito in Honduras was established as a private, nonprofit institution in 1968, but became an autonomous public institution in 1976, whereas Educrédito in Venezuela is still a private institution. In some countries, however, student loan programs are administered within national banks. In Mexico, for example, a student loan fund is administered by the Bank of Mexico on the basis of an agreement between the bank and the federal government. Similarly, in Jamaica the Student Loan Fund is administered by the Bank of Jamaica.

Table 2–6. Number of Student Loans Awarded in Brazil, Colombia, Ecuador, Panama, and Venezuela, 1976–78

Country and institution	Number of students in higher education (1978)	Number of students receiving loans (1976–78)
Brazil (FNDE)	1,251,116	388,415
Colombia (ICETEX)	211,302	56,422
Ecuador (IECE)	235,274	14,271
Panama (IFARHU)	34,302	4,502
Venezuela (Educrédito)	282,074	2,202

Source: Woodhall (1983).

There are also numerous private loan institutions. In Brazil commercial banks have loan schemes; one private, nonprofit institution set up by a trade union, the Associação do Profissionais Liberais Universitarios de Brasil (APLUB), administers the APLUB Foundation for Educational Credit. In addition, a semi-independent agency within the Ministry of Labor and Social Security provides loans and scholarships to the dependents of trade union members.

Some private loan funds are administered by individual universities, for example, the Catholic University in Chile and Sociedad Administradora de Crédito Educativo para la Universidad de Oriente (SACUEDO) in Venezuela. A fund in Costa Rica, Departmento de Formento Nacional de Prestamos para Educación (FONAPE), is administered by a commercial bank. In addition, several Mexican universities have loan schemes for students.

The variations in the formal structure of loan institutions in Latin America are matched by considerable variation in the way they are funded. The government is the main source of funds for most of the national educational credit programs, but in some cases the finance comes from general government revenue, in others from taxes earmarked for educational credit. Many of the institutions have received loans from the Inter-American Development Bank (IDB) or USAID, but in such cases the national government is required to contribute to the financing through matching funds, or in some other way. Central or commercial banks are a major source of funds in Colombia, Costa Rica, and Mexico. There are also nontraditional sources of funds, including national lotteries. Private donations are significant in some countries, and these are often encouraged by governments through fiscal incentives.

Finally, loan repayments provide some of the financing, although the proportion varies and is very small in some of the newer institutions. The main source of funds for ICETEX is the government, followed by loans from commercial banks, which, as a result of a resolution of the Central Bank, are authorized to make rediscountable loans to ICETEX at only 2 percent interest. In addition, ICETEX administers funds for private and public enterprises and uses this money to finance loans for professional and technical training. In Argentina, INCE receives half of its funds from the government and half from commercial banks. In Brazil, national lotteries contribute to the financing of two loan funds, administered by FNDE and by the Federal Savings Bank (Caixa Económica Federal); the state-owned oil company, Petroleo Brasileiro, also contributes to their financing. Oil revenues are an important source of finance in Ecuador, where a payroll tax also contributes to Instituto Ecuatoriano de Crédito Educativo (IEC), while in El

Salvador there is a loan fund financed entirely by the Central Bank. Barbados, Colombia, Costa Rica, Dominican Republic, Honduras, Jamaica, Panama, and Trinidad and Tobago have all received loans from USAID or IDB for on-lending to students. As is evident from this list, many of the educational credit institutions in Latin America have been able to exploit nontraditional sources of revenue, including private contributions, such as donations, loans from commercial banks, national lotteries, and other public and private sources.

The length of repayment period of student loans in Latin America and their repayment terms vary greatly. These are summarized in table 2-7. In some cases (for example INCE in Argentina), the

Table 2-7. Repayment Terms of Student Loans, Latin America, 1978

Country	Interest (percent) During study	Interest (percent) During repayment	Length of repayment (years)	Grace period (months)
Argentina	Linked[a]		Same as borrowing	12
Bolivia	5	5–15	Maximum 10	3
Brazil				
APLUB	5	10	Same as borrowing	6–12
Caixa Economica Federál	12+	12+	Variable	12
Colombia				
ICETEX	3–14	6–16	Variable	3–6
Costa Rica	6–8	6–8	n.a.	2–6
Chile				
Catholic University	Linked[b]		6	12
Ecuador	Variable		6	Variable
Honduras	8	8	8	3–6
Jamaica	6	6	9	12
Mexico				
Banco de México	n.a.	8.5–12	7	12
Nicaragua	3	6	n.a.	12
Panama	n.a.	5	15	n.a.
Dominican Republic	12	12	3 times borrowing	Variable
Venezuela				
Educrédito	8		Variable	6
SACUEDO	3–8	3–8	2 times borrowing	6–12

n.a. Not available.
a. Linked to cost of living and bank rate.
b. Linked to cost of living.
Source: Woodhall (1983).

loan must be paid back in the same period of time as the student's borrowing period, whereas other programs (for example, SACUEDO in Venezuela) allow the borrowing period to be twice as long or (as in the Dominican Republic) even three times as long. Where a specific period of time is prescribed, it ranges from two years in Peru (Instituto Nacional y Becas y Crédito Educativo), to four years in some private programs in Mexico, to fifteen years in Panama (Instituto para la Formación y Aprovechamiento de los Recursos Humanos).

All the loan programs allow a grace period before repayment must begin, usually six months or a year. In some cases it is possible for borrowers to postpone repayments or renegotiate repayment terms if they are in financial difficulties because of illness or unemployment, for example, but in no case is this automatic (as it is in Sweden). The method of making repayments also varies. In most cases, borrowers are required to pay through banks or to send payments directly to the loan institutions, but in some cases deductions may be made from employees' salaries by either public or private employers; for example, ICETEX is authorized to require this, in some cases. Interest rates vary among countries, but are invariably below market rates of interest and usually below the central bank discount rate.

Most loan programs require a personal guarantee from borrowers. In some cases they must promise to work in a particular occupation or region after completing their studies, and those who obtain a loan for study abroad must promise to work in their own country. For example, the Student Loan Fund in Dominica that obtains assistance from the Caribbean Development Banks states: "If the applicant is in the public service or teaching service, he must, after completing his studies, undertake to work at least five years in such service, if the course of study is for a period of one year or more. In all other cases, the applicant must undertake to work, after completing his studies, for at least three years in any of the less developed member states of the bank" (Woodhall 1983, p. 44).

Because the proportion of student loans that have not yet become due for repayment is high in many countries, it is difficult to find reliable evidence on the extent of default in Latin America. Many individuals, particularly opponents of loans, refer to high rates of default, and some countries have experienced high default rates, but this is by no means a universal problem. A review of IDB experience with loans to educational credit institutions suggests that the problem of defaults has been serious in some Caribbean countries. In Trinidad and Tobago, 67 percent of the borrowers who had begun to repay their loans were late in their installments.

**Table 2–8. Percentage of Debts Due for Repayment
in Arrears or Default, Latin America, 1978**

Country and institution	Percent
Brazil (APLUB)	2.0
Colombia (ICETEX)	11.0
Costa Rica (CONAPE)	0.5
Ecuador (IECE)	19.0
Honduras (Educrédito)	9.0
Jamaica (Students' Loan Bureau)	7.0
Mexico (Bank of Mexico)	5.0
Peru (INABEC)	22.0
Venezuela	
Educrédito	30.0
SACUEDO	8.0

Source: Woodhall (1983).

Jamaica at one time experienced a 50 percent default rate. On the basis of this experience, IDB now requires educational credit institutions to limit installments to no more than 10 percent of a borrower's earnings. In the case of Colombia, ICETEX had an average 5 percent annual loss owing to defaults between 1953 and 1968. Considering the length of experience, history of good management, and breadth of program of ICETEX, this is regarded by some experts as the lowest rate of loss that can be expected. In Honduras, where the collection experience of Educrédito is described as good, it has been found that lower-income students have the better repayment records. There is evidence that high default rates often indicate some other, underlying problem, such as high rates of wastage and dropout or unemployment. Of the debts due for repayment, the percentage in arrears or default in some Latin American countries is shown in table 2-8.

Africa

A number of small loan programs can also be found in Asia, Africa, and the Middle East.

Ghana. The student loan program in Ghana was short-lived; it was introduced in June 1971, but abandoned in October 1972 because the government that introduced it was overthrown. The new head of state was opposed to the idea of student loans.

Nigeria. Nigeria used to have a small federal government loan scheme, together with a system of tuition fees plus grants, but this system was fundamentally changed in 1977–78, when tuition fees were abolished and the responsibility for grants and loans was transferred from the federal government to the states. Some states still have small loan schemes, but in general loans are available only for students who are studying abroad, and even then they are regarded as a supplementary source of funds for those who have already begun a course of higher education abroad but have encountered financial difficulties.

Kenya. The government of Kenya introduced a loan scheme to cover students' living expenses in 1974. From the mid-1970s until 1981, a total of KSh20 million was provided to students in the form of loans. Graduates must begin to repay their loans after a grace period of two to four years, and the normal repayment period is about seven or eight years with interest at 2 percent.

The experience with collecting loan repayments has been disappointing, and it is estimated that half of all students who should have begun to repay their loans by 1982 were late or in default; in several cases, this was because students had dropped out of universities before completing their programs. The original regulations of the student loan scheme made no provision for this. Another weakness of the original design of the scheme was that no effective machinery was established to collect repayments. It is recognized that the main problem is one of keeping records, since students or graduates may change addresses frequently and may even change their names. A recent attempt by the government to introduce a clause whereby parental land should be used as collateral for the loan provoked student demonstrations in 1981.

Asia

India. Student loans were introduced on a small scale in India, but have never been a major source of finance for higher education, although the Planning Commission argued in 1966 that greater emphasis should be placed on loans, which after "a period of initial investment [would] develop into a self-generating, self-perpetuating fund." However, there has never been a comprehensive loan program in India.

Sri Lanka. The small-scale loan scheme in operation in India was one factor that persuaded the People's Bank in Sri Lanka to establish a loan program "with a view to easing the indebtedness of the people and to accelerate the development of the country." The university loan scheme of the People's Bank was set up in 1964. It provides loans at 4 percent interest, and graduates are expected to start repaying as soon as they have a job. The loan scheme is known to be used by low-income families. However, a high proportion of the borrowers were found to be unemployed for long periods after graduation. This helps to explain the poor repayment record of the scheme. In 1978 loan repayments amounted to only 12 percent of the total that had been lent to students. The problem of unemployment, which is common in many developing countries, and the fact that many graduates had to wait long periods before finding a job, suggest that the grace period allowed in many loan schemes may be insufficient.

Pakistan. Commercial banks operate a student loan scheme in Pakistan, where the banks are nationalized. This is the Qarz-e-Hasna scheme, launched in 1980–81 to replace a federal government student loan scheme introduced in 1974. The government provided half the finance for this scheme and the commercial banks the other half. The Qarz-e-Hasna program provides interest-free loans for study in Pakistan or abroad, in scientific or technical subjects or medicine. The loans are means-tested, and may fall into three categories: comprehensive loans to cover all tuition and living costs; partial loans, to supplement a scholarship or other aid that is insufficient; and travel loans, to provide assistance for those who are studying abroad. The scheme is administered by the nationalized banks under the direction of the Pakistan Banking Council. Repayment normally starts after a grace period of two years, but unemployed graduates may have a longer grace period. The normal repayment period is ten years.

Middle East

Egypt. There is a small loan scheme in Egypt, but a survey carried out for the International Institute for Educational Planning (Sanyal 1982) showed that only 5 percent of the students questioned had received a government loan and about 2 percent had received a nongovernment loan. The majority (nearly 80 percent) relied on their families for financial support, but 18 percent had a scholarship.

Israel. There is a long-established student loan scheme in Israel. The fund was set up in 1964 to give students financial help with tuition fees. Higher education is not free in Israel, although fees are not intended to cover full costs; fees are 25 percent higher for students whose fees are paid by their employers.

The Student Loan Fund is financed in part by the government and in part by six major banks. According to the budget of the fund for 1980–81, the banks were expected to provide 50 percent of the income of the fund, the government 40 percent, and loan repayments the remaining 10 percent. However, actual expenditure was less than planned, and thus the government contribution was less than 40 percent. In 1977–78, more than 6,000 loans were provided, which represented 12 percent of the total student population. More than one-third of these students were from disadvantaged families. In 1980–81, 5,833 loans were awarded.

The loans are administered by the banks, on behalf of the Student Loan Fund. The loans have a low interest rate, but must be repaid within two years. Students must pay a small contribution to a loan insurance fund that covers loans written off due to disability. Between 1964 and 1977, the Student Loan Fund awarded nearly 70,000 loans and reported that repayment in arrears was only 4 percent, and loans in default or written off were negligible.

The Israeli scheme has one feature that is unusual, if not unique. A student who is awarded a loan may opt for a grant of 35 percent of the value of the loan instead of the loan. This figure presumably represents the subsidy provided for borrowers in the form of low interest rates. This subsidy varies from 25 percent to more than 50 percent in some Latin American programs. In Israel the subsidy is less because of the short repayment period, but there students have the choice, not usual in other countries, of receiving this subsidy as a grant or as a loan.

Scholarship Plans

Individual Scholarships

Numerous scholarship (grant) plans in developing countries provide funds to selected individuals to further their education. In some cases, the scholarship is for study at a designated school— private or public. In others the choice of school is left to the receiver of the scholarship. These arrangements can be illustrated by the Regular Training Program of the Organization of American States (OAS).

The fundamental objective of this program is to further the economic, social, technical, and cultural development of the Latin American peoples. Under the policy established by the council of the OAS, priority is given to studies, research, and training necessary for the expansion of productivity; scholarships are granted to candidates who have advanced training in the field for which the scholarship is requested.

The candidates must be citizens or permanent residents of an OAS member country, with a university degree, or they must have demonstrated ability to pursue advanced studies in the field chosen. The scholarships can last from three months to a maximum of two years and are tenable in any of the OAS member countries, outside of the candidate's own country. They cover travel expenses, tuition fees, study materials, and subsistence allowance.

Group Scholarships

Scholarships to groups of students give funds for education at a school of the individual's (or the parents') choice. Group scholarships can be compared to food stamps: they provide the means to education, without specifying the provider. Although associated with Milton Friedman, the idea is older than the University of Chicago and goes back at least to Thomas Paine. Writing in the 1790s, Paine proposed a reduction of government expenditure from US$8 million to US$1.5 million. He advocated a distribution of US$4 million, according to the size and age of the family. The government was to pay

> to every poor family . . . four pounds a year for every child under fourteen years of age; enjoining the parents of such children to send them to school, to learn reading, writing and common arithmetic; the minister of every parish, of every denomination to certify jointly to an officer, for that purpose, that this duty is performed (Beales and others 1967).

Although incorporated in British legislation in 1870 and subsequently promoted by British Catholics ("A Scholarship for Every Child"), the idea has made little progress outside Vermont (McClaughry 1984), mainly because of the bitter opposition of educationalists who prefer that decisions about children's education be made by professional educators, rather than be based on parental preferences. However, a similar scheme worked smoothly and successfully when, after World War II under the so-called G.I. bill, demobilized U.S. servicemen were given grants that could be spent on any educational course meeting prescribed standards.

The only developing country to apply this idea is Chile, where local authorities pay approved non-fee-paying schools a specified amount for each day that a child attends, with the schools being allowed to compete for enrollments. The value of this payment is on the order of US$100 a year, which may be one-fifth or one-sixth of the fees charged by equivalent private schools in Chile.

Nevertheless, the amount has been sufficient to enable groups of teachers—and parents—to establish some new public schools. The Chilean voucher cannot be used to supplement fees in private schools. The system was introduced in the 1940s as part of a reorganization that devolved responsibility for the schools from central government to the counties. It was revised in the 1970s. No comprehensive evaluation of the Chilean voucher system appears to have been published.

The Role of the Government

The roles of the private and public sectors in the provision of services can be shown diagramatically on a matrix such as the one in figure 1-1. The top quadrants represent the private sector as "buying" services, and the bottom quadrants, public sector "buying." The right-hand quadrants represent the private sector acting as "producers," and the left-hand quadrant represents public sector "production." If this matrix was applied to education, the spread of activities between the public and private sectors might appear as it does in figure 2-1.

The matrix indicates that, although governments have large roles in education, the private sector can fulfill most of them without governmental assistance. In particular, where a government role is deemed necessary—for example, to protect children from bad parental decisions—it is not necessary for the education services themselves to be provided by government. Governments can assist by providing encouragement, legislation, punishment, inspection, and even money, without getting into the business of building schools and hiring teachers. Even such functions as the testing of students can be privately provided. Furthermore, a government can have a major influence on private education: it can determine the curricula to be taught and, by means of an inspection system, influence teaching standards.

Some assert that governments can, and should, determine the mix of skills to be taught to ensure the availability of trained personnel for all "essential" purposes. This is not the place to assess the merits or failures of manpower planning, but the existence of millions of educated unemployed suggests that this particular form of planning claims more than it can deliver.

This is not to say that governments should be neutral about education. Economic and social development can be accelerated by the spread of knowledge, and many governments wish to support education for this reason alone. Others have other reasons; for example, they may wish to promote social cohesion or to relieve poverty. But governments can act in many ways. By select-

**Figure 2–1. Government and Private Sector as Buyer
and Producer of Education Services**

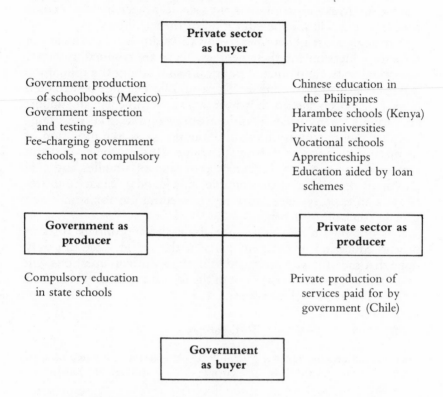

Government production
   of schoolbooks (Mexico)
Government inspection
   and testing
Fee-charging government
   schools, not compulsory

Chinese education in
   the Philippines
Harambee schools (Kenya)
Private universities
Vocational schools
Apprenticeships
Education aided by loan
   schemes

Compulsory education
   in state schools

Private production of
   services paid for by
   government (Chile)

ing candidates for government service on the basis of written, competitive examinations, the rulers of China did much to encourage literacy and education.

To the extent that it may be necessary to spend more on education than people can afford to pay of their own accord, there are numerous ways of targeting public funds to buy the required services from the private sector. But conditions vary so much from one country to another that it is impossible to generalize about a private-public mix in education. Each society should determine the roles to be shouldered by its own government to improve the education of its citizens.

Conclusion

This brief review of private sector activities in education shows that such activities exist throughout the world and can be traced far back in time. The extent and quality of education differ from society to society and higher economic development tends to be associated with longer training periods and with increased specialization. Most impressive are the sacrifices made by low-income people to provide for the education of their children.

Although most governments nowadays are united in being in favor of education for their peoples, there are conflicting views, associated with fundamental political issues, about the role of the private sector in providing it. These conflicts cannot be explored here. It has been shown, however, that governments can support education in many ways, ranging from benign neglect (for example, in Chinese education in the Philippines), to the provision of financial assistance to private providers (for example, in Latin America) and direct government provision of supplies and employment of teachers (for example, in Uganda). Most countries allow a mix of systems, that is, state education for some, and private education for others.

It is not possible to generalize about the appropriate roles of private education in different parts of the world. One can only hope that the officials concerned with these difficult questions will make their decisions in the light of the relevant evidence from their own countries as well as others.

References

Ahmed, Zulficar, and Munawar Mirza. 1975. *The Financing of Privately Managed Schools in the Punjab*. Paris: Unesco International Institute for Educational Planning.

Anderson, John E. 1973. *Organization and Financing of Self-Help Education in Kenya*. Paris: Unesco and International Institute for Educational Planning.

APICE (Asociación Panamericana de Instituciones de Crédito Educativo). 1979. VIII Congreso, Panamericano de Crédito Educativo. Bogotá.

Beales, A. C. F., and others. 1967. *Education: A Framework for Choice*. London: Institute of Economic Affairs.

Calaway, Archibald. 1973. *Nigerian Enterprise and the Employment of Youth: A Study of 225 Businesses in Ibadan*. Nigerian Institute of Social and Economic Research Monograph Series 2.

Castle, E. B. 1966. *Growing Up in East Africa*. London: Oxford University Press.

Chitnis, S., and C. Suvannathat. 1984. "Schooling for the Children of the Urban Poor." In *Basic Needs and the Urban Poor: The Provision of Communal Services*, ed. P. J. Richards and A. M. Thomson. London: Croom Helm.

du Sautoy, Peter. 1968. *Choice: Lessons from the Third World*. London: Institute of Economic Affairs.

Heyneman, Stephen P. 1983. "Education during a Period of Austerity: Uganda, 1971–1981." *Comparative Education Review*, 27(3):403–13.

Lloyd, P. C., A. L. Mabogunje, and B. Awe. 1967. *The City of Ibadan.* Cambridge, Eng.: Cambridge University Press.

Mathur, Y. B. 1973. *Women's Education in India, 1813–1966.* New York: Asia Publishing House.

McClaughry, John. 1984. "Who Says Vouchers Wouldn't Work." *Reason* 15(9):24–32.

Naik, J. P. 1967. "The Role and Problems of Private Enterprise in Education." In *The Christian College and National Development.* Madras: Christian Literature Society.

Orr, Kenneth. 1977. *Appetite for Education in Contemporary Asia.* Canberra: Australian National University.

Rawski, Evelyn S. 1979. *Education and Popular Literacy in Ch'ing China.* Ann Arbor: University of Michigan Press.

Sanyal, Bikas C. 1982. *University Education and the Labour Market in the Arab Republic of Egypt.* Elmsford, N.Y., and Oxford, Eng.: Pergamon.

Sheffield, James R., and Victor P. Diejomash. 1972. *Non-Formal Education in African Development.* New York: African American Institute.

Tan, Jee-Peng. 1985. "Enrollment and Expenditure on Education: Some Macro Trends." *International Review of Education.* Paris: Unesco.

Thompson, Kenneth W., Barbara R. Fogel, and Helen E. Danner (eds.). 1976. *Higher Education and Social Change: Promising Experiments in Developing Countries.* Vol. 2, Case Studies. New York: Praeger.

Waggoner, George R., and Barbara Ashton. 1971. *Education in Central America.* Lawrence, Kan.: University of Kansas Press.

Woodhall, Maureen. 1983. *Student Loans as a Means of Financing Higher Education.* World Bank Staff Working Paper 599. Washington, D.C.

Yates, Barbara A. 1984. "Comparative Education and the Third World: The Nineteenth Century Revisited." *Comparative Education Review* 28(4):533–49.

3

Electricity

An enterprising man reasoned that, if he provided television, people would come to his coffee shop and drink and eat while they watched. He ran it with a generator which made lines on the screen because the generator was sometimes strong and sometimes weak. (No one in Sakathiam ran a television set from a car battery as they have done in other parts of Thailand before the coming of electricity.) The coffee shop set was on from 8:00 to 9:30 in the evening and also in the daytime on Saturday and Sunday. At least three channels were available. Before the coming of electricity no one else wanted to make an investment in television. When electricity came, teachers were the first to have television in their homes.

—JASPER AND FERN INGERSOLL, "CHANGE
IN ENERGY USES IN VILLAGE THAILAND"

UNLIKE EDUCATION, HEALTH, AND WATER SUPPLY, electricity is a relatively new arrival. Although electricity was used for telegraphy in the 1830s, it was not until the development of the dynamo in the 1850s that electricity could be used on a commercial scale. Development was rapid thereafter. By 1855 an electrical railcar was in operation but was destroyed in Scotland by operators of steam trains. In 1876 Paul Jablochkov, a Russian officer, invented the "electric candle," which was the first electric arc lamp. In 1879 and 1880 Edison in the United States and others in Europe in-

For help in the preparation of this chapter special thanks are due to Richard Dosik, Alfred Gulstone, Gilbert Hunt, Ted Minnig, Hilda Ochoa, Donal O'Leary, and Robert Saunders, the World Bank; John Eustis, the Department of Energy; Amnon Manor, Feuchtwanger Industries Ltd.; I. C. Price and W. B. Gillett, Sir William Halcrow and Partners; Jeffrey Kenna, Intermediate Technology Power Ltd.; James Lay and Paul Clark, the National Rural Electrical Cooperative Association; Walter Primeaux, University of Illinois; Jeff Coburn, Jan Gessler, Michael Starr, and Ricardo Zuloaga.

vented the electric light bulb and solved the practical problems of its manufacture. In 1881 Edison established the first public electric supply station, on Pearl Street in New York. By 1887 New York City had six electric companies, and by 1905 Chicago had forty-five, only one of which had an exclusive franchise granting the sole rights to serve a territory. Thus, electricity supply was first introduced to the world as a competitive service provided by private enterprise.

In other parts of the world, electricity supply was started by private companies: in London and Shanghai in 1882; in Valencia (Venezuela) in 1885; in Colombo in 1895; in Calcutta in 1899; and in Dairen (Manchuria) in 1902. By 1914, electric light and power were available throughout the world. By 1981, the latest year for which data are available, the average annual production per person in 100 developing countries ranged from 12 kilowatt hours in Burundi, to 4,952 in Suriname (see table 3-1).[1]

Electricity is now used for so many activities—manufacturing, cooking, lighting, heating, education—that consumption differences generally reflect real differences in living standards. How electricity is used when first introduced in a country varies greatly in different parts of the world, but an idea of the uses afforded by electricity can be obtained from a survey of 173 residences in the Nicoya peninsula of Costa Rica in 1976 (Lay and Hood 1978): 42 of these residences were found to be directly connected with a business enterprise and 17 were part of a farm operation. The uses recorded were as follows:

173 (100 percent) had one or more electric bulbs or neon lights
132 (76 percent) had electric irons
102 (59 percent) had television sets
 75 (43 percent) had refrigerators
 34 (20 percent) had electric blenders
 25 (15 percent) had electric radios (most households had
                  portable radios)
 23 (13 percent) had electric stoves
 21 (12 percent) had electric fans
 16 (9 percent) had stereo equipment or record players
 15 (9 percent) had washing machines

1. Power planners in the United States assume that one person uses the output of a 1,000-watt (1-kilowatt) electric power supply (1 kilowatt can power fifteen electric lights or one small electric heater). Therefore a 100-kilowatt power station can serve 100 people (say, 50 homes) and 1,000 kilowatts (or 1 megawatt) of power can serve 500 homes. A city of 500,000 would require the output of a 1,000-megawatt generator.

Table 3–1. GDP and Electricity Production in 100 Developing Countries, 1981,

Country	Population (thousands)	GDP per capita (U.S. dollars)	Electricity produced per capita (kwh)
East Africa			
Angola	7,784	900	192
Botswana	930	1,021	431
Burundi	4,229	264	12
Comoros	358	n.a.	31
Djibouti	381	n.a.	289
Ethiopia	31,800	134	21
Kenya	17,363	327	112
Lesotho	1,372	291	71
Madagascar	8,969	322	55
Malawi	6,241	208	68
Mauritius	971	1,166	486
Mozambique	12,485	358	104
Rwanda	5,346	235	20
Seychelles	60	—	850
Somalia	4,392	421	25
Sudan	19,242	528	68
Swaziland	641	1,018	775
Tanzania	18,600	281	51
Uganda	13,047	792	26
Zaire	29,777	181	144
Zambia	5,842	597	1,034
Zimbabwe	7,190	911	1,020
West Africa			
Benin	3,595	266	32
Burkina Faso	6,325	186	18
Cameroon	8,668	834	193
Cape Verde	300	218	30
Central African Rep.	2,379	292	29
Chad	4,549	87	14
Côte d'Ivoire	8,505	1,019	217
Congo, People's Rep.	1,658	1,128	99
Equatorial Guinea	346	—	75
Gabon	669	5,210	863
Gambia	604	349	73
Ghana	11,830	2,356	456
Guinea	5,571	302	89
Guinea-Bissau	790	167	38

Table 3–1 (continued)

Country	Population (thousands)	GDP per capita (U.S. dollars)	Electricity produced per capita (kwh)
West Africa (continued)			
Liberia	1,941	544	571
Mali	6,881	161	13
Mauritania	1,560	451	81
Niger	5,704	300	52
Nigeria	87,603	883	83
São Tomé and Príncipe	115	25	96
Senegal	5,862	433	124
Sierra Leone	3,574	323	65
Togo	2,664	332	95
East Asia and Pacific			
China	991,300	267	312
Fiji	646	1,962	491
Indonesia	149,659	521	73
Kampuchea, Dem.	7,090	n.a.	32
Korea, Rep. of	38,880	1,661	1,204
Lao People's Dem. Rep.	3,501	101	29
Malaysia	14,200	1,793	676
Philippines	50,348	730	390
Solomon Islands	237	688	n.a.
Thailand	47,500	759	355
Viet Nam	55,707	n.a.	72
South Asia			
Bangladesh	89,515	134	33
Burma	34,109	168	44
India	690,183	239	191
Nepal	15,029	161	19
Pakistan	84,501	334	190
Sri Lanka	14,988	295	124
Europe, Middle East, and North Africa			
Afghanistan	16,349	203[a]	63
Algeria	19,602	2,134	361
Cyprus	623	3,318	1,704
Egypt	43,290	584	549
Jordan	3,370	1,098	367
Morocco	20,891	710	269

(Table continues on the following page.)

Table 3–1 (continued)

Country	Population (thousands)	GDP per capita (U.S. dollars)	Electricity produced per capita (kwh)
Europe, Middle East, and North Africa (continued)			
Portugal	9,826	2,403	1,688
Romania	22,353	2,540	3,216
Syrian Arab Rep.	6,314	1,636	421
Tunisia	6,528	1,268	463
Turkey	45,529	1,267	577
Yemen Arab Rep.	7,251	394	92
Yemen, People's Dem. Rep.	1,957	380	158
Yugoslavia	22,516	3,074	2,653
Latin America and Carribean			
Argentina	28,174	4,405	1,444
Barbados	251	3,693	1,396
Belize	149	1,108	557
Bolivia	5,721	1,252	293
Brazil	120,507	2,356	1,167
Chile	11,292	2,927	1,203
Colombia	26,425	1,412	873
Costa Rica	2,340	1,123	1,009
Dominica	74	796	243
Dominican Rep.	5,592	1,292	702
Ecuador	8,605	1,613	438
El Salvador	4,671	759	333
Guatemala	7,477	1,159	223
Guyana	796	766	625
Haiti	5,104	297	73
Honduras	3,818	689	250
Jamaica	2,194	1,340	953
Mexico	71,215	3,365	957
Nicaragua	2,777	930	429
Panama	1,877	2,046	1,790
Paraguay	3,057	1,840	275
Peru	17,031	1,366	619
Suriname	353	3,044	4,952
Uruguay	2,929	3,972	1,205

n.a. Not available.

a. 1980.

Source: World Bank.

10   (6 percent) had electric floor polishers
 9   (5 percent) had electric pumps for household water
 6   (3 percent) had electric mixers
 5   (3 percent) had electric sewing machines
 4   (2 percent) had thermoheaters for their showers (bath)
 3   (2 percent) had one each of the following items: electric
         skillets, electric ovens, air conditioning, elec-
         tric tools, juice extractors
 2   (1 percent) had electric clothes dryers; also had one each
         of the following items: hot water tank, hair
         dryer, electric clock, tape recorder, and elec-
         tric massager.

One can see from the above data that the provision of electricity involves much more than switching from candles or kerosene lamps to electric light bulbs. Electricity opens to its users many new opportunities and new activities that may not even have been considered before. Interestingly, television was not the most widely owned electrical appliance in the working-class households in Costa Rica. It was the electric iron.

Electrification in North Yemen

How the private sector can supply electricity, even under unfavorable conditions, can be illustrated by the experience of the Yemen Arab Republic (North Yemen), one of the poorest countries in the world, which not only lacks a modern infrastructure but also has a difficult terrain. Until the middle of this century it was governed by a theocracy that did little to encourage technical development. In 1950, however, the old Imam was overthrown and, following a decade of war, a forward-looking government was established.

By the early 1960s electricity was being produced in the main cities on a small scale by government agencies and private individuals. The source of this electricity was small diesel-powered generating sets. Some of the private producers supplied their own homes and those of their immediate neighbors. These small generating and distribution schemes were gradually combined, and in 1963 the General Electricity Company of Sana'a was established as an independent private company, owned by the city government (75 percent), the Yemen National Bank (15 percent), and private shareholders (10 percent). In the same year, the Taiz Electric Company was established as a private company owned by the local government (17 percent), the Yemen National Bank (23 percent), and private citizens (60 percent). Then in 1965 the Hodeidah Electricity and Water Company was established as a wholly owned subsidiary of the Yemen National Bank. These companies developed along completely independent lines. All lacked qualified technical and managerial staff, with the result that construction, maintenance, and planning were poor. The chronic shortage of generating capacity inhibited growth.

After the civil war, the shareholders of the companies asked the government to buy their holdings. The government responded in 1975 by establishing the Yemen General Electricity Corporation (YGEC), with the former three companies as its nucleus. The corporation was entrusted with the generation and distribution of electricity to the three main cities of Sana'a, Hodeidah, and Taiz, as well as to twenty-eight other towns and rural centers. Although the YGEC was granted sole responsibility for generating and distributing electricity, generation for own use was permitted with a license from the ministry in charge. In 1975 the YGEC was generating 42 percent of the national total (43.3 million kilowatt-hours) compared with the estimated 58 percent (60 million kilowatt-hours) being provided by private suppliers.

Despite a rapid expansion of the YGEC's facilities, however, the public system was unable to meet the tremendous growth in demand for electricity. During the economic boom of the 1970s, a great many small generators were imported for own use, for small private utilities, and for a few cooperatives. World Bank staff estimated that about 33 percent of the population had electricity in 1981, compared with only 4 percent in 1975. Between 1975 and 1981, the public supply increased from 43.3 to 228 million kilowatt-hours; the rate of increase averaged 31.9 percent a year. But in the same period the supply generated by the private sector (for own use and for sale to the public) increased from 60 to 400 million kilowatt-hours; here the annual rate of increase was in excess of 39 percent.

Thus, between 1975 and 1981 the share of the private sector increased from 57 to 66 percent. This was largely due to village initiatives financed by money remitted from relatives working abroad and assistance from the government and the Confederation of Yemeni Development Associations. The technical and safety standards of the private suppliers were generally poor, however, and the prices paid to the private sector were about three times as high as the tariff of the public sector. Nonetheless, many people received electricity rapidly, despite difficult conditions. The experience of Yemen shows that, as in the West, the private sector in developing countries can meet public demand for electricity.

The central question in this chapter is: how can the private sector best be encouraged to increase the supply of electricity, especially to those who at the moment have no access to it? This question cannot be answered, however, without some idea of the industry and the reasons behind the conventional view that electricity should be provided either by a public agency or by a regulated franchise having a monopoly over its territory.

The Structure of the Industry

The process of providing electricity consists of three stages (see figure 3-1): generation at the power source; transmission, usually at high voltage, to the consumption area; and distribution to the customers. To understand how these stages are related, it is useful to distinguish between *isolated supply* and *interconnected supply*.

"Isolated supply" means that electricity is produced at a single point to serve the needs of a locality. Electricity is generated and distributed locally and does not have to be transmitted over long distances. This is typically the case in North Yemen, Papua New Guinea, and other places where the terrain is difficult.

"Interconnected supply" means that two or more generating units serve one or more areas. These are interconnected by a network of transmission lines known as a grid. Certain standards must be followed when electricity is generated into a common grid; for example, all participating stations have to generate at the same voltage (or use transformers) and at the same cycle frequency. Because the points of power generation are dispersed, the total reserve capacity required is less than it would be if each area being served was linked to a single generating station and was unable to draw on spare capacity available at the other generating points. There are other advantages to dispersed generation; for example, a dispersed system is less susceptible to sabotage than a system depending on one generating point only. Furthermore, a network of separate power stations, each able to buy from the grid or sell to it at a price designed to equate supply and demand at any time, can offer significant system economies. (This point is discussed in more detail in the appendix to this chapter.)

Interconnected supply gives operators, whether private or public, considerable flexibility in choosing the generating units to be employed at any particular time, depending on the demand for power and the maintenance needs of the equipment, among other factors. Where some of the power supplied is "interruptible" (for example, where the contracts with industrial customers allow the

Figure 3–1. Elements of an Electric Power System

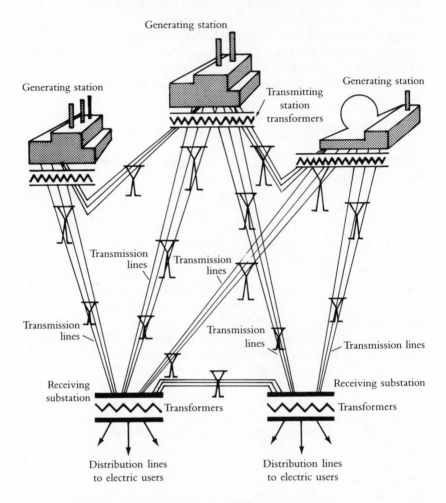

Source: Economic Regulatory Administration (1979).

service to be cut off in times of heavy demand), the operators of the power system also have some leeway in deciding which demands to meet.

But the transmission facilities required for interconnection are expensive to build. The cost of putting up transmission lines over long distances, particularly in mountainous regions, can range from $15,000 to $25,000 a kilometer in the United States. Maintenance costs may also be considerable (Clark 1982). Thus, where loads are small and widely scattered, large centralized power plants generally cannot compete successfully with small plants. The choice between isolated development or interconnection with the central grid depends on a number of factors that must be evaluated site by site and country by country to identify the least-cost option.

Interconnected systems can accommodate a mixture of private and public generators; similarly, isolated generators can be either publicly or privately operated. It is notable that a large number of private, isolated units were responsible for spreading the supply of electricity in Europe and the United States in the first decades of the industry and that integration into a public grid did not come until after World War II.

Power may be generated in two ways for sale to the public grid:

- Cogeneration, whereby electricity is produced simultaneously with other useful forms of energy, such as mechanical or thermal energy
- Self-generation, whereby electricity alone is generated by units that can be independent of the public utility.

Both of these forms of dispersed generation offer substantial savings in real resources and have therefore attracted wide interest ever since the energy crisis of the 1970s.

Cogeneration

The fundamental difference between a conventional energy system and a cogeneration system (see figure 3-2) is that the former produces either electricity or thermal energy, whereas the latter produces both simultaneously (U.S. Department of Energy 1978). By recapturing and using some of the thermal energy that is normally discharged from an engine, a cogeneration system can reduce fuel consumption by 10–30 percent. Cogeneration thus offers significant energy savings.

Cogeneration is not a new concept. It has been in use since the 1880s and is thus almost as old as the electric power industry itself. A well-known example was the district heating system built in London during the 1930s, which used surplus heat generated by the Battersea Power Station (before it was closed down) to heat dwellings. In the United States, the Franklin Heating Station in Rochester, Minnesota, which was built in 1927, provides both

Figure 3–2. Typical Cogeneration System

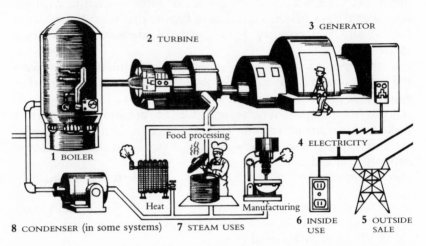

Note: A company burns fuel in a boiler (**1**) to turn water into steam. The steam flows to a turbine (**2**), where it rotates blades attached to a shaft that extends into an electric generator (**3**). As the shaft spins, electricity is produced in the generator. The electricity (**4**) is then sold to an electric utility (**5**) for distribution over power lines, or it is used in the company's own plant for lighting or to power machinery (**6**).

The steam that was fed into the turbine retains much of its energy and is piped to equipment that uses it for heating or other industrial or commercial purposes (**7**). After that, the spent steam has either become water or is turned back to water in a condenser (**8**). The water is piped back to the boiler and the process is repeated.

The system is nearly identical to that in a conventional electric generating plant, except the steam is used for work after it leaves the turbine instead of being discarded as waste heat. The process also allows the fuel in the boiler to do double work—thus the term "cogeneration."

After the extra cost of equipment, maintenance, and other expenses, cogeneration typically saves a business about 30 percent over the cost of using two fuels for two tasks—whether the energy is generated by the company internally or purchased from outside providers.

electricity and power for a clinic, a hotel, and a hospital. Previously, all three had maintained their own heating plants and purchased electricity from the municipal power company. By 1972, the percentage of total electric power produced by cogeneration was 18 percent in Italy, 16 percent in France and the Federal Republic of Germany, 12 percent in the Netherlands, and 2.5 percent in the United States (U.S. Department of Energy 1978).

Orly, one of the two major airports serving Paris, installed a cogeneration plant in the early 1970s; here the electricity was generated with diesel engines and the exhaust used to heat the terminals. Another cogeneration system recently installed in Paris is at Porte-Malliot. Four diesel-generator sets supply part of the electrical demand of this giant convention center and shopping complex. The remainder of the power needed is purchased from the utility grid in varying amounts, in accordance with a sliding time-of-day rate scale. Both these cogeneration installations power their diesels with natural gas, but have the capability to switch to diesel oil.

The extent to which developing countries have made use of cogeneration has varied greatly. In some, the private production of electricity for sale is prohibited by law. In others, such as Brazil, it is encouraged. In a number of countries—Indonesia is one—large industrial concerns use cogeneration for their own purposes, but the electricity produced is not sold to the public. Korea is one of the few countries in which electric power cogenerated by private firms is sold to the public grid.

One of the most interesting applications of cogeneration in tropical countries is in the production of surplus electricity from sugarcane. Sugarcane is processed into sugar in two stages: juice is extracted from cane stalks and the juice boiled until sugar crystals form. The extraction requires mechanical power while the boiling requires heat energy in the form of low-pressure steam, since it is mainly an evaporation process. Steam is obtained by burning the residue, called bagasse, from the extraction process. In most cases, enough bagasse is produced to provide the steam needed to run the factory.

In the early days of the industry, factory designers were interested only in producing enough steam at the lowest possible cost to provide enough motive power and enough heat to process the juice. They relied on low-pressure steam boilers, 100 to 150 psig (pounds per square inch gauge). Because steam turbines are not very efficient at these low pressures, it was not economical to use them for generating electricity. Gradually, as factories became larger and it became necessary to modernize equipment and improve efficiency, there was a shift toward boilers of larger capacities and higher steam pressures (175 to 250 psig). At these pressures, the generation of electricity became practicable, and many modern factories used electricity for the production process. But the objective of the factory designers remained to generate just enough electrical power to satisfy the production needs of the factory.

This attitude changed in the aftermath of the 1973 oil embargo. Many sugarcane producers realized that bagasse was an underused and undervalued resource, particularly in the sugar factories that had enough capacity to produce electrical power for export. Suddenly the objective of self-sufficiency was eclipsed by the desire to exploit to the maximum a natural resource that was readily available. Paturau (1982) recently pointed out that on a world basis it would theoretically be possible to produce more than 50 kilowatt-hours of *surplus* electrical energy for every metric ton of cane processed; this would add up to 22 billion kilowatt-hours of extra energy a year. At present, 4.5 billion kilowatt-hours could proba-

Table 3–2. Developing Countries in Which Sugarcane Is Grown

Central America and the Caribbean	*Asia*	*Africa*
Barbados	Bangladesh	Angola
Belize	Burma	Burkina Faso
Costa Rica	China	Cameroon
Cuba	India	Chad
Dominican Republic	Indonesia	Congo, People's Rep.
El Salvador	Iran	Côte d'Ivoire
Guadeloupe	Iraq	Egypt
Guatemala	Malaysia	Ethiopia
Haiti	Pakistan	Gabon
Honduras	Philippines	Ghana
Jamaica	Sri Lanka	Guinea
Martinique	Viet Nam	Kenya
Mexico	Thailand	Malagasy Rep.
Nicaragua		Malawi
Panama	*Oceania*	Mali
St. Kitts	Fiji	Mauritius
Trinidad and Tobago	Western Samoa	Morocco
		Mozambique
		Nigeria
South America		Rwanda
Argentina		Senegal
Bolivia		Somalia
Brazil		South Africa
Chile		Sudan
Colombia		Swaziland
Ecuador		Tanzania
Guyana		Uganda
Paraguay		Zaire
Peru		Zambia
Suriname		Zimbabwe
Uruguay		
Venezuela		

Source: World Bank.

bly be produced if all the surplus bagasse was to be utilized. A significant amount of surplus energy is already being produced by the cane sugar industry in several countries, including Hawaii and Mauritius, but how much surplus power is produced worldwide by sugar factories is not known as the data are not usually available. In any case, the examples set by Hawaii and Mauritius indicate that the energy shortage in tropical countries could be significantly reduced by the cane sugar industry. In many instances, however, sugar factories are not allowed by law to supply power to the local utility grid, or the price they are offered for their energy is unattractive. (See table 3-2 for a list of countries in which sugarcane is grown.)

As an example of what might be done, the World Bank, in response to a request from the government of Guyana, asked the consultants of CORE International to identify an energy conservation project that could use bagasse as a fuel. The consultants selected the Enmore sugar mill for a feasibility study and recommended a $10 million investment for the addition of a bagasse drying system, modification of two 83,000-pound-per-hour boilers, a new 7.5 megawatt turbo-alternator, a water cooling system, a 14-kilometer, 11-kilovolt transmission line, and a transformer with switching and control equipment. The excess electricity to be generated at Enmore could be sold to the public grid and would enable the Guyana Electricity Corporation to reduce its load-shedding program and manage the public electricity requirements more effectively. Financial rates of return were expected to exceed 24 percent a year. Proposals to generate electricity from bagasse for sale to the public grid have also been made in the Dominican Republic.

Self-Generation

Whereas cogeneration produces electricity in conjunction with mechanical or thermal energy, self-generation produces only electricity. In some cases, the producing firm uses the electricity for its own purposes, and in others, some of the power is sold to the public grid. Following recent legislation in the United States, thousands of small private facilities have been built for the sole purpose of selling power to the public grid.

Large-scale self-generation by the private sector can be illustrated by the operation of the Tata Electric Companies (TEC) of India, which have had a long and successful history in many industrial, mercantile, service, and nonprofit enterprises. The TEC consist of three companies: the Tata Hydro Electric Power Supply

Company Limited (Tata Hydro) formed in 1910, the Andhra Valley Power Supply Company Limited (Andhra Valley) formed in 1916, and the Tata Power Company Limited (Tata Power) formed in 1919. These are private companies that are separately owned by public shareholders but that operate as a group under the same management. They form a part of the Tata group of enterprises, which have substantial financial resources, an excellent credit rating, and highly efficient management. Each company operates its own hydro plant under an individual license (the Bombay Hydro Electric License issued in 1907, the Andhra Valley Hydro Electric License issued in 1919, and the Nila Mula Valley Hydro Electric License issued in 1921). The companies also own and operate jointly the 800-megawatt Trombay thermal power station and a 1,400-kilowatt high-voltage transmission system. They employ a common managerial and technical staff of about 3,000 people.

Before 1954, the more populous areas of Maharashtra were supplied by private entities operating under license. But in 1954 the Bombay State Electricity Board was formed, and it took over much of the responsibility for the supply of electricity. In 1960, it was divided into the Gujarat Electricity Board (GEB) and Maharashtra State Electricity Board (MSEB). The private electricity firms in the area were gradually taken over, and the principal ones now remaining are the Tata Electric Companies and the Bombay Suburban Electric Supply undertaking (BSES). The private companies operate under license within their own concession areas. Licensees other than the TEC merely distribute electricity (they buy their power in bulk from the MSEB and TEC). The TEC are the largest licensees and operate their own generating stations, which have a total installed capacity of more than 11,000 megawatts. They serve 114 industrial consumers (such as textile mills) and also sell in bulk to the local authorities and to the private companies that distribute in the area under license. In addition, they supply about 70 megawatts to Indian Railways and about 350 megawatts to the MSEB.

The TEC, which obtained loans from the World Bank in 1977 and 1984, are well-managed concerns but, in accordance with India's Electricity Supply Act of 1948, they are not allowed to earn a clear profit in excess of a reasonable return. This restriction inhibits their growth, and they are always short of electric power. In fact, the TEC have to buy more power from the MSEB than they sell to it. This is not unusual in India, which has experienced chronic power shortages since its independence and has seen the demand for power grow twice as fast as the economy. According to a study by the Federation of Indian Chambers of Commerce, the shortage of electric power is crippling industrial growth. The study suggests that the private sector should be encouraged to set up generation facilities and utilities on a scale large enough to meet the country's power requirements.

Relevance of Criteria for Public Sector Provision

Natural Monopolies

Before electricity can be switched on—whether in factories, in people's homes, or in the systems lighting the streets—it has to be generated, transmitted from the power station, and distributed to users. Although electricity can be generated in many ways, all require the input of power. The most common power sources are machines that burn fuel or that are driven by running water, but power can also be obtained from the sun, wind, and other sources. Natural monopolies are not involved in the generation of electricity. A company distributing electricity to the public or using electricity for its own purposes, can, in principle, acquire power from various sources, and generally does so by using the least costly method for regular operations and the more costly method (for example, old equipment) as a reserve or to meet peak demands. Although few countries have gone as far as the United States, which has rules that public distribution networks must buy electricity from small private producers that use renewable energy as their main source of power, some countries (for example, India and the Republic of Korea) do allow power to be purchased from outside sources.

Unlike electricity generation, transmission and distribution can be regarded as a natural monopoly. It is less costly, for example, to cover an urban area with one electric grid than with two overlapping ones. However, the consumer does not necessarily benefit from having access to only one network. Primeaux (1985) has reported that communities in the United States that are served by competitive services (for example, Lubbock, Texas) do not pay more for their power than consumers in other cities where there is no competition.

Arrangements could also be made to pass on to the customers some of the lower costs associated with single systems, while allowing some degree of competition. Costs could be reduced, for example, if utility poles carried the lines of more than one company; indeed, the same poles could be used to carry electricity and telephone lines. Even if the transmission or distribution of electricity is a natural monopoly, this is no reason to protect monopolies from competition. Furthermore, if competition is bound to fail, why go to the trouble of prohibiting it? Electricidad de Caracas was never protected from competition, and neither consumers nor producers suffered as a result.

Externalities

Consumers generally recognize that electricity is tremendously useful and expect to pay for the service. It would be difficult to argue that, because of its externalities, electricity should be offered at a subsidized rate that only a public authority can provide. Even if there were externalities, it would always be possible to contract with private companies to supply this service.

Inability to Charge or to Exclude Nonpayers

In general, charging for electricity or cutting off the supply of those who do not pay does not present a problem. Consumption is usually recorded on electric meters, and the fear of instant electrocution discourages most people from trying to bypass their meters. The timely collection of electricity charges over a large area is a difficult task, but not an impossible one. Electricity can also be supplied through prepayment coin meters, which enable consumers to buy electricity in small quantities, as and when required. With one significant exception, it cannot be claimed that electricity cannot be charged for.

The exception is street lighting, because there is no way of making it available to some people and not to others. Thus street lighting has to be provided as a community service, whereby the community pays the electricity supplier and recovers the costs through taxation. But the need to supply public street lighting does not imply that electricity should be publicly provided. Street lighting can be provided by private firms under contract to local authorities, as is the case in parts of New York City.

Merit Goods

Does electricity have the characteristics of a merit good? That is to say, do the users fail to appreciate its real value and thus would they fail to consume enough of it unless it was subsidized through public supply? The advantages of electricity are so well known that electricity cannot be considered a merit good.

Scale Economies

There are undoubtedly scale economies in both the generation and transmission of electricity, in the sense that unit costs can fall as the size of the generators or the transmission cables increases. In the United States, for example, the unit costs of a 550-megawatt oil-fired generating station are estimated to be some 20 percent less than the unit costs of a 225-megawatt station; and a 250-megawatt nuclear reactor can be expected to cost 50 percent or so more per kilowatt than a 1,000-megawatt reactor (Dunkerley and others 1981).

But this in itself is not a sufficient argument for public supply: although it might be cheaper to manufacture bread in one bakery that is large enough to supply a whole city, rather than in individual bakeries, this is not generally regarded as a sufficient reason for granting a monopoly to a municipal bread organization. Scale economies of this kind can be handled by economic markets, and generally are. To the extent that there are scale economies in bread manufacture, some bakeries amalgamate. At the same time, some bread factories with their own distribution systems compete with individual bakers. The situation is similar in the production and supply of electricity. To the extent that bigger plants provide cheaper electricity, they may be built to provide cheap service. In fact, this was the case in many countries (for example, Venezuela and the United States) before the 1973 energy crisis: power plants of increasing size produced electricity at steadily declining costs and prices. But in developing countries, where investment programs are less responsive to consumer needs, the more economic, larger systems are not always provided, with the result that many millions receive poor service, or none at all, and can expect service to improve only through the development of local, small-scale supplies. It may not have been helpful to prohibit a villager in North Yemen from buying electricity from his neighbor's generator on the ground that a nationwide system would have been cheaper in the long run.

Thus, the supply of electricity does not appear to involve any substantial externalities that would justify public provision; it is possible to charge for the service and to exclude nonpayers; the product is not a merit good in the sense that people do not realize its value; and there is no natural monopoly in electricity generation. There are scale economies in generation, but these do not seem to be significant enough to justify the prohibition of private, competitive supply. In contrast, the scale economies in transmission and distribution can be important enough to constitute natural monopolies and justify production or regulation by the public sector.

Private Sector Involvement

Opportunities for the Private Sector

Given the structure of the electricity industry outlined above, the private sector seems best suited for a role in the generation stage, particularly under conditions of interconnected supply, when the supply can be competitive. But, as will be seen later, private sector generation is more prevalent in cases of isolated supply, despite the possible abuse of monopoly power. Competitive transmission of electricity, which could involve wasteful duplication, is unusual in developing countries. Where private transmission occurs (for example, in India or Venezuela), it is usually part of a franchised operation. The same is true of local distribution. In contrast, in the United States the transmission of electricity is both private and competitive, and local competitive distribution (alternative suppliers on separate networks offering service to domestic users), though rare, exists in about twenty urban areas.

The following roles for the private sector can be identified:

- Competitive distribution, whereby final consumers have a choice of suppliers. Some examples of competitive electricity provision can be found in the United States (see table 3-3), but none have been located in developing countries.
- Unregulated (or, rather, self-regulated) private supply in major urban areas, whereby consumers have no choice of supplier. This is the situation in Venezuela (the system in Caracas is described below).
- Private sector provision of a franchised operation, subject to regulation by a public authority. In this situation consumers have no choice of supplier, but the supplier is a regulated private firm rather than a public sector agency. Although many of the private companies providing electricity on a franchise basis have been taken over by the public sector, some entities of this type remain, for example, in the Caribbean area.
- Private sector generation of electric power for sale to a publicly operated electric grid. Although about 15 percent of power in the United States is supplied to public utilities by private firms, far less is supplied in this way in develop-

ing countries. The example of the Tata Electric Companies in the Bombay area has already been mentioned.

- Provision by consumer cooperatives.
- Small independent hydroelectricity suppliers. Small hydro-electric generators, ranging in capacity from 100 kilowatts to 10 megawatts. Manufactured in North and South America, Yugoslavia, and other countries; they can provide power independently of national distribution systems and are to be found throughout the world. (Some that are operated by the private sector and by local cooperatives are described below.)

Table 3–3. Communities in Which Electric Utilities Directly Compete, May 1982

State and city	Type of competitive firm	State and city	Type of competitive firm
Alabama		Ohio	
Tarrant City	MP	Cleveland	MP
Troy	MC	Columbus	MP
		Hamilton	MP
Illinois		Newton Falls	MP
Bushnell	MP	Piqua (outskirts)	MP
Iowa		Oklahoma	
Maquoketa	MP	Duncan	MP
Michigan		Pennsylvania	
Bay City	MP	East Stroudsburg	PP
Dowagiac	MP	Stroudsburg	PP
Ferrysburgh	MP		
Traverse City	MP	South Carolina	
Zeeland	MP	Greer	MP
Missouri		Texas	
Poplar Bluff	MP	Electra	MP
Sikestown	MP	Floydada	MP
Trenton	MP	Lubbock	MP
Kennet	MP	Seymour	MP
		Sonora	MP
		Vernon	MP

Note: M indicates municipally owned, P indicates privately owned, and C indicates cooperative ownership (U.S. Federal Power Commission, *Typical Electric Bills,* January 1966).

Source: Primeaux (1985).

- Generation from renewable energy. The use of bagasse to generate electricity has already been mentioned. Examples of private generation from timber, sunlight, wind, and biogas are described below.

Competitive Distribution of Electricity

Primeaux (1985) has identified twenty-nine communities in the United States in which households have a choice of electricity supplier (see table 3-3). No such cases have been found elsewhere. In the United States they occur, for example, when a municipality decides to start its own service without buying out the existing supplier, which might be a firm supplying more than one community. These systems tend to be popular with consumers and (despite conventional wisdom) they are not more costly than monopolistic systems.

Unregulated Private Supply, Caracas

Electricity was introduced in Caracas, the capital of Venezuela, at a time when the country was poor and disrupted by civil war. The results illustrate the potential of private enterprise even under the most adverse circumstances. The principal figure in this history was Ricardo Zuloaga, who was illiterate until the age of twelve because his family could not afford to buy him shoes so that he could go to school. (It is typical of the man that, when later in his life he provided schools for neighborhood children, he decreed that all children should attend without shoes to avoid embarrassment of this kind.) In 1883, when Zuloaga was a seventeen-year-old successful engineering student, the municipal theater was illuminated by electricity to celebrate the first centenary of the birth of Simón Bolívar. The demonstration impressed young Ricardo and all who saw it, but the system of direct current used in 1883 had limited commercial applicability, because it was not possible to transmit it economically over long distances. Nevertheless, in 1888 public electric lighting was inaugurated in Valencia, the first South American city to use electricity for public lighting. The power was insufficient for industrial uses.

In 1891, Zuloaga—then a qualified engineer of twenty-five— came across a magazine article describing how electricity generated as an alternating current could be transmitted at high voltage over long distances with minimal losses and was inspired to go to Europe to learn more. While in Switzerland, he engaged in an intense study of all aspects of electricity. On his return, he devoted his energies to establishing an electric system for Caracas. He found a suitable site for a hydroelectric plant (at El Encantado, ten miles from Caracas) and set about raising the necessary funds. In July 1895, he bought the land at El Encantado, and on November 12 of the same year the Compañia Anónima la Electricidad de Caracas was constituted at the first meeting of its shareholders in Caracas. To be able to attend, Zuloaga had to ask his brother to lend him a decent suit and two bolivars to pay for the coach fare. The initial capital of the company was 500,000 bolivars, 300,000 of which was in cash; the remainder was to compensate Zuloaga for his studies, contracts, land, and other expenses.

In December 1895, Zuloaga visited Europe again to arrange for the purchase of generators and other equipment that could not be manufactured in Venezuela. On his return he managed every detail of the construction of the plant and contracted with the municipality and with local factories for the sale of electricity. Despite numerous setbacks, the plant was completed, and the inaugural ceremony took place on August 8, 1897, in the presence of the president of the republic and other ministers and important personalities. After the speeches, a switch was operated and the machinery started to run without a hitch.

The plant at El Encantado consisted of two vertical-axis turbines, made by Escher Wyss in Switzerland, with a generation capacity of 240 kilowatts. These turbines were used until 1911, when they were replaced by a single 400-kilowatt unit. The power was carried to Caracas at 5,000 volts. Two days after the inauguration of the plant, the company took on its first full-time employee who served as accountant, cashier, money collector, and secretary. The office was a small room in a private house. Under the guidance of Zuloaga, the company expanded rapidly. It paid its first dividend—9 percent a year—in 1904, and it continued paying monthly dividends almost without interruption for eighty years. The demand for electric light and power grew as new industries were established and as old ones switched to electricity. The company's capital expanded to 3.45 million bolivars by 1911, 15 million by 1926, and 21 million by 1932, the year of the death of its founder. By 1984 the capital exceeded 1 billion bolivars.

Electricidad de Caracas never had a formal concession; although its rates were not regulated, they declined steadily as the city expanded and the company was able to take advantage of scale economies. The rates in Caracas were about the same as in the United States. For many years, the government was in fact urging

Electricidad de Caracas to raise its rates to enable its own company to increase its revenues. Electricidad de Caracas not only refused to do this, but also supplied the poor people living in the "ranchos" at concessional rates. By all accounts, Electricidad de Caracas was extremely well run as a private company (Ruhl 1978).

Through no fault of its own, the company's financial situation deteriorated in the 1980s, and its future as an independent entity is now in doubt. The reasons for this are instructive. First, it was unable to obtain payment for power supplied to the municipality and to government departments. Because the supply to the municipality included the street lighting for the city center, the accumulated debt was substantial, and one official of the company spent all his working time trying to collect the government debt. To add insult to injury, the company was required to pay a 4 percent turnover tax on electricity that it had sold but that had not been paid for. Second, the company was required by the government to invest US$800 million in new generating facilities. This money had to be borrowed and repaid in U.S. dollars. However, the devaluation of the bolivar in 1983 effectively tripled the burden of this loan and made it almost impossible to repay. For these reasons, Electricidad de Caracas became technically bankrupt and lost much of its independence.

Private Sector Concessions (Franchises)

When private firms are granted concessions to operate an electricity service on a monopoly basis, they are generally subject to regulation by a public agency. As the price for protection from competition, the public regulating agencies determine the prices that may be charged for electricity. Inflation has taken its toll on many concessionaires in the developing countries. Squeezed between rising costs and the inability to maintain the real value of their revenues, most were forced to give up their concessions and were taken over by governments whose policies made their independence impossible.

A further problem with regulated electricity suppliers, at least in all countries that follow the practice of the United States, is that the remuneration of the concessionaire is given as an allowable return on the capital invested in the business. This induces concessionaires to invest as much as possible in order to increase the rate base. Furthermore, there is little incentive to reduce other costs, as the regulators tend to remunerate concession holders on a cost-plus basis. For these reasons, private concessions to supply electricity have become less and less popular, and only a few remain—

for example, in Barbados and the Cayman Islands in the Caribbean, in Equador (Guayaquil Private Power Company), and in the Philippines (Manila Electric Light Company).

The problems of regulated electrical companies in Latin America can be seen in a study of conditions in Brazil, Chile, Colombia, Costa Rica, and Mexico during the 1950s (Cavers and Nelson 1959). In all these countries rates were kept low in order to provide cheap electricity; the "cheap electricity" resulted in "low earnings and poor service"; and "the effective cost to the economy [was] often . . . very high in terms of inconvenience, delay, and damage, plus the extra cost of private plant." The study team concluded that

> Every country studied has suffered from acute electric power shortages at some time or other since World War II. In several important supply areas, shortage has been the rule and abundance the exception. Even when generating capacity has been adequate, service to ultimate consumers has often deteriorated because of bottlenecks in distribution capacity. The rapid rate of installation of private plant in some of the most important industrial areas of Brazil and Colombia points to an almost continuous struggle to obtain enough public utility electricity, and frequent statements of government officials and industry leaders testify to the shortage of capacity . . . It seems clear that Latin America's need is for *more* electricity and not for *cheap* electricity. (Cavers and Nelson 1959, p. 29.)

By contrast, electricity in Venezuela was provided by an unregulated private sector. The situation there at about the same time was described in an internal World Bank report.

> The control of rates by some form of a commission is now being considered. Since the current level of electricity rates is reasonable, the mission sees no pressing need for such control. Development plans of the private companies, although not the subject of review by the Government, are most satisfactory. The private companies on the whole have been progressive and have adequately served.

The fact that unregulated companies provided better electric service than regulated ones in Latin America is instructive, but it does not necessarily imply that private, unregulated electric companies would be appropriate in all developing countries. Consumers facing monopoly suppliers can have serious problems. But these may be met in other ways than by perpetuating monopolies protected and regulated by government (Houston 1985). One way is to form consumer cooperatives that enable the users of public services to exercise the powers of ownership.

Electrical Cooperatives

Argentina and Chile provide the earliest examples of electrical cooperatives in Latin America. Another pioneer in this respect was the United States, where forty-six electrical cooperatives were organized between 1914 and 1930; most of these were small projects serving from 10 to 360 members. The spread of electrical cooperatives was encouraged by the New Deal. In 1933 the Tennessee Valley Authority (TVA) Act authorized the TVA board to give preference in the sale of surplus electric power to "cooperative organizations of citizens or farmers." The first rural electric cooperative in the TVA area, the Alcorn County Electric Power Association, was established on June 1, 1934, with headquarters at Corinth, Mississippi. It was followed by the Rural Electrification Administration (REA) established in 1936. REA loan funds were available to stimulate electric service in rural areas, and thus many farmers formed new cooperatives to obtain these loans. The first such loan was made on October 1, 1936, to assist a cooperative in Minnesota. In 1937 the REA drafted the Electric Cooperative Corporation Act, a model state law for the formation and operation of rural electric cooperatives. Since then the number of electrical cooperatives has increased rapidly, and there are now more than one thousand. In 1942 the leaders of the movement organized the National Rural Electric Cooperative Association (NRECA), with headquarters in Washington, D.C.

Readers who do not consider the United States to be a developing country may wonder what bearing this information has on the problems of Africa, Asia, and Latin America. The connection is that the first general manager of the NRECA, Clyde Ellis, conceived the idea of an international program. Following approaches to President-elect John F Kennedy and to the new Secretary of State Dean Rusk, Ellis persuaded the NRECA board to export the idea of rural cooperatives with the aid of funding from USAID. A contract between NRECA and USAID was signed in 1962; but, even before that, NRECA had sent a man to Nicaragua to help organize a rural electric cooperative there. By 1981 the AID-NRECA teams had financed more than 196 rural electric systems serving more than 11 million consumers in fourteen countries (see table 3-4).

Electrical Cooperatives in the Philippines. The NRECA's efforts in developing countries have been focused mainly on the Philippines,

Table 3–4. Cooperatives Helped by NRECA and USAID, September 1, 1980

Country	Number of rural electric systems	Number of meters	Number of consumers
Brazil	12	13,000	84,500
Chile	15	22,000	143,000
Colombia	1	14,000	91,000
Costa Rica	4	29,000	188,500
Bolivia	5	70,000	455,000
Ecuador	1	10,000	65,000
Nicaragua	5	42,000	273,000
Peru	1	13,000	84,500
Venezuela	1	2,000	13,000
Philippines	120	1,400,000	9,100,000
India	5	115,000	747,500
Viet Nam	3	27,000	175,500
Bangladesh	13	1,000	6,500
Indonesia	10	3,800	24,700
Total	196	1,761,800	11,451,700

Source: Bennet (1981).

where the NRECA worked for thirteen years before moving on to other countries. The changes in the electrified areas have been dramatic. Not only has the birth rate declined among populations with electrified homes, but cottage industries dependent upon electricity are flourishing and the scholastic performance of students is improving. School buildings can be used at night, and farmers can expect two or three harvests a year rather than one as a result of irrigation by electrically powered pumps. Refrigeration, running water, and hot water, in addition to improving household living, have made it possible to form new enterprises, such as commercial poultry farms. La Unión Eléctrica Co-op, 140 miles northwest of Manila, is providing power for 30,000 homes and 100,000 people. It is also sponsoring rural water projects and has pioneered the employment of women to wire village homes.

Not all of the Filipino electrical cooperatives are financed by USAID. Eighteen miles southwest of Manila, in Cavite Province, is a small hydro project, financed by a loan from China (which is reported to have some 100,000 30-kilowatt minihydro projects). It provides cheap power for seventy homes (Bennet 1981).

Electrical Cooperatives in Santa Cruz, Bolivia. Santa Cruz in eastern Bolivia is famous for its cooperatives. On November 14, 1962, when it was a poor, crowded city of about 80,000 inhabitants, a group of Santa Cruz businessmen, professionals, teachers, and farmers met in the city hall to discuss what could be done to improve the city's electric service. At that time, the electric voltage in parts of the city was not high enough to keep the light bulbs burning brightly, and outright failures were an everyday occurrence. The group decided to send a representative to a meeting of the Organization of the Cooperatives of America and, as a result of the contacts made there, obtained a US$7 million USAID loan; US$3.5 million went to the national utility for generation and the construction of transmission lines, and the remaining US$3.5 million went to the local Cooperativa Rural de Electrificación (CRE) for building a new distribution system in the city and four nearby towns. When the new system was energized in 1970, the co-op had 8,500 members. Five years later, USAID provided a further loan of US$13 million, which enabled the cooperative to electrify eighty-four villages and towns.

By 1981, the co-op had 50,000 members and had become one of the largest in the world. The city had grown to 300,000; that growth was powered in part by electricity. Among the recent developments is an industrial park on the outskirts of Santa Cruz that contains sixty tenants, including the largest textile mill in South America, Santa Cruz's largest newspaper, a sawmill, and a soy oil plant. The countryside north of the city has processing plants for cottonseed, sugarcane, and timber; very few such rural industries existed in the area before the coming of electricity. Also newly established are medical and dental clinics, hospitals, and night classes in the schools for children and adults who work during the day. Television sets are common, and the University of Santa Cruz operates an educational program (Gallant 1981).

Many cooperatives are able to provide electricity at a remarkably low cost by relying on small hydropower systems. This technology can be applied in many developing countries.

Small Hydroelectric Systems

Small hydroelectric plants (for example, those generating 1–1,000 kilowatts) can provide affordable, reliable electric power to many areas that are now without electric service, particularly in isolated communities where the cost of transporting fuels or building transmission lines is high. Hydropower uses falling water to produce electricity and does not depend on fossil fuels such as petroleum or coal. Although the initial costs of hydroplants may be somewhat higher than the cost of diesel or gasoline generators of similar capacity, the river water that is required to operate them

is free and abundant in many areas of the world. The technology
of small hydroelectric plants has been well developed for many
years, but at present the emphasis is on low-cost, mass-produced
turbine generator sets that require relatively little care and maintenance. This equipment is manufactured in many countries, including China, Colombia, India, and Yugoslavia. (Some examples of
the costs of small hydroelectric plants are presented in table 3-5.)

**Table 3–5. Installation Costs for Small Hydro Plants
in Developing Countries**

Country	Capacity (kilo- watts)	Head (meters)	Cost per kilowatt[a]	Equip- ment as percent- age of cost	Comments
Thailand	800	40	$2,850	15	Concrete construction for civil works
Ecuador	400	40	2,200	36	Lined canal; imported equipment
Ecuador	400	19	2,700	30	Lined canal; direct intake; im- ported equipment
Nepal[b]	200	58	900	36	Partly lined canal; loose-packed rock dam
Nepal	120	14	900	21	Masonry-lined headrace
Indonesia	120	15	1,300	58	No headrace; local turbine
Thailand	100	79	950	21	Concrete construction for civil works
Philippines[b]	100	27	750	38	Local construction materials and turbine
Indonesia	90	19	1,050	54	Concrete-lined headrace
Nepal	80	16	1,650	23	Local materials and turbines
Nepal	80	34	1,050	31	Local materials and turbines
Nepal	25	22	650	28	Existing irrigation works
Indonesia[b]	15	22	600	30	No headrace or governor, used alternator
Thailand	15	10	2,350	41	Earth dam and headrace
Thailand	10	6	1,500	27	Lined canal; local turbine
Pakistan[b]	10	—[c]	270	61	Local materials and equipment
Nepal	9.5	9	600	46	Local materials and equipment, except penstock
Pakistan[b]	7.5	—[c]	320	60	Local materials and equipment

a. Not including transmission and distribution costs.
b. Projects implemented and managed locally.
c. Precise heads unknown, but generally between 5 and 10 meters.
Source: Clark (1982).

Clark (1982) has pointed out that small unsophisticated hydro-electric systems, especially those with a capacity below 100 kilo-watts, can be substantially cheaper to run than conventional systems, as shown in figure 3-3. Clark cited four reasons for this difference in cost: (1) the technology is simpler and can be easily grasped by villagers; (2) greater innovation in design is possible; (3) maintenance is simplified, since the materials are provided locally; and (4) community participation, on which this approach is based, reduces labor, engineering, and management costs and provides greater assurance of long-term success. Clark suggested that local participation is particularly important in that it improves the chances of success, since power plants are more likely to respond to the needs of consumers when this approach is used. The local provision of hydroelectric power can be illustrated by examples from Colombia, Nepal, and Sri Lanka.

The Dormilon Power Project. In 1982, Intermediate Technology Industrial Services (ITIS) of the United Kingdom funded a water-powered sawmill and electric generator at the small village of El Dormilon in the province of Antioquia in central Colombia (the information on this project is based on Burton and Holland 1983; and Holland 1982). The objective was to demonstrate that water power can be cheaper than any alternative source and can have an important effect on rural development. The project was executed by the members of the community themselves with support from the nongovernment rural development organization Comunidad por los Niños led by Alvaro Villa, which had already helped to set up fish farms, biogas plants, and small microhydro plants. Technical direction came from John Burton, who had been teaching at universities in Colombia for more than ten years with the support of the British Council.

The El Dormilon community consists of some twenty small subsistence farming families living in the valley of the Dormilon River. The main economic activities are cutting timber from the forest, extracting aggregate and ballast from the river, cattle farming, and coffee growing. Although these families were enthusiastic about the idea of having electricity for lighting and cooking, the poorer members of the community could not afford the payments for a hydro plant used only for domestic power. A way had to be found to earn some income with the power that the plant would be producing twenty-four hours a day. Possible industrial applications included coffee hulling and sugarcane crushing, but the one villagers cited as being most useful was timber sawing. Timber, which was then sold at the roadside as logs for processing else-

Figure 3–3. Cost Comparisons of Selected Power Plants

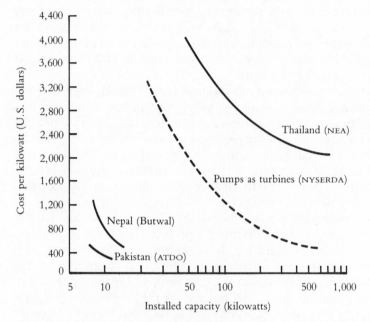

Note: ATDO = Appropriate Technology Development Organization; NEA = National Electrical Authority; and NYSERDA = New York State Energy Research and Development Authority.

Source: Clark (1982).

where, could be sawed into planks and then used for packing cases, broomsticks, building materials, and even furniture.

A study of the value added by a small sawmill and the repayment cost for the whole plant showed not only that the cost of the sawmill and hydro plant would be amply covered by the income from the sawmill, but that there would be a substantial surplus. The electric generator and transmission lines would be paid for by a fixed tariff, equivalent to the amount villagers would save in kerosene and candles.

Further savings, in time if not necessarily in cash, could eventually accrue through the use of electricity for cooking. Because the plant was small, however (its size was limited by the flow of the nearby Quebrada Mulato River and the power it could generate), it was not possible for each household to have a 1- or 2-kilowatt electric cooker and for all of them to cook simultaneously (as they normally would). The solution was to use heat storage cookers; these cookers have a very low wattage and store energy as heat in a cast-iron block for twenty-four hours a day, which can be extracted when needed. Enough heat can be stored to meet the cooking needs of most households. Once all cooking is done electrically, the community should save close to 4,000 hours a year in fuelwood collecting time.

Microhydro technology is familiar in Colombia, even if it has not been widely used in recent years. Old Pelton wheel turbines are commonly used to drive cane crushers or sawmills, but the idea of having a community-owned installation provide domestic electricity as well as industrial power was new. The objective behind ITIS's involvement was to help persuade funding institutions such as development finance corporations to support this type of scheme.

The Comunidad por los Niños had helped to set up regular community meetings to discuss the project. The villagers drew up a legal document establishing the community as a legal entity with its own bank account and thereby committed themselves to the joint ownership of the sawmill hydro plant and formally agreed to repay the loan. All the construction work for the microhydro plant on the river diversion, pipeline, and powerhouse was undertaken by the community. Records were kept of the number of hours each person worked, and those who did not participate but who subsequently wanted to be connected to the electrical supply had to pay cash in lieu of labor or were charged a higher-than-standard tariff. The community committee decided how the plant should be operated and fixed the tariff for domestic power. Sawmill operators were trained by an instructor from SENA (the national technical training organization). One year of grace was allowed before the first payment on the loan was due; during that time income from the sawmill would build up.

The turbine was designed and manufactured by C.CH.LG. of Bogatá (director, Jaime Lobo-Guerrero). An electronic load governor from Evans/GP Electronics of the United Kingdom was used for speed control, and thus flow control was not needed. The generator is connected all the time, and the load control governor controls the saw speed (which is important for good cutting) and dumps the excess power as heat. The saw is connected to the turbine via a chain coupling, so it can be disconnected when not needed.

The storage cookers are fed on a separate transmission line from the main electrical connection to each house. Thus the main line can be disconnected when power is needed for sawing. At the same time, a constant load is available to power the storage cookers during the day and night; the remaining power is used to drive the saws during the day and to provide lighting at night. A transformer provides each house with a fused electrical supply (110 volts, 60 Hertz, the standard domestic voltage in Colombia).

A conservative estimate of the load factor (the ratio of power available to power usefully used) is 40 percent. On this basis, the cost of power works out to be considerably less than half the cost of diesel power and is also roughly equivalent to the grid tariff, if there is no connection charge. (For communities more than a few kilometers away from an electric grid, the cost of connection makes that alternative unattractive.)

The cost of the project, including a two-year maintenance contract, was US$28,000. The cost of the microhydro system without the sawmill was US$18,400 (US$613 per kilowatt). Both figures were within the budget. The income from sawed timber is expected to be US$29,000 a year, and savings on candles and firewood should be about US$3,200. Total annual capital and maintenance costs are US$2,900. Thus the earning capacity of the community has increased considerably. One year after the installation was completed, the community was selling timber for construction work (such as shuttering) and was using the offcuts to make tomato crates. The income from these sales exceeded predictions.

Cogeneration in Nepal. Nepal is a country with few roads, a scattered but dense population in certain parts of the country, rugged terrain, many deforested areas, and no oil reserves. Faced with these conditions, the Nepalese see decentralized hydropower as a promising option in their struggle to achieve economic development. But the government approach to installing small hydropower plants in Nepal manifests some of the same characteristics encountered in other countries: bureaucratic delays, high costs, and a growing dependence on external financing to cover these costs.

In the 1960s, Balaju Yantra Shala (BYS), a private machine shop in Kathmandu established under a Swiss aid program, undertook to design, fabricate, and install several propeller turbines to drive grain-milling machines. This effort encouraged another group— the United Mission to Nepal (UMN), through its Butwal Engineering Works Private Limited (BEW) and Development Consulting Services (DCS)—to become involved not only in designing, fabricating, and testing turbines and associated hardware, but also in developing a viable, virtually nonsubsidized approach to the field implementation of small water-powered mill installations. (These and the following details are based on Inversin 1982.)

The United Mission to Nepal, which is at the root of these developments, is a private voluntary organization with headquarters in Nepal. It consists of nearly forty Protestant mission groups and church-related aid agencies. In addition to working in the health and education fields, it carries out rural and industrial development projects under the aegis of its Economic Development Board. The first such undertaking was the Butwal Technical Institute (BTI), begun in 1963. As this project grew beyond its original function of apprenticeship training in its machine shops, new organizations were created. BTI was subsequently redefined as the holding organization for the various workshops that were formed into private limited companies. Among these were the Butwal Plywood Factory, the Butwal Power Company, the Gobar Gas and Agricultural Equipment Company, the Butwal Wood Industries, and the Himal Hydro Construction Company. The mechanical workshop became the Butwal Engineering Works Private Limited. Another organizational structure, Development and Consulting Services, now carries out most of the nonworkshop-oriented consulting and field work. The private limited companies and DCS are located in Butwal, a small Nepalese town at the base of the foothills of the Himalayan range.

The Nepalese have long been accustomed to harnessing their water resources. For centuries, they have tapped the country's streams and rivers for irrigation. Thus canals—many of them kilometers long—crisscross the hills and valleys; some are perched on steep mountain slopes, and a few even tunnel through rock. Rice, corn, wheat, and other crops are grown on the irrigated plots. Until recently, the Nepalese processed much of their produce by hand, using rudimentary tools. This is how they hulled rice, milled grain, and expelled oil from seed. However, they had some mechanical assistance by way of their vertical-axis waterwheel used to drive the millstones for milling grain. Thousands of these water-powered mills dot the countryside.

Recently, diesel-powered mills that perform all three of these tasks were introduced in the mountains. Although these mills cost more to operate than the water-powered mills, they have proved popular. They can now be found throughout the country in areas distant from the main roads and population centers. As the cost of diesel oil became increasingly burdensome, however, BYS decided to use water power as an alternative source of motive power for these mills. It therefore fabricated and installed propeller, and later cross-flow, turbines.

During the initial phases of this project, progress was slow because only materials available in Nepal and the Indian subcontinent could be used. Thus many items had to be designed and manufactured in Nepal, whereas it would have been far easier to import them. In 1977, the first three mills powered by water turbines were installed in the hills of Nepal. Eleven more were installed in 1978, and the numbers increased in subsequent years. A total of sixty-five mills had been installed by 1982.

Although most of the hydropower plants were used to power food-processing machinery, mill owners were also interested in generating electricity for lighting. As a result, a cogeneration system was developed to use the falling water to produce electrical power for lighting as well as mechanical power for milling. The electrical system selected for lighting was a 24-volt direct current.

One of the problems in designing a system for use in the hills of Nepal is that most mill installations are several days' walk from the road and few people know anything about electricity. Certain basic design criteria therefore had to be established. First, the system had to have sufficient power to light a minimum of six bulbs. Furthermore, a lead-acid battery—which is both heavy and requires maintenance—could not be part of the system. In addition, the voltage output of the alternator would have to remain constant over the wide range of speeds at which the turbine actually runs, and the system had to be reliable.

The system that finally evolved utilizes an automobile alternator and a DCS-designed voltage regulator. An alternator manufactured in Bombay and costing about US$100 was used initially, but a source of alternators costing only US$40 was later found. This 12-volt alternator is connected in such a way as to generate 24 volts, with the result that the unit can generate twice the power that would otherwise be available. Incandescent bulbs running at 24 volts are widely used on the Indian railway system and are readily available—not, it is hoped, by removing them from railway carriages.

The voltage regulator was designed to maintain the voltage output at a nearly constant level over the wide range of speeds to which it is exposed. Most of the components are mounted on a laminated, printed plug-in circuit board designed by DCS and manufactured in India. The difficulty of performing good soldering in the hills of Nepal, away from any source of electricity, necessitated this change. The alternator is driven off the same pulley that powers the mill machinery. The alternator pulley drives the alternator at 3,000 revolutions a minute when the turbine is running at design speed.

By 1982, seven mill-lighting units had been installed. A standard installation with a total of eight incandescent lights cost about US$420. In addition to the basic installation, optional items were available. These included additional wiring (with a maximum of twelve bulbs), electric fans, fluorescent tube lighting, and an electric horn. The horn is necessary to notify the villagers that the mill is open for business.

In this manner, a small quantity of "safe" (24-volt) electricity has been made available for lighting the mill, so that work can continue in the evening and may possibly be available for homes in the vicinity of the mill. Several mill owners have expressed an interest in using a 240-volt AC alternator of sufficient capacity to provide power for the villagers, primarily for lighting. Although the private generation and supply of electricity is technically feasible, legal questions regarding it still have to be resolved, even in Nepal.

Small-Scale Power Plants for Rural Industry in Sri Lanka. There are hundreds of disused microhydro plants in need of renovation on the tea estates of Sri Lanka. These plants were installed fifty to sixty years ago to run the tea factories by mechanical drive or by DC generators and were abandoned in recent years when mains electricity was introduced. Today, because the grid electricity supply is failing to meet demand and electricity prices are rising rapidly, the tea estate corporations are making every effort to rehabilitate these old plants. (The shortfall in electrical supply is expected to continue even after the large Mahaweli scheme is completed.) The repair of equipment at the Alupolla and Kataboole tea estates provides examples of low-cost private enterprise rehabilitation. (The information on Sri Lanka is based on Holland, 1982.)

From 1926 to 1975, the factory at Alupolla was powered by a Gunther Francis turbine, directly driving an 80-kilowatt DC generator. A transmission line took this power to the factory, where two DC motors drove the line shafting. After 1975, the tea-processing machines (roller, roll breakers, withering fans, and so on) were driven by AC motors fed from the grid, and the turbine was neglected; it ran at about 5 percent capacity to provide only lighting.

In 1982 Intermediate Technology Industrial Services (ITIS) helped Brown and Company, a Sri Lankan engineering firm, to rehabilitate the turbines. New Pelton wheels were installed, and the hydraulic governors were replaced by electric load controllers. The total cost of reactivation was about US$60,000 per estate, and the annual electricity saving about 380,000 kilowatt-hours, or

US$44,000. Thus, the cost of rehabilitation was recovered in less than two years.

The work on the tea estates led to a separate rural development project with the Norwegian Save the Children Foundation (Redd Barna). This project involved resettling landless farmers in the jungle north of Matale. The farmers had planted cardamom, a highly valued spice that grows well in the semi-jungle at that altitude. Having purchased an electric dryer, Redd Barna approached Brown and Company for a small hydro plant to run it, since a grid extension was too expensive to build. The new plant was installed with ITIS technical assistance to optimize the control of the dryer and make the best use of the limited power available.

Generation from Renewable Energy

Brazil is rich in many resources, but not in petroleum. The government is therefore encouraging firms to produce electricity from renewable energy. In 1981, it passed a law allowing private firms to generate electricity and sell it to public distribution systems. One of the private firms responding to this initiative is SATHEL Usinas Termo Hidro-Eléctricas S.A. of the northern state of Rondônia.

SATHEL manufactures (under license) a Swedish type of wood-fired steam turbine. It decided to sell electric power made by its equipment and contracted with the city of Ariquemes (population 25,000) to sell bulk power at an agreed rate per kilowatt-hour. The contract is for ten years; at the end of that time the city will have the option of renewing its contract or buying the equipment from SATHEL at a price agreed to in the contract.

SATHEL uses timber to power its turbines and has gone into forest management to ensure that the timber used in its operations is more than replaced. It currently has three electricity supply contracts in the state of Amazonas, two in Rondônia and three in Acre. The contracts, all for "isolated" systems, provide for a minimum quantity of power to be sold each year but do not give SATHEL a monopoly. The company is eager to expand its operations, both in Brazil and elsewhere.

Photovoltaics—Electricity from the Sun

Visitors to the 1984 Khartoum International Fair were fascinated by the solar water pump on display at the Renewable Energy Research Institute stand. They discovered that, by casting enough shadow on the solar panels that powered the pump, they could stop the flow of water from one barrel into another. As soon as they moved back, the water started to flow again. Inside a nearby stall they could see lights, fans, an air cooler, and a refrigerator all driven by an array of solar panels on the roof that provided power to a bank of batteries, which in turn provided power for the nighttime operation.

The technology that made all this possible is known as "photovoltaics," the conversion of light directly into electricity. The conversion occurs when particles of light strike a specially treated wafer of silicon and cause the electrons within the silicon to flow. When these wafers are connected together in a panel, small amounts of electricity can be collected into a usable current. Originally, this was done to provide current to charge the batteries of space satellites. As a result of recent research, this technology can now be used to generate electricity at prices that are beginning to compete with the costs of operating the more usual oil-, diesel-, and gasoline-powered generators. Sales have increased, and economies of scale in manufacture have brought down the price of solar electricity to US$10 per peak watt, or one-tenth of what it cost in 1964. "Peak watts" are the maximum amounts of power per square meter of the earth's surface. At present, solar panels can turn about 10 percent of this power into electricity. The hotter the cells, the less well they work; conversely, they perform very well in cold mountain areas, such as the Himalayas or the Alps, where the light is very bright (Winter 1984).

Is this space-age technology relevant to poor people living in developing countries? Indeed, it is. The majority of the 10 million villages in developing countries have yet to be connected to national electricity grids. Rural electrification has long been a priority objective, and vast sums are being spent annually on increasing capacity. But load factors are often low, and operational and administrative problems abound. Photovoltaic generators would in many cases provide an attractive means of meeting rural electricity demands, since they are simple to operate and maintain, require no fuel, and last for many years. Moreover, being modular, the systems can be made small at first and then extended in subsequent years as the load builds up. Most of the developing countries concerned have ample sunlight and usually enough open land for the photovoltaic arrays.

There are already many hundreds of small stand-alone photovoltaic systems operating throughout the world. In addition to solar-powered calculators and their small microelectronic units, systems commercially available in the power range up to 1 kilowatt include battery chargers, lighting units, water pumps, refrigerators, alarm systems, cathodic protection systems, emergency telephones, television sets, remote beacons, and other navigation aids.

The first solar-powered television set was installed in Niger in 1968. Since then more than 123 schools in Niger have been similarly equipped, as have schools in several other countries. Photovoltaic systems have generally proved more reliable and cheaper to operate and maintain than the large primary batteries or gasoline-engine generators previously used.

One problem with photovoltaics is that electricity is difficult to store. Rechargeable batteries can be used, but they are expensive to buy, heavy to transport, and difficult to maintain, as most automobile owners know. Photovoltaics are therefore ideally suited for applications where the final product itself may be stored (for example, water in a tank or ice in a refrigerator) or where the power can be dispensed with when the sun is down (for example, ceiling fans). Small solar-powered pumping systems designed for water supply and irrigation have long been considered to have great potential for improving living conditions and raising agricultural output in developing countries. A good market for solar pumps that can serve remote cattle-watering points has opened up in the southern part of the United States, in Brazil, and in many other countries where the cost of regularly servicing engine-powered pumps is prohibitive.

In view of the great importance of water pumping, the United Nations Development Programme in 1978 initiated a global project to test and demonstrate small-scale solar pumps. The World Bank was appointed executing agency and consultants were engaged to review the available technology and carry out laboratory and field testing along with extensive economic and system design studies. Detailed reports on the conclusions of this project and a handbook on solar pumping are available from Intermediate Technology Publications[2] to help potential purchasers determine whether solar pumping is appropriate for their circumstances and how to procure suitable equipment.

With the development of straightforward photovoltaic pumping systems, complete water treatment packages that are self-contained and simple to operate are now becoming available. Photovoltaic-powered desalination units using the reverse osmosis process have also been demonstrated. In addition, photovoltaic refrigerators have been under development for a number of years, and several types are now available commercially. The World Health Organization has been supporting projects concerned with

---

2. 9 King Street, London WC2, England.

the development of suitable medical refrigerators for storing vaccines and other medical supplies (WHO 1981). Costs are still too high for major sales, but as technical development proceeds, performance should continue to improve and the need for batteries may be eliminated.

With cells embedded in rooftiles, photovoltaics can be used to provide electricity to houses. A 500-watt system would be sufficient to power three lights, two ceiling fans, and a television set where battery storage is designed to suit the climate and use required. Such a system could run entirely on direct current at 24 or 48 volts and thereby avoid the extra cost and complication of an inverter, but this may not be acceptable in the longer term as the residents would want to be able to operate ordinary domestic appliances requiring alternating current at the national voltage and frequency. However, many appliances could be designed to work from low-voltage DC supplies, as noted earlier in the case of Nepal.

If photovoltaic systems were to become a significant energy resource for a country, its government might wish to build up a local manufacturing capability and not be dependent on imports. Some developing countries are already establishing their own photovoltaic industry, notably Brazil, India, Mexico, and China. Wherever the manufacturing of photovoltaic cells is not yet practicable, a high proportion of the cost of photovoltaic systems can be met by local input. For example, most subsystem components (such as electronic controllers, batteries, pumps, and motors) may be obtained from local sources, and in this way a fledgling photovoltaic industry may be established to produce competitively priced systems with 60 percent or more local content (Starr 1984).

Wind Power as a Source of Electricity

Wind machines have pumped water and ground grain for centuries, but they have been less widely used as electric power generators. Although wind turbines were a common sight on isolated farms in the United States between the early 1900s and the 1930s, they could not compete economically with inexpensive fossil fuels, and they eventually passed from the American scene. Now conditions have changed, and wind energy is staging a comeback (*Energy Researcher* 1981). The main problem with wind as a power source, as with solar energy, is its variability. Except in places like Cape Horn (which tend to be underpopulated), winds do not blow steadily enough to provide reliable power sources for the generation of electricity.

One way of dealing with this problem is to have the windmill tricklecharge a battery, but most commonly available generators cannot do this because they are designed to run at high speed. Intermediate Technology Power Ltd. has recently designed a new generator of simple, robust construction that is reliable and suitable for small-scale local manufacture. Because it utilizes few specialized parts and can be driven directly by a windmill rotor without any step-up in speed, costs can be kept to a minimum. The unit is currently being tested and, if successful, will be manufactured in Kenya.

Another solution is to connect the wind-generated power to a public grid, which would "bank" the surplus electricity made available by production from wind power by buying the surplus and selling it back when the wind dies down. Arrangements of this kind have been worked out in the United States and in Canada. A dairy farm with a 10-kilowatt turbine, for example, may be able to generate one-quarter of its annual electricity needs. (In a strong wind it would generate excess power; in periods of calm it would generate no power.) The local utility would provide power during the windless periods and purchase the windy day excess.

Several utilities are experimenting with large wind turbines to assess their performance and to determine how these machines could best be integrated into utility power systems. Southern California Edison is one such utility. Since October 1980, Edison has encouraged private developers to build wind parks and to sell the electrical output to Edison. Since June 30, 1984, agreements have been reached on fifty-two projects in the Tehachapi and San Gorgonio Pass areas for a total of 804 megawatts. From the inception of the program through May 31, 1984, Edison had purchased 37 million kilowatt-hours from wind parks. In the Tehachapi area, Edison has interconnected thirteen wind parks consisting of a total of 1,225 machines with a capacity of 70 megawatts. In the San Gorgonio Pass area, there are six wind parks consisting of a total of 311 machines with a capacity of 18 megawatts.

Outside North America, wind power is exploited by the private sector in Kenya. Windpumps are being manufactured and installed by Bobs Harries Engineering Ltd., in collaboration with IT Power Ltd.

Biogas

Biogas is a mixture of methane and carbon dioxide that is produced by the fermentation of human or animal manure. It is widely used in Asia and the South Pacific as an alternative fuel. The residue left behind during fermentation makes good fertilizer.

A mixture of organic materials, usually consisting of pig manure, night soil, and crop by-products or grasses, is commonly used in family-sized digestors for the production of gas. In the rural areas of China, all types of human and farm wastes have been used as fertilizers for centuries. According to one estimate, in 1962, 70 percent of the night soil and 60 percent of all farm manure produced in China were used for fertilizer. Because of the importance of organic fertilizer in Chinese agriculture, the advantages of biogas production as an improved method of treating organic wastes has been especially significant (Taylor 1982).

Although most digestors are used by families to produce fuel and fertilizer, community units can drive pumps or power units for cottage industry, so that even poor people can use them profitably. The Chinese have been particularly successful in promoting and exploiting biogas, especially since 1958–59, the years of the Great Leap Forward.

According to Taylor (1982) most community digestors in China are built to provide fuel for internal combustion engines or electricity generation. When electricity is desired, modified diesel engines are hooked up to small asynchronous generators. In Sichuan, special generator units with capacities of 3, 5.5, and 7.5 kilowatts have recently been put into mass production for use in biogas systems.

A total of 301 small biogas power stations with a combined capacity of 1,494 kilowatts have been built in Sichuan. The smallest station has a capacity of 3 kilowatts, and the largest station has a capacity of 120 kilowatts. A recent report from Jiangsu Province states that the 8-kilowatt biogas power stations built there were completed in only one to two months, at a cost of about 4,500 yuan (about US$340) per kilowatt. In the suburbs of Guangzhou (Canton) in Guangdong Province, a large electricity generation system, employing a series of digestors with a total volume of 6,000 cubic meters, has recently begun to generate power on a test basis. The system has a total installed capacity of 500 kilowatts.

The Role of the Government

Inasmuch as electric power was developed privately in a number of countries, from Argentina and Bolivia to Yemen and Zaire, it is difficult to argue that the government has to play a direct role in the provision of electricity. At the same time, the government may have to determine technical standards, such as voltage and cycle frequency, that make it possible to link systems and buy consumer goods. (Those who have lived in different parts of England may remember the box of alternative electrical plugs and light bulbs that had to be kept on hand when cities were served by a variety of voltages and associated outlets.) It is also appropriate for government to determine and enforce safety standards: for example, to ensure that electrical systems are properly grounded, that live wires are color-coded and safely insulated, and so on. In the long run, competition may bring about appropriate standards, but at a heavy and avoidable cost.

In situations where a single distributor obtains a monopoly to supply electricity so that consumers do not have the choice of switching to another supplier, the government must ensure that prices reflect costs and that consumers are not victimized. However, the necessity of monopolistic distribution has been questioned in the United States and should not be taken for granted without site-specific investigation. Governments may have a similar role where there is a monopoly in long-distance, high-voltage transmission. But in electricity generation, the case for competition is strong, and governments might follow the examples of the United States and Brazil by passing laws that require public distributors to buy from those who offer cheap electric power, even if they are independent suppliers.

Although the United States is widely regarded as a bastion of competition and free enterprise, its power sector is generally organized as a system of public utilities, which are regulated monopolies. Federal laws, notably the 1978 Public Utilities Regulatory Policies Act (PURPA), were recently passed to increase efficiency and competition in electricity generation, particularly through the use of renewable energy sources—hydro, solar, and windpower— and the encouragement of cogeneration. Countries that do not depend on regulated monopolies for their electricity may not need PURPA-type legislation. For example, in India, a company called Energy Development Ltd. was formed in 1981 to exploit renewable energy resources in Karnataka State. It was to generate power using "microhydro"-generating stations and feed the power so generated to the state-owned grid. The state utility was to pass on the extra power to the participating industries, wherever it was needed. The Karnataka Power Corporation made a survey of the potential sites for microhydro stations and pinpointed some 248 such sites among medium-size irrigation dams, canal drops, and weirs. The corporation estimated that these stations would have a potential output of 400 megawatts (*Modern Power Systems,* December 1981).

Before 1978, such transactions were difficult to organize in the United States for the following reasons (O'Leary 1982):

- Electricity utilities were not required to purchase electricity generated either "as available" or on a firm contract basis even if the electricity was offered at a favorable rate.
- Backup power that was sold to small power producers, who usually met all or most of their own needs, was generally priced at a discriminatory high rate.
- Even if a small power producer was permitted to supply energy to a utility, the producer ran the risk of being deemed a utility and thereby being subject to a plethora of federal and state regulations. Compliance with such regulations was often much more costly than any economic benefits that might accrue from the sale of electricity.

Section 210 of the PURPA act dealt with these problems in several ways. First, electricity utilities were *required* to buy power from any new qualifying small power production facilities if offered at a price less than the "avoided costs" to the utility of generating the power itself or of buying it from another source. To be a qualifying facility, a production unit had to have a capacity of 80 megawatts or less and had to produce electricity primarily from renewable resources. Second, utilities were to sell power to a qualifying facility at the same prices and conditions that applied to other, similar customers. Third, qualifying facilities were to be exempted from all federal and state laws and regulations pertaining to electrical utilities.

The act defines the "avoided costs" that utilities have to pay for power as "the incremental costs to an electric utility of electric energy or capacity or both which, but for the purchase, from the qualifying facility or qualifying facilities, such utility would generate itself or purchase from another source." The actual levels of this cost have to be determined by the regulatory agencies in the states concerned. In practice, the amounts paid have been in the range of 4–8 cents per kilowatt-hour.

As a result of these changes, the electrical utilities in the United States have been flooded with offers of electric power from individuals and companies anxious to produce electricity for sale. Eighteen such applications were received in 1977, but by 1981 the number had jumped to 1,800. The proposed projects are scattered throughout the country at places such as abandoned textile mills, irrigation dams, and locks in major rivers. The process can be illustrated by the experience of Barbara and George Mallett, who founded the Mom and Pop Power Company of Weaverville, California.

When they made their application, the Malletts already owned a small hydroelectric generator that produced 60 kilowatts for their resort business. Basing their claim on the PURPA law, they proposed to expand their power plant to a capacity of 600 kilowatts, at a cost of $190,000. They got their permit, found the money (US$18,000 of their own, the rest borrowed), and installed a new turbine, generator, and switch gear. With a plant earning US$80,000 a year, the couple expected to pay off the investment in three years. In typical Californian style, the Malletts then decided to augment their livelihood by helping others to generate hydropower. They formed a support group, the Small Power Producers Association of California, traveled, lectured, and offered workshops and consulting services.

Should other developing countries wish to follow the example of the United States and introduce similar laws—Brazil has already done so—they might consider the possibility of making them less restrictive than PURPA. In many situations, the private sector could be encouraged to provide power using not only generators of less than 80-megawatt capacity, but also any form of power, not necessarily renewable energy.

There certainly seems to be no reason for government agencies themselves to go into the electricity-generation business, that is, to construct power stations and employ the staff that provide the service.

Conclusion

As noted earlier, large sections of the developing countries are still without electricity, especially the rural areas. In some cases private companies, individuals, and cooperatives have been able to supply power needs, be it for small villages or for large cities. In some situations—for example, where hydropower is available—electricity has been provided at low cost by local people. Although small isolated systems can be an expensive means of providing power, they may be the cheapest solution in rural areas and, for many people, are often better than nothing. However, even where large interconnected supply grids exist, the private sector can play a major role in the generation of electricity.

An important role for the government in this industry is to set safety and other standards and to protect consumers who have no choice of suppliers. As the examples in this chapter have shown, there is no need for governments to intervene directly in the generation and pricing of electricity or to determine who should be allowed to generate electricity. Because of natural monopoly characteristics, there may be a case for public sector transmission or distribution of electricity, but even this is open to question in the light of experience in the United States.

Appendix: Equating Electricity Supply to Demand in Real Time

T. W. Berrie

An electricity grid consists of a transmission network plus power stations and bulk customers. The stations and customers may be private or public entities, and each may be able to buy from or sell to the grid at a price designed to equate supply to demand over a period close to real time. Such grids can offer very large economies in the electricity supply sector. Furthermore, with the development of the small, inexpensive, reliable microcomputers, microcontrollers, and microprocessors, it is now also technically possible to balance—or bring under "homeostatic" control—the supply of and demand for electricity over periods close to real time so that the market is always "sold out." This means that electricity supply authorities can implement a range of electricity prices, previously given only theoretical consideration, starting with industry (where the seeds of such pricing have already been sown through existing energy and load management schemes) and ultimately extending to commercial and domestic users. Thus considerable savings can be passed on to the national economy, to the electricity sector, and to customers. It has been estimated that a utility might save as much as 1,000 million monetary units a year[3] out of a turnover of, say, 7,000–8,000 million monetary units. This appendix describes the general case; actual savings will depend upon individual circumstances.

The practical application of true homeostatic control of electricity supply systems—whereby supply and demand are treated as having one single joint value—will also require a revolutionary change in electricity supply sector policies with regard to management and probably ownership patterns. Such a change cannot take place overnight. Nevertheless, experience with electricity sector load management schemes already indicates that the spread of such homeostatic control through real-time pricing is inevitable, if only

3. See the editorial, *Electrical Review* 209(8):11 (September 1981).

as an extension of load management schemes. Pioneers of real-time "spot" pricing in the electricity supply sector began talking about the possible savings here as early as 1970 and have continued to do so ever since,[4] but there has been little public discussion of the implications of a real-time market for electricity. Therefore, if the level of savings mentioned above is to be realized, these ideas need to be publicized more widely.

Preview of Past Experience

Throughout its history the electricity supply sector has had to use what commodity sectors would call "artificial" rules for planning, pricing, and investment, because it has not been possible to balance supply and demand in real time. The problem is that electricity has to be manufactured the instant it is demanded, since the storage of any amount is prohibitively expensive. Over the years electricity utilities have collectively devised sets of rules to permit planning, pricing, and operating criteria to be used that are at least indirectly linked to the demand at any given instant. These rules are based on actual past demand together with forecasted demand, which is also based on past demand, with the result that electricity prices are prescribed to a large extent by assumptions made about the electricity sector in the future. Such prescribed prices are known to have their limitations, although most electricity utilities try to keep them to a minimum in their planning, pricing, and operating activities. The problem can be seen, for example, when new power stations are being installed. These stations are designed to meet the maximum expected future demand, but consumers demand is not related in any real way to the investment costs imposed on the economy or the electricity supply utility. Also, electricity production by a process plant (cogeneration), by a privately owned small generating plant that may have been installed for standby purposes (autogeneration), or by unusual energy sources such as solar power is presently discouraged by the low buying price set for such electricity if purchased by central utility. Under the present prescribed pricing, a distinction has to be drawn between fully expectable (firm) supplies of electricity and not fully expectable (nonfirm) supplies.

Despite the effort that has gone into planning electricity supply systems and setting tariffs according to the best economic and

4. See the many publications on homeostatic system control by the MIT Power Systems Laboratory, Cambridge, Mass.

financial principles, many believe that, as a result of prescribed pricing, safety margins have been built into planning, operating, and pricing and that these margins cater to uncertainty in a fore-casted market for electricity rather than to a real-time market. Thus the emphasis has been on generation and transmission; how-ever, this emphasis is at odds with the growing concern about energy conservation and with the view that optimal use must be made of resources.

Potential

As noted earlier, modern technology together with efficient communications circuits has made it possible to change the ap-proach to planning, pricing, and operation of the electricity sup-ply. These activities can now be oriented toward a real-time mar-ket. If electricity spot prices can be quoted close to real time, preferably by some independent market-maker (as will be ex-plained later), electricity produced by cogeneration, autogenera-tion, and renewable energy sources will have a value equal to that of electricity being produced by the main utility. Under such spot pricing, the market for electricity will be "cleared" at each instant in time; that is, all demands will be met at a worthwhile price. Before this can happen, a shortage premium will have to be added to the incremental cost of production to make up the normal spot price whenever a shortage appears likely at generating plant. This premium must be high enough to keep demand within the limits of supply. Such a premium will also indicate to consumers and producers when it may be necessary to invest in (1) additional generating plant by all electricity producers; (2) a generating plant that differs from the present plant (for example, by having a different ratio of capital to operating costs or by burning different fuels); (3) additional consumption plant by consumers; or (4) a consumption plant that differs from the present plant. Thus spot pricing will for the first time enable the electricity market to have a direct effect on investment decisions.

Electricity and Commodities

For most commodities, especially everyday consumables, avail-ability, price, and usage basically follow the laws of supply and demand; that is, they exist in a near-perfect marketplace in which products and consumers themselves individually and automati-cally adjust their buying and selling prices and quantities at any instant without reference to a central control. The literature contains a great deal of information about the optimal behavior of sectors in which the atmosphere of a near-perfect marketplace prevails, and the ground rules for ensuring optimal behavior in such circumstances are well understood. When the electricity supply sector begins to operate in such a near-perfect marketplace under spot pricing, many concepts now taken for granted in the sector will need to be reexamined. Some of the changes that will have to be considered have already been mentioned; for example, pricing and operations procedures will have to cater to uncertainty about the future and the present prescribed prices will have to be replaced by spot prices in a real-time market set by a "market-maker" for any instant in time, whether the electricity is produced by main utilities, cogenerators, autogenerators, or renewable energy sources. Furthermore, the preferred ownership pattern for electricity generation, transmission, and distribution utilities will also have to be reconsidered.

Plant Investment

Under spot pricing of electricity, investment rules may differ somewhat from those presently being used in the electricity supply industry. By and large, a plant will be worth investing in if

- Investment costs are less than the savings in the total costs of running the electricity supply system over the life of the equipment to be invested in. This is likely to be the normal criterion for all the electricity producers, that is, main electric utility, cogenerators, autogenerators using renewable energy sources, and large consumers.
- Investment costs are less than the savings in the summated "electricity shortage premium" over the life of the equipment to be invested in. This is likely to be the normal criterion for the market-maker, for example, the electricity transmission or grid operator or owner.

Remote Control and Switching

When electricity supply systems are small, consumers can be given individual attention with respect to the prices to be charged and control over their supplies. As supply systems become larger, this simple interface tends to disappear, and prices of electricity tend to be set remotely and without much consideration for the circumstances of individual electricity consumers. With the introduction of electricity load management schemes over the past ten years, the individual requirements of large consumers have again begun to be taken into account as an integral part of electricity supply system planning, pricing, and operation. Under these schemes, the consumer is asked to agree beforehand to being charged a lower-than-normal price for *not* taking up load at a restricted time, for example, at a time of peak demand on the supply sector. Similar schemes being tested for small consumers would, by prior agreement, enable the main electricity utility to switch the consumer's apparatus off and on using radio links, telephone lines, television cables, or signals sent through the electricity supply conductors. Although rather expensive at present, such load management and control devices will cost considerably less once economies of scale can be achieved through large batch production.

Although most of the devices described above are one-way systems, from producer to consumer, the trend is toward two-way systems (Crawley 1985). The microprocessors that are now available not only make it economic to use two-way communication devices with spot pricing, but also ensure that the producer will be continuously informed of consumers' views (possibly through the market-maker) with respect to both quantity and price. With instantaneous two-way communication of the demand and supply position, producers and consumers will invest more wisely, and prices will be set more optimally. Two-way interactive control has several other benefits: for example, meters can be read remotely for all public utility services (electricity, gas, water, telecommunications). The cost of such meters can also be expected to decrease rapidly once manufacturers go into large batch production.

Possible Savings

The type of savings that might be expected from electricity spot pricing can be seen in table 3-6.

Institutional Aspects

Spot pricing of electricity is feasible under all practical patterns of ownership and degrees of regulation of the electricity supply sector. A large number of ownership patterns of generation, transmission, and distribution authorities are physically possible, and many of these combinations already exist in many parts of the world. Two common examples illustrate the opposite extremes: (1) all the generation may be owned by a single, heavily regulated, publicly owned monopoly that also owns and operates all the transmission and distribution systems; and (2) there may be several

Table 3-6. Possible Annual Savings for Electricity under Spot Pricing

Type of saving	Plant margins (percentage points)	Megawatts	Millions of pounds sterling
From direct fuel savings	—	—	600
From providing extra capacity when uncertainty is eliminated in assessing:			
Plant breakdown	18	9,000	210
Demand[a]	10	5,000	110
Both of the above	28	14,000	320
From operating extra capacity when uncertainty is eliminated in assessing:			
Plant breakdown	16	8,000	180
Demand[a]	5	2,500	50
Both of the above	21	10,500	230
From remote meter reading (electricity, gas, water, telecommunications)	—	—	200
Total	—	—	1,000–1,400[b]

— Not applicable.

a. Actual demand is above forecast.

b. To be viewed against an operating profit made by the electricity supply sector of, say, about £300 million and an income of about £7,500 million.

Source: Berrie (1981).

government-regulated public and private generating utilities, each a monopoly in its own geographical area. Such utilities may be only loosely interconnected, and various other public and private utilities may own and operate the transmission and distribution systems.

A pattern that is not yet common is one in which a number of publicly and privately owned electrical utilities freely compete for the same spot electricity market; such an arrangement is perhaps ideal for spot pricing. It has been suggested that spot pricing systems could operate most efficiently where generation is competitive. But, in a completely unregulated market, a handful of utilities might be able to take over the producers and then artificially manipulate prices. Complete deregulation of generation could thus lead to serious problems unless care is taken to safeguard the competitive process.

When electricity is being provided to a spot price market by a number of competing authorities (public or private)—whether from main generating utilities, cogenerators, autogenerators, or renewable energy sources—each generating source will look at the current spot price as well as the forecasts for spot prices to make an independent decision about how much electricity to generate or consume and sell or buy. If this system is to work properly, there must be a government-regulated "market-maker," preferably in the marketplace itself, to assess and mark up (or down) the spot price from instant to instant. The presence of such an authority will keep the spot market buoyant, so that all groups producing electricity can work together satisfactorily. There must be room for all sizes and types of generation sources—not only the main generation utilities, but also cogenerators, autogenerators, and sources of renewable energy. Also, some of the smaller generation utilities that have smaller outputs and that may have access to lower-cost technology than the larger utilities must be able to benefit accordingly. Such an arrangement will encourage competition in the spot marketplace. Whatever the type of generating utility or its needs, all must be able to benefit and remain buoyant in the marketplace.

Because, in practice, the operators of the main transmission systems, especially those of a national interconnected grid, are normally the ones responsible for efficiently "dispatching" the supply of generating units to meet the demand requirements, it seems "natural" for these operators to take on the duties of setting the spot price, thereby earning enough to finance their own needs. Even in smaller systems some transmission must always exist to connect electricity buyers and electricity sellers. Thus, for practical reasons, the transmission utility would seem to be the best authority to set the spot price. The transmission authorities for all systems constitute the interface between the electricity marketplace and the consumer, and between the generation source and the marketplace, with respect to billing, public relations, marketing, and so on. Because no single generating utility among the many feeding into a network can bill any consumer supplied from the network, no generation utility knows precisely which consumer it is supplying. This again points to the usefulness of having transmission authorities set the spot price. The network market-makers would also be responsible for keeping the national grid electricity transmission network operating safely and satisfactorily.

Forward and Future Markets: Agents

Not all electricity generation utilities will make the same assumption about what the spot price is going to be. One pumped-storage electricity utility might buy electricity for pumping, thinking that spot prices will go up in the next few hours. Another pumped-storage electricity utility might sell electricity because it expects spot prices to go down in the same period. Others might make similar assumptions within a longer time frame, for example, with respect to what is considered the most financially profitable use of fuels by different generation utilities.

At least in the early stages of spot pricing, each generation utility will tend to make independent forecasts of spot prices and the share of the total electricity market that the utility in question is likely to achieve at these prices. These forecasts will be based on past experience. Each utility will also have to guess how its rivals will behave, a healthy activity to encourage in any competitive business situation. Both electricity producers and electricity consumers could buy-in such forecasts of both electricity spot prices and likely market shares from an agency set up especially for that purpose, as is done in most commodity sectors. Many argue that such an agency would probably be more efficient than a system that relies on separate forecasts by individual utilities, because the latter forecasts nearly always tend to be heavily biased. Forecasting agencies could also act as clearinghouses for advance information on generation and network plant availability, which is essential to the efficient operation of an electricity supply sector.

Investment decisions would have to be based on spot price forecasts for months or even years ahead. An aid to such decisions would be "forward" buying and selling of electricity. That is, electricity to be produced or consumed in the future would be bought or sold in the present. The forecasting agencies mentioned above, or other agencies set up especially for the job, could handle such transactions. Actual futures markets in electricity might even be the most efficient way of handling these transactions. For example, electricity producers and consumers of all types could set up contracts for the buying and selling of electricity for future periods, and the contracts themselves could be bought and sold commercially. Commodities are often traded on forwards and futures markets, both of which help to keep a near-perfect competitive marketplace.

References

Bennet, Douglas J. 1981. "New Direction for the Partnership." *Rural Electrification* 39(5):20–21, 38–39.

Berrie, T. W. 1981. "Interactive Load Control." *Electrical Review* 209(8): 4.

Burton, John, and Ray Holland. 1983. "Micro-hydro Power as an Energy Source for Rural Colombia." *Appropriate Technology* 10(3):25–27.

Cavers, David Farquhar, and James R. Nelson. 1959. *Electric Power Regulation in Latin America.* Baltimore, Md.: Johns Hopkins University Press.

Clark, Paul J. 1982. "Cost Implications of Small Hydropower Systems." Paper presented at a Workshop on Small-Scale Hydropower in Africa, Abidjan, March 1–5, 1982. Washington, D.C.: National Rural Electric Cooperative Association.

Crawley, D. F. 1985. "Load Management—Physical Systems." Paper read at the Symposium on Energy Policy and Strategy, Imperial College, United Kingdom, March 25–29.

Dunkerley, Joy, and others. 1981. *Energy Strategies for Developing Nations.* Baltimore, Md.: Johns Hopkins University Press.

Economic Regulatory Administration. 1979. *The National Power Grid Study.* Vol. 2, DOE/ERA-0056-2. Washington, D.C.: U.S. Department of Energy.

Energy Researcher. 1981. "Wind Power." February, pp. 1–4.

Gallant, Frank K. 1981. "Cooperation Comes to Santa Cruz." *Rural Electrification* 39(5):12–15.

Holland, R. 1982. "Energy for Rural Development." *Water Power and Dam Construction,* December, 29–32.

Houston, Douglas A. 1985. "How to Short-Circuit the Utility Monopoly." *Reason,* April, 34–38.

Inversin, Allen R. 1982. "Private Sector Approach to Implementing Micro-Hydropower Schemes: A Case Study." Washington, D.C.: National Rural Electric Cooperative Association.

Lay, James D., and Joan H. Hood. 1978. "Evaluation Report: Rural Electric Cooperative of Guancaste, R.L. and Rural Electric Cooperative of San Carlos, R.L." Washington, D.C.: National Rural Electric Cooperative Association.

O'Leary, Donal. 1982. "The Contribution of Legislative Initiatives Such as PURPA Towards Involving the Private Sector in the Development of Small Hydroelectric Power Plants in Developing Countries." Washington, D.C.: National Rural Electric Cooperative Association.

Paturau, J. Maurice. 1982. *By-Products of the Cane Sugar Industry: An Introduction to Their Industrial Utilization.* Sugar Technology Series 3. 2d ed. rev. New York: Elsevier.

Primeaux, Walter J. 1985. "Total Deregulation of Electric Utilities: A Viable Policy Choice." In *Unnatural Monopolies.* Santa Barbara, Calif.: Reason Foundation.

Ruhl, Juan. 1978. *Ricardo Zuloaga 1867–1932.* Caracas: C.A. La Electricidad de Caracas.

Starr, M. R. 1984. "Small-Scale, Stand-Alone Photovoltaic Systems: An Overview." Paper presented at the 166th Meeting of the Electrochemical Society, New Orleans, La.

Taylor, Robert P. 1982. *Decentralized Renewable Energy Development in China.* World Bank Staff Working Paper 355. Washington, D.C.

U.S. Department of Energy. 1978. "Co-generation: Technical Concepts, Trends, Prospects." Washington, D.C.

WHO (World Health Organization). 1981. *Solar Refrigerators for Vaccine Storage and Icemaking*. Geneva.

Winter, P. 1984. "Photovoltaics—An Appropriate Technology for Sudan?" London: Renewable Energy Development Company Ltd.

World Bank. 1960. *The Economic Development of Venezuela*. Baltimore, Md.: Johns Hopkins University Press.

4

Health

They answered, as they took their fees,
"There is no cure for this disease."

—HILAIRE BELLOC, "SELECTED
CAUTIONARY VERSES"

THE HEALING PROFESSION, if not the oldest profession in the world, is certainly one of the oldest. The practice of midwifery—helping mothers to give birth—goes far back in time. Sumerian clay tablets dating from 2500 B.C. describe Nintur, "Midwife of the Gods," together with her equipment, incantations, and rituals. Chinese medical inscriptions are known from as early as 1800 B.C. and the Book of Rites written in the Zhou dynasty (1100–800 B.C.) records four medical specialities: nutrition, internal medicine, surgery, and veterinary medicine (Pei 1983).

In India the medical system known as Ayurveda (the science of life) was well developed by the time of the Gupta dynasty in the early centuries of the Christian era (Basham 1976). Unani medicine, which is widely practiced in Pakistan and India, traces its origins to the system of Galenic (Greek) medicine that was preserved and developed in the Middle East during the Arab civilization (Said 1983). Unlike the old Chinese, Greek, and Indian systems, traditional African medicine tends to be localized, with practices and observations handed down from generation to generation, either verbally or in writing. Eighty percent of Africa's

Many helped in the preparation of this chapter, especially David de Ferranti and K. V. Ranganathan, the World Bank; Drs. Abraham Drobny and Harold Sadin, Washington, D.C.; Drs. Kathleen Elliot and Carmel Goldwater, London; Maureen Lewis, the Urban Institute; Victor Rodwin, New York University; Dr. W. Stinson, the American Public Health Association; Dr. John B. Tomaro, the Program for Appropriate Technology in Health; and Dr. Susan Ueber Raymond, Center for Public Resources.

population is reported to depend on these traditional, privately provided, medical services.

Except for the health care offered to the armed forces, medical services have been mainly privately provided throughout history. In every society, certain individuals obtained skills in healing or in drug preparation and made these available to their neighbors in exchange for compensation that most could afford. This is still the situation among the populations of Africa and Asia and in many parts of Latin America. The institution of government-financed social security and the "right" to free medical care is a fairly recent phenomenon, which originated in Germany in the 1880s (Roemer 1971).

In the nineteenth and twentieth centuries, great advances took place in the medical sciences, water supply and sanitation, education, and housing, and governments became better able to implement countrywide public health programs. As a result, health in industrialized countries dramatically improved, as is evident from the increased longevity and the reduction or virtual elimination of many diseases (for example, tuberculosis). But conditions in the developing countries are far different.

Health Conditions in Developing Countries

By any criterion, health conditions in the developing countries, especially in Africa, are deplorable. Each year 16 million children in the developing world die from or are crippled by six diseases that can be prevented through inoculation: tetanus, measles, polio, diptheria, whooping cough, and tuberculosis. In 1982, the life expectancy of a man in Western Europe, Australia, or North America was seventy-one years, whereas it was only sixty-one in China and India, and less than fifty in many countries of Africa. The number of children who died before reaching one year of age were, per thousand births, 10 in Western Europe, Australia, and North America; 78 in China and India; and 100 in many African countries (World Bank 1984). Furthermore, many of those who survive in developing countries suffer from illnesses that disrupt normal activities for roughly one-tenth of their time (World Bank 1980). These differences are undoubtedly associated with differences in income and with the consequent availability of modern sanitary and medical facilities.

Private health services still play a leading role in all developing countries. Many people in Sub-Saharan Africa, for example, prefer the traditional, indigenous systems, and use modern facilities (where available) only as a last resort. Private provision, both traditional and modern, is also important in Asia, North Africa, and Latin America. According to a report made to the U.S. Agency for International Development (Merrill and others 1980) on the use of health services by the Thais, private sector expenditure for health care in Thailand was estimated to have been four times the amount spent by the government on health. Fifty percent of curative health care was delivered through private pharmacies and a further 20 percent by traditional healers and injectionists.

A broader picture emerges from the work of de Ferranti (1985), who studied the levels of private expenditures on health as a proportion of total expenditures in different countries. Some of his findings are summarized in table 4–1. Although these data have to be treated with care, there can be no doubt that private health providers are important in developing countries, often more important than in the industrialized countries. Particularly striking

Table 4–1. Private Expenditure as a Percentage of Total Health Expenditure, Various Years

Country and Year	Percent	Comments [a]
Developing countries		
Afghanistan, 1976	88	Payments by individuals only
Argentina	69	
Bangladesh, 1976	87	Payments by individuals only
Botswana, 1978	48	Payments by individuals account for 21 percent
Brazil, 1976	31	
Brazil, 1981	33 or more	Rough estimate
Burkina Faso, 1981	24	24 percent if contributions to social insurance are included; excludes private foreign aid
Burkina Faso, 1982	19	
China, 1981	32	Payments by individuals only
Colombia, 1978	33	68 percent if contributions to the social insurance system are included
Ghana, 1970	73	
Haiti, 1980	65	Payments by individuals account for 57 percent
Honduras, 1970	63	

Table 4–1 (continued)

Country and Year	Percent	Comments [a]
Developing countries (continued)		
India, 1970	84	
Indonesia, 1982–83	62	64 percent if contributions to government insurance scheme are included
Jamaica, 1981	40	
Jordan, 1982	41	
Korea, Rep. of, 1975	87	
Lebanon, 1982	50 or more	Rough estimate
Lesotho, 1979–80	12	Does not include expenditures on traditional practitioners and private non-PVO services
Malawi, 1980–81	23	
Mali, 1981	54	
Mexico, 1976	31	
Pakistan, 1982	71	72 percent if contributions to social security are included; payments by individuals account for 58 percent
Peru, 1982	53	Rough estimate
Philippines, 1970	75	
Rwanda, 1977	37	Does not include expenditure on traditional practitioners and nonhospital modern care; payments by individuals account for 13 percent (or 15 percent of recurrent expenditure)
Senegal, 1981	39	Does not include expenditure on traditional practitioners
Spain, 1976	39	
Sri Lanka, 1982	45	As percentage of recurrent expenditures only
Sudan, 1970	41	
Swaziland, n.d.	50	
Syria, n.d.	76	
Tanzania, n.d.	23	
Thailand, 1978	79	
Thailand, 1979	70	

(Table continues on the following page.)

Table 4-1 (continued)

Country and Year	Percent	Comments [a]
Developing countries (continued)		
Togo, 1979	31	Does not include expenditure on traditional practitioners or nonhospital modern care; payments by individuals account for 28 percent
Tunisia, n.d.	27	
Venezuela, 1976	58	
Zambia, 1981	50	Payments by individuals account for 27 percent, missions 3 percent, and services funded by mining enterprises 19 percent
Zimbabwe, 1980–81	21	Payments by individuals account for 17 percent
Industrial countries		
Australia, 1974–75	36	
Canada, 1975	25	
France, 1975	24	
Germany, Fed. Rep., 1975	23	
Italy, 1975	9	
Japan, 1976	10	
Netherlands, 1974	29	
Norway, 1976	4	
Portugal, 1976	24	
Sweden, 1975	8	
Switzerland, 1975	34	
United Kingdom, 1974–75	7	
United States, 1974–75	57	

a. There is no comment for some countries because source provides only limited information on definitions or data used.

Except as noted, "private" includes, in principle, expenditures on health services by (1) individuals, excluding regular contributions to government insurance schemes (such as payroll deductions for social security), (2) employers on behalf of their employees, (3) private voluntary organizations (such as mission hospitals), and (4) private practitioners—all taken net of government subsidies and other transfers (items 2, 3, and 4 should be net of fees collected). In practice, however, many figures are crude approximations. "Total" health expenditure encompasses all private, public, and quasi-public (hence government insurance scheme) outlays—again in net terms.

Source: de Ferranti (1985).

are the figures from Asia: in 1970 private health expenditures accounted for 84 and 75 percent of total health expenditures in India and the Philippines, respectively, and for 75 percent in the Republic of Korea in 1975. These high percentages pertain not only to traditional medical services but also to those offered by the increasingly available modern health facilities, which are less prevalent in Africa.

The questions to be addressed in this chapter are: What roles, if any, can private health services play in reducing the incidence of disease among the world's poorest populations? If substantial roles can be identified, one can then ask under what circumstances public policy should encourage private activities in this sector, keeping in mind considerations of efficiency and equity. What does economic theory have to say about the appropriate mix of public and private health services?

Appropriate Mix of Public and Private Provision of Health Services

De Ferranti's (1985) classification of health services as "curative" and "preventive" (see table 4–2) provides a useful starting point in considering the appropriate roles of the private and public sectors in the provision of health services. Preventive services, which account for about one-quarter of total expenditures, can be subdivided into patient-related, which typically absorb two-thirds of the costs of preventive services, and nonpatient-related, which typically absorb one-third. How do the criteria for judging the appropriateness of public and private provision presented in Chapter 1 relate to these types of health service?

Natural Monopolies

There do not appear to be any significant natural monopolies in the supply of health services.

Decreasing Costs

Although some items used in health care (such as X-ray machines) are so expensive that they can be justified only by intensive use, and the specialized services provided by hospitals may be justified only on a provincial or district basis, the tendency of costs to decrease as health services increase is not sufficient to warrant government involvement in their provision. To the extent that

Table 4-2. A Taxonomy of Health Services

Services	Percentage of total expenditure on health[a]
Curative	70–87
Personal services (outpatient and inpatient care)	
Sale of medicines	
Preventive	
Patient related	10–20
Maternal and child health care (such as immunization)	
Other (such as home visits by village health promoters)	
Nonpatient-related	3–10
Disease-control programs (such as spraying for malaria)	
Sanitation	
Education on and promotion of health and hygiene	
Control of pests and zoonotic diseases	
Monitoring (such as for epidemics)	

Note:. Includes family planning (under "Preventive, Patient related").
a. Rough estimates because of definitional differences among countries.
Source: de Ferranti (1985).

scale economies exist, they can be captured on a voluntary basis by independent private practitioners. This is what happens when doctors set up a group practice to use common facilities.

Externalities

Significant externalities are associated with health services. For example, the presence or absence of a communicable disease in one person will affect the welfare of others. To the extent that the welfare of infants—both before and after birth—depends on the health of their mothers, there are strong public policy grounds for measures to improve the health of mothers; such measures can be classified under patient-related preventive services. Public disease-control programs (for example, vaccination and immunization programs) can also be justified on this basis, as can many other preventive services, such as health education.

Pure Public Goods

A number of nonpatient-related preventive services can be characterized as pure public goods. As noted earlier, these are goods that have to be provided to an entire community or not at all; nonpayers cannot be excluded, and beneficiaries cannot be forced to pay. Many disease control programs are in this category: it is of little benefit to a private owner to rid his property of mosquitoes if the neighbors do not do likewise. Government support for such services can therefore be justified.

Merit Goods

Some medical services can be considered merit goods. That is, they have special merit but, if left to market choices, they would be purchased in insufficient quantity. One obvious example of such a service is the treatment of infants. In the most formative periods of their lives, human beings have neither the knowledge on which to base choices nor the power to exercise them. The extent to which parents make the right choices for their children is a point that is widely debated in all societies, but there can be no doubt that there are at least *some* situations in which children could benefit from medical advice and treatment (such as immunization) for which parents are unable or unwilling to pay. Hence there is a case for the public support of prenatal and postnatal clinics and other facilities that help pregnant and lactating women and their infants.

The extent to which adults, when left to their own devices, choose to have less medical care than is in their own interest is another debatable point, but it need not be pursued here. The opposite argument is sometimes heard that individuals, if left to themselves, spend "excessive" amounts on medicines. To the extent that this is true, health services exhibit characteristics of "demerit goods," which justify public intervention to ensure that scarce medical resources are not wasted. Indeed, some people oppose medical insurance and the freedom of the rich to buy medical services on the ground that the associated health expenditures are wasteful. For this reason, private medical practice was banned for a period in parts of Turkey (UNDP 1983).

The argument that medical services are merit goods can be extended to the notion that "consumers" of medical services (the sick) are in no position to judge the suitability of alternative treatments, such as surgery. But this difficulty exists whether services are publicly or privately provided. The important point here is that an element of trust is essential for good doctor-patient relations. This trust is more likely to exist when patients have the freedom to choose their doctors than when they are denied this choice.

It may be concluded that preventive medical services exhibit the characteristics of externalities, pure public goods, and merit goods that justify public intervention. The case for public intervention in curative services (which make up the bulk of health expenditures) is less strong and probably applies only to contagious diseases and the treatment of the very young, the infirm, and others incapable of making sound decisions for themselves.

It does not necessarily follow that public intervention has to involve governments in the direct provision of services by salaried officials. The options of employing private doctors, fumigating firms, laboratories, and so on may also be available. For example, a twenty-year program in India to overcome iodine deficiency by iodizing common salt failed when implemented by public sector companies, which manufactured iodized salt but did not succeed in selling it, even in areas where iodine deficiency was a serious health problem. In reviewing the program, the government of India decided to allow private salt manufacturers to produce and sell iodized salt. The revised program is currently being implemented and reviewed (Samuel Paul, personal communication 1986).

Examples of Private Sector Provision

The private sector has been extensively involved in the provision of health services in developing countries, and the literature on the subject is correspondingly large. To narrow the information down to manageable form, the examples presented in this chapter are organized under the following headings:

> Modern services
> Traditional healers in modern health services
> Medicines and medical appliances
> Health insurance
> Employer-provided health care.

The objective in all cases is to identify examples of services to low-income people, who in developing countries constitute most of the population. That the better-off can obtain private medical services in developing countries is well known, but not of special interest to this study.

Modern Services

Throughout the developing world, modern health facilities are available to those with the inclination and money to use them. Some of these facilities also cater to poor people—for example, ten of the eighty-five private hospital beds in Legazpi City, the Philippines, are "charity beds." The Apollo hospitals in Madras and the Jaslok hospital in Bombay have excellent reputations, as have numerous private facilities in Latin America.

Private health care in the Middle East goes back many years. Well-equipped hospitals were founded in Baghdad in 981; in Damascus in 1154; and in Cairo in 1284 (Burgel 1976). In more recent times, the roles of the private and public sectors in providing health care in the Middle East and North Africa (particularly Egypt, Jordan, Lebanon, Morocco and Tunisia) have been studied in great detail by the Center for Public Resources (Raymond and Glauber 1983). This report showed that, in the early 1980s, the private health sector was strong and growing in all five countries. In Jordan, 50–60 percent of health care delivery was in the private sector; in Tunisia and Egypt about 50 percent; and in Lebanon about 80 percent. In Morocco, more than half the doctors and virtually all the pharmacists engaged in private practice, but 90 percent of hospital beds were in the public sector.

An example of a private sector hospital is the Alsalam Hospital in Cairo (Raymond and Glauber 1983, p. 92):

Opened in October 1982, the 100-bed Alsalam Hospital was conceived and executed by a small group of private Egyptian physicians. In addition to servicing the individual patients of its staff physicians, the hospital:

- Has contracts with 24 companies (local and foreign) to cover employee health services; a total of 9,000 employees are thus covered;

- Has an agreement with the Ministry of Health to provide fixed rate services to patients referred from the public system for kidney disorders;

- Provides fixed-rate services for employees of the General Agency for Land Reclamation/Ministry of Agriculture.

Comprehensive studies of private participation in health care in other developing countries are still to be done, and there are doubtless many successes—and failures—to report.

Another point that should be mentioned, but that cannot be explored here in depth, is the role of multinational companies (Micou 1985).

- Pfizer Inc., for example, has worked closely with Brazilian officials on a major demonstration project to control schistosomiasis, a waterborne disease that affects the liver and is prevalent in many underdeveloped areas.
- Along with twelve other American-based firms, Pfizer has also established a system in Gambia for distributing pharmaceuticals and improving health care. Working with the Gambian medical and health department, the firms have helped the government develop efficient procurement policies, stock-management systems, and distribution networks.
- CIBA-Geigy has joined with the government of Egypt in providing technical assistance and financing for a project to control skin disease in that country, particularly leprosy. In addition to supplying drugs, the company has provided personnel to design and evaluate the project and to improve diagnosis and treatment.
- Hindustan Lever Ltd., a subsidiary of Unilever PLC, offers health education, financing, and agricultural services to more than thirty-five villages in India.

Traditional Healers in Modern Health Services

The developing world contains an enormous variety of private health care providers; most are unqualified to practice medicine in the "Western" sense and many are even illiterate. This situation may be illustrated by a World Health Organization (WHO) survey conducted in Bangladesh in 1976–77 (Claquin 1981). The survey was designed to determine the distribution of private health care providers, who were defined as individuals not employed by the government health service who were perceived by the community as providing resources and assistance in illness. Health care providers were divided into seven categories:

- Allopathic (that is, modern) practitioners with M.B. or B.S. degrees or medical board licenses.
- Practitioners without medical degrees or licenses who use allopathic drugs, including antibiotics.
- Practitioners using homeopathic medicine who are institutionally trained or self-taught.

- Ayurvedic or Unani practitioners who are institutionally trained or self-taught.
- Traditional midwives (*dais*) who learn their craft by apprenticeship and personal experience.
- Spiritual healers who do not use medicine but heal through chanting, amulets, and charms.
- Others, such as bone setters, who do not fall into any of the above categories.

The numbers in each class, as given by Claquin, are shown in table 4-3.

Traditional practitioners are preferred by ordinary people for many reasons, a principal one being that the treatments are more familiar and more comprehensive, in that spiritual as well as physical problems are often covered. Sometimes the traditional practitioners charge less (or accept payment in kind instead of in cash), but they do not do so invariably. There are many recorded cases of patients preferring to pay a fee to a traditional practitioner rather than obtain free service at a Western-type clinic or hospital. And some of the traditional experts in Africa are so well known that patients cross international frontiers to seek their advice.

Many attempts have been made—with the encouragement of the WHO—to integrate the traditional and modern health systems. Significant progress has been made in this direction in China and

Table 4–3. Distribution of Health Care Providers

Practitioner	Number	Percentage of all private practitioners	Population per health provider	Health providers per 100,000 population
Qualified allopathic	57	2.6	35,413	2.8
Unqualified allopathic	764	36.0	2,642	37.8
Homeopath	482	22.7	4,188	23.8
Ayurvedic or Unani	218	10.2	9,259	10.7
Traditional midwife	274	12.9	7,367	13.5
Spiritual healer	288	13.5	7,009	14.2
Other	37	1.7	54,556	1.8
Total	2,120	100.0	952	105.02

Source: Claquin (1981). Copyright © 1981, Pergamon Press, Ltd.; reprinted with permission.

India and some in Africa, where the needs are most acute. But there are difficulties.

First, many in the "modern" camp will have nothing to do with the traditional practitioners. This attitude is found not only in developing countries; it was, and is, not unusual for the medical establishment in many Western countries to attempt to exclude from the profession those with low qualifications. Indeed, this attitude is present in most professions. Second, many in the "traditional" camp see modern medicine as a threat to be resisted, rather than as an opportunity to be embraced for the benefit of all. Third, most of the traditional practitioners are private, self-employed professionals, who expect to earn their living by receiving fees for services rendered. If integration means that these individuals are to become salaried employees of state organizations, various conflicts are bound to arise.

But, on the positive side, many of the traditional practitioners are eager to improve their skills by taking courses offered by the modern sector. In Ghana, as a part of projects designed to link traditional systems with the modern training sector, traditional birth attendants (TBAs) received special training. Neumann and Lauro report (1982) that, after completing the training program, some of the TBAs felt they should be salaried by the Ministry of Health. Although this was clearly not the aim of the program, the ministry did encourage TBAs to charge higher fees, provided they implemented their new skills. In addition, the villagers were informed that certain features would indicate that TBA skills had indeed improved and were encouraged to increase remuneration for services accordingly.

Even in societies where traditional medicine is strong, modern medicine is considered better for certain ailments. Whereas the traditionals are considered better at dealing with spirits and with mental problems in general, modern medicine is better when surgery is required. Many traditional practitioners recognize the existence of germs and the value of aseptic procedures. Being in a competitive business, they have much to gain by improving their services, and many sell Western remedies—although sometimes in traditional wrappings.

The Gandhigram Institute of Rural Health and Family Welfare was founded in 1962 by K. V. Ranganathan (subsequently a staff member of the World Bank's Economic Development Institute) with the objective of promoting rural health and breaking down the barriers between the traditional and modern health sectors. The institute holds meetings that both traditional and modern practitioners attend. As a result of these meetings, both camps understand the strengths and weaknesses of the other and refer patients, if appropriate, to healers in other sectors.

Similar work is also being done in Africa. For example, the Association of Rwandan Tradipractitioners of Bare was formed in 1977 to upgrade the standards of the profession. Information on remedies is exchanged (despite the tradition of secrecy), strict hygiene is promoted, and patients with certain complaints (such as hepatitis) are sent away for Western treatment. From time to time, patients are referred to the association by Western practitioners (Telesphore 1982).

In certain Andean regions of Peru more than 60 percent of the people—in some places as many as 80 percent—are treated exclusively by local healers (*curanderos*). In an effort to lead the population progressively toward modern medicine, the chief physician of a health center in southern Peru decided to collaborate with the curanderos of his region by inviting them to his center for instruction in the basic principles of hygiene and first aid. Each of the participants in his "courses" received a first aid kit. These curanderos then returned to their communities and became local health educators. After some years under their influence, the change in the health behavior of the people was reported to be "visible" (Bannerman, Burton, and Ch'en 1983).

Medicines and Medical Appliances

The role of the private sector in providing medicines and medical appliances may be discussed under three headings: the traditional, the modern, and the modern informal.

Traditional. Of the 500,000 or so species of flowering plants that exist on the earth, about 10 percent, or 50,000 species, are thought to have been used therapeutically at one time or another (Farnsworth 1980). Scientific studies have shown that about 500 of these have real therapeutic value when used in extract form by humans. Many have proved to be worthless and some even harmful.

Traditional healers have always been associated with traditional medicines, many of which they make themselves. The medicines are invariably sold—even when the consultations are not charged for—and provide an important source of income for the practitioners. Some of these remedies are also produced on a large scale in special institutes (as in China) and factories (as in India).

In China and India, as in Europe and the Middle East, many of the prescriptions are published in reference books and can be copied by others, to the extent that copyright and trademark laws allow. Where information is transmitted by word of mouth, as in parts of Africa, many of the remedies are secret. This means that they cannot be critically reviewed or widely used if found to be beneficial.

The collection and publication of information on all traditional remedies would undoubtably benefit users everywhere and enable practitioners to improve their services. This may not be a profitable activity for the compilers, but it could be a suitable task for governments and for international organizations. Indeed, WHO is supporting a data base (NAPRALERT, Natural Products ALERT) designed to shed more light on this subject.

Modern. In many industrialized countries the demand for pharmaceuticals is increasing, rather than diminishing, as living and health standards rise, and the production and marketing of them is a major industry. Although there has been no comprehensive study of the industry in developing countries, a glimpse of its potential can be obtained from Raymond and Glauber (1983, p. 46), who give the following example from Jordan:

> The Arab Pharmaceutical Manufacturing Company, Ltd. (APM), Jordan's oldest and largest domestic drug company, is capitalized at JD4 million [Jordan dinars] as of 1982. This is twenty times its capital at the time of its 1962 registration. The public sector owns only 5.5% of APM's shares; the remainder are spread among 22,000 shareholders. The company is governed by a nine-member board of directors, with public sector representation from the Ministry of Health and the Armed Forces.
>
> In 1982, the company's sales volume totaled $17.4 million, up 13% from 1981. This total sales volume was distributed as follows:
>
> - Sales to Government: 1.4% of total 1982 sales, an increase of 12.6% over 1981;
>
> - Sales to the private local market: 17.2% of total, up 17.8% over 1981;
>
> - Exports: 71.4% of total sales.

The company's export market is largely in the Arabian peninsula and East Africa. However, export expansion to West Africa is planned after the completion of a new factory in mid-1983. This new facility, to be called the Al-Buheira Pharmaceutical Manufacturing Company, Ltd., will have twelve times the production capacity of APM's current factory. The factory is being built by a British company with a total construction and equipment cost of nearly JD9 million.

Currently APM manufactures 17 product groups and over 100 individual products. The new factory will expand that product group line to 47.

APM employs a labor force of over 400, exclusive of managers and technicians. That number will more than double with the 1983 opening of the new plant. The company operates two shifts per day to satisfy product demand.

The proliferation of modern pharmaceuticals in developing countries can have harmful effects. In the countries of origin, the use of these medications is usually limited by laws that regulate sales and require that certain products be taken under the supervision of physicians or other licensed practitioners. Traditional drugs, also, are specifically prescribed by the traditional dispensers. But in many developing countries medical practitioners do not exercise any control over the use of modern prescription drugs such as antibiotics, as do practitioners in the developed countries. Throughout Latin America, for example, prescription medications, usually manufactured by multinational pharmaceutical firms, can often be purchased over the counter in pharmacies or shops or from medicine vendors. The link between healer and healing resource is not always present, and the products are frequently available in the absence of physicians or other trained practitioners (Ferguson 1981).

Taylor (1976) has reported that, in some regions of India, indigenous practitioners supply modern medicines on a large scale. In Mysore and the Punjab 80 percent of the medicines are modern, and 50 percent of the patients receive penicillin injections, generally from unqualified practitioners supplied by pharmacists. Taylor considered the greatest source of hazard to be the tendency of "pseudo-indigenous practitioners" to use the most powerful drugs possible, such as chloramphenicol, to obtain quick results. Similar systems of "pharmaceutical medicine" have been reported in Ethiopia (Slikkerveer 1982).

There does not appear to be any easy solution to this problem. Possibly the manufacturers could exercise better control over their distribution channels and, with the assistance of the governments concerned, could take action against those who sell their products for inappropriate uses. Publicity campaigns, in which both manufacturers and governments have a role, could also be used to alert customers about the dangers of misusing pharmaceuticals. Without doubt, health professionals in pharmacology need better training.

Modern Informal. Mention must also be made of the numerous secular and religious charitable organizations concerned with the provision of low-cost medical facilities to poor people in developing countries. Specialist organizations working in the health field include the Appropriate Health Resources and Technologies Action Group Ltd. (AHRTAG) in London, the Program for Appropriate Technology in Health of Seattle, Washington, and Die Christoffel Blindermission of Benshein, Federal Republic of Germany, which specializes in assisting the blind. Most of these organizations are privately financed, often on shoestring budgets. They are involved in the development of such products as solar-powered refrigerators for the storage of vaccines; oral rehydration kits for treatment of diarrhea; pedal-powered grinding equipment for the production of low-cost spectacles in areas where there is no reliable electricity supply; and artificial limbs, including some with knee-joints that enable the users to squat and to cross their legs.

Health Insurance

Individuals cannot predict the incidence of disease or accident and therefore effective health coverage must include insurance against expenses arising out of medical emergencies. Insurance can take many forms. In some villages in India it is the custom to donate part of the harvest to the local practitioner to ensure that medical service is available in times of need. In the Indonesian village of Ngesti Rahayu, each family pays for the services of trained health workers. In more developed societies, there are a variety of insurance schemes, some run by the state, some by private insurance companies.

Insurance in Lalitpur, Nepal. An example of health insurance between these two extremes in seen in the schemes provided in the Lalitpur district of Nepal (Donaldson 1982). The annual premium for membership in two health posts is equivalent to US$1 per household per year. This figure is based on the cost of a cigarette in Nepal, which is equal to one-twelfth of a dollar; it is believed that households can forgo one cigarette a month in order to purchase health insurance, which covers the costs of these health posts over and above a subsidy received from the government. At a third post, which does not receive a government subsidy, the premium is set at US$2 per household per year, which is intended to cover all of the costs. People who take the insurance have the option of paying in installments or of contributing labor equal to the price of the insurance premium. Membership in the insurance schemes entitles beneficiaries to free medical services and drugs at the posts; to outpatient services costing up to US$4 a visit at a local hospital; and inpatient services costing up to US$8 a stay.

Cooperative Insurance in India. One of the world's outstanding cooperatives is the National Dairy Development Board program that started in Kaira District, Gujarat, in the mid-1940s (NCIH 1984). It has steadily expanded to the point that it now comprises 4,500 cooperatives with more than 2 million members. The success of this nongovernmental cooperative scheme has been ascribed to the flexibility, imagination, and personal leadership of Verghese Kurien, who was able to develop a solid financial base and create the mutual trust necessary for true cooperation.

The services of the milk cooperatives include health care for the animals, which led some milk producers to express the hope that in their next incarnation they would be a buffalo so that they could have three meals a day and receive the tender loving care of first aid workers and veterinary doctors. On hearing this, cooperative managers became aware that villagers needed more health care education and facilities. The demand and determination grew to find a way of using the cooperative structure to build a health care program with emphasis on mothers and children.

In the early 1970s a consultant team was engaged to consider how to use the cooperative structure for a new service function. It concluded that the dairy program in cooperatives worked because of the zeal of its well-paid professional management and recommended that the new health services should be run by professional managers. Thus, a program was created whereby the co-op system provided basic prepaid health care to its members, especially for mothers and infants in villages.

The Tribhuvandas Foundation, a charitable, non-profit trust, was formed in 1975 and began operations in 1980. Maternal and infant health services became its top priority, backed up by a supplementary feeding program. In the maternal and infant care scheme, village health workers provided basic treatment while mobile health care teams made regular visits to each participating village. By 1982, eighty-two villages were participating in the maternal and infant care scheme and thirty villages had supplementary feeding programs for malnourished children under the age of five. In order to participate, a village has to appoint a health worker and agree to pay the costs out of the sales of milk. The milk cooperative also has to form a health care subcommittee consisting of a managing committee of interested village women and local physicians.

After the women health workers are selected, they are trained by the foundation, first in the classroom and then on the job with other village health workers. After her training, the health worker returns to the foundation, at first once a week and then once every two weeks, to learn new techniques. The health worker dispenses medicine, keeps accounts, manages supplemental feeding programs, and helps organize income generating activities for women. The field staff carry out vaccinations and health education in addition to family planning and hospital referral services.

Health Insurance in Rural China. Contrary to common belief, health care in the People's Republic of China is not centralized, nor is it free (Hu 1976). Three main types of health care insurance are available in China:

- Public expense medical insurance for state cadres and students. This scheme, which is free, covers 2 percent of the population.
- Labor medical insurance for workers in factories and state-owned firms. This scheme, which is also free to the direct beneficiaries (dependents have to pay 50 percent of treatment costs) is financed by the employing enterprise and covers 10–12 percent of the population.
- Cooperative medical services for those who live in rural areas—about 80 percent of the population.

A typical cooperative medical service works in the following manner. Participation in the cooperative medical services is voluntary. The main beneficiaries of these services are poor and lower-middle-class peasants. In the early period of the service, commune members had the option of joining or not joining the system; although a commune can still decide whether to join, once it does join everyone in the commune has to participate.

The annual membership fee varies among and within communes over a period of time. The fee is based on the commune's expenditures for treatment and medicine in the previous year. For instance, in 1972, Pu-chiang Commune, Chekiang Province, had fewer serious illnesses than before, and because the commune has used herbal medicine extensively (a major cost-saving factor), the annual membership fee was reduced from 1 yuan (equivalent to U.S.45 cents) in 1972 to 0.35 yuan in 1973. About fifteen communes across the country reported their annual membership fees; these ranged from 0.35 to 3.60 yuan per person in 1973, the average being about 1.5 yuan per person per year. The average size of a family is five persons; thus, annual expenditures for membership fees were about 7.5 yuan per family, about 1.5 percent of the family's disposable income. Incomes and health insurance premiums vary considerably among the communes, but 1.5 percent of annual disposable income seems fairly representative. This is not an insignificant figure for poor and lower-middle-income peasants, as most visitors to China have claimed. In fact, there are reports that peasants in some poor areas avoid participation in the cooperative medical services, save the membership fee, and chance staying healthy.

In addition to collecting a fee from commune members, the cooperative obtains funds from each production team, which pays from its collective welfare funds for each member subscribing to the medical services. The production team's contribution varies, depending upon agriculatural production during the year and the extent to which its commune members have used the medical services in that time. Each commune has a "public accumulated fund" contributed by production teams. This fund comprises reserve and welfare funds. The reserve fund, which is about 7–10 percent of the gross income, may be used to buy farm equipment or to finance hospital construction, which is supplemented by state funds. The welfare fund, which is about 2–3 percent of the gross income, is used to pay for education costs, cooperative medical services, and social welfare assistance. These figures vary among communes.

Once the peasant or his family join the cooperative medical service, they pay a fee of 0.05–0.10 yuan for each visit to the brigade health station. This helps to pay maintenance expenses incurred by the station (excluding the salaries of barefoot doctors and public health workers, which are paid from production team funds). The registration or visit fee also serves to discourage indiscriminate use of available services. During the early days of cooperative medical services, when registration fees were not charged, certain communes reported overutilization, such as unnecessary visits and requests for tonic herbs. As a result, large deficits built up, and several commune cooperative medical services had to be discontinued.

To help control health costs, the brigade uses barefoot doctors for referring patients to provincial or city hospitals. If patients seek care at these hospitals on their own initiative, they cannot receive reimbursement from brigade health funds. Conversely, if the barefoot doctors refer a patient to these hospitals, part of the patient's medical expenses will be reimbursed by the brigade health fund.

Some communes pay 50 percent of the costs, and others pay fixed amounts of 30–40 yuan; the remaining expenses, including the food costs, are paid by the patients themselves.

Insurance Provided by Companies. Private health insurance can be a profit or nonprofit service provided by individuals or by groups. Group insurance is cheaper to administer, and in most cases premiums are paid, at least in part, as a fringe benefit by an employer. Either the employer or an employee organization can serve as the collective agent in purchasing a group policy from an insurance company. Most private health insurance companies operate as business enterprises. Although private health insurance is in principle purchased on a voluntary basis, employers who purchase group insurance policies for their employees and pay part of the premium as a fringe benefit may nevertheless require contributions from employees.

Even in countries that have compulsory health insurance schemes, it is possible to give contributors the choice of using an approved private company instead of a government fund. Contributors in Chile, for example, have had this choice since 1981.

It is not possible, in the space and time available, to discuss in depth the achievements of private health insurance companies in developing countries. Table 4-4 gives some information about companies identified in Latin America.

Employer-Provided Health Care

Employer-based health care systems can be divided into three categories (ILO 1985). First, national laws may require, or give financial incentives to, employers to provide full or partial health care. Second, employers may be required to provide health care as a result of labor union contracts, especially in countries with strong unions and a shortage of skilled labor. Third, employers may provide health care on their own initiative in order to attract skilled expatriate or local labor when operating in remote areas. Examples can be found in the mining and construction industries of Latin American countries.

Employer-based systems have contributed in differing degrees to the overall availability of health care. Their net contribution has been questioned, however, on the grounds that a large portion of health care provided by employers is tied in with occupational and environmental health hazards. Table 4-5 gives some examples of health provision activities of employers in Sub-Saharan Africa.

(Text continues on page 153.)

Table 4-4. Selected Companies Providing Health Insurance in Latin America

Country and company	Number of members, years in operation	Coverage	Rates
Argentina			
Omint S.A.	11,107 policies (average 4 members per policy) Medical insurance 16 years	Full	US$700 a year (family plan), US$400 a year (individual), or 4,500 pesos a month
Tim S.A.	5,000 families, 10,000 policies, 16 years, 2 clinics fully owned	Closed system, basic plus orthodontia and psychiatry, full coverage 15 years (special)	US$600 a year (family plan), US$400 a year (individual)
Galeno Provision Médica	14 years, 26,000 members	Full	US$650 a year (family plan), US$480 a year (individual), or 5,000 pesos a month
CEMIC (Centro de Educación Médica e Investigación Clínica)	25 years, First Insurance Co-Foundation (nonprofit)	Full, only for open scheme (own plus other hospitals)	US$500 a year (family plan), US$400 a year (individual)
Medicus S.A.	11 years, operates with 10 not-owned hospitals, 10,000 policies (3–4 family members each)	Basic and full	3,300 pesos a month (family plan), 4,000 pesos a month (individual), 5,600 pesos a month (full)
Skill S.A.	16 years, 30,000 members	Closed system and full	2,400 pesos a month (closed), 4,500 pesos a month (full)

(Table continues on the following page.)

Table 4–4 (continued)

Country and company	Number of members, years in operation	Coverage	Rates
Argentina (continued)			
Otamendi	Private (hospital)	Work with private health insurance companies (such as Salud S.A.) and social security members	Market prices, but subject to Ministry of Health approval
Apsot (owned by Tech Int Corp.)	8,000 members, Tech Int S.A. medical insurance for its corporate staff	Full	Fringe benefit for Tech Int's salaried staff
Chile			
Cia. de Seguros Consorcio Nacional de Seguros	3,000 (health), 20,000 (life)	Life and health, 55–80 percent reimbursement, pharmaceuticals	300 pesos (US$33) a month package price to enterprises
Cia. de Seguros La Chilena Consolidada	200,000	Life with health coverage for emergencies, 50 percent reimbursement for surgery	200 pesos (US$22) a month; life and oncology insurance US$300 a year
La Sudamerica Cia. de Seguros	700 firms	To enterprises only, basic health plan and supplements	US$111 a month, comprehensive life insurance
Colombia			
Compania de Seguros Generales y de Vida	n.a.	Accidents, medical expenses (related only to emergencies)	Rates approved by Suprintendencia Nacional de Seguros

144

Aseguradora Gran Colombiana	25 years, 1,400 firms (more than 25 members each)	Hospital rooms and services, surgery, medical visits, and diagnosis	Rates approved by Superintendencia Nacional de Seguros; family plan 62,000 pesos (US$609) a year, group rate is lower
Costa Rica			
Agencia de Seguros Edwin Garro	20 years, 150 policies (individual), 20 enterprises (group insurance for companies with more than 8 staff up to 55 years old)	Hospital, maternity, surgery reimbursement up to 70 percent of medical expenses	Instituto de Seguros sets tariffs and prices of medical expenses
Ecuador			
Sucre Cia. de Seguros	44 years	Accident expenses, 100 percent coverage	n.a.
La Nacional Cia. de Seguros	n.a.	Emergencies and accident-related medical services only.	n.a.
Ecuasanitas	16 years in Quito (32 years in Spain), 16,000 policies or approximately 50,000 people insured	100 percent coverage on 44 specialities, medical and accident coverage up to 75,000 sucres.	300 sucres (US$5) enrollment costs, 700 sucres (US$11) a month for each family member
El Salvador			
Pan American Life Insurance Co. (PALIC)	70 years, 8,000 (group)	Tied to life insurance, hospitalization, surgery, X rays, accidents; group insurance, 80 percent reimbursement	1,400 colones a year (US$560), premium set by actuarial appraisal and competition

(Table continues on the following page.)

Table 4-4 (continued)

Country and company	Number of members, years in operation	Coverage	Rates
Guatemala			
Compania de Seguros Granai y Thompson	12,500 members (group), 125 enterprises with more than 15 staff members, 8 years	Illness, hospitalization coverage, 80–100 percent reimbursement	457–700 quetzal (US$457–700) a year for maximum insurance
La Comercial Aseguradora Suizo Americana	60 new members a month	Hospitalization and emergencies only 250 quetzal a week	72.50 quetzal (US$72.50) a year, Superintendencia de Bancos
Mexico			
Banamex Seguros America Banamex S.A.	Group and individual policies	Coverage of medical expenses based on salary; three plans. Coverage: staples 30 percent, medical expenses 15 percent, pharmaceuticals 10 percent, Coinsurance at own expense	Premiums are the same for the three plans
Seguros Monterrey Serfin S.A.	Since 1942	Major medical expenses, 1 percent deductible, 20 percent coinsurance; group insurance, same coverage; Reimbursement scheme: up to US$1600 for surgery, up to 20 percent for anesthesia; US$80 a day for hospital, US$30–60 a visit	Approved by the Comisión Nacional Bancaria; 7,272 pesos (US$38) a year for individuals; 6,000 pesos (US$32) a year for group insurance

Seguros Bancomer	Group insurance (firms) and individuals	Medical expenses (surgery, hospital visits, ambulance, pharmaceuticals) related to illness or accident; accident (medical coverage)	Premium: husband, 24,187 pesos (US$123) a year; wife, 33,869 pesos (US$173) a year; child, 7,654 pesos (US$39) a year
Panama			
La Aseguradora Mundial		Life and accident (medical services insurance) up to 5 percent of agreed coverage amount (fixed with user)	Market prices
Cia. Internacional de Seguros S.A.	40 enterprises, 1,000 members	Hospitalization and medical coverage, two plans: basic and 80 percent reimbursement	Premiums approved by Ministerio de Comercio, Oficina Regulación de Precios
British-American Insurance Co., Ltd.	n.a.	Hospitalization, life, and accident only; hospital coverage up to US$1,500 a day, surgery coverage US$1,500 per intervention	Premiums approved by Ministerio de Comercio, Oficina Regulación de Precios, US$85–90 a month
The Continental Insurance Co.	n.a.	Emergencies, accidents, surgery only; reimbursement system	Premiums approved by Ministerio de Comercio, Oficina Regulación de Precios, US$68 a month
Cona Seguros	n.a.	Health insurance reimbursement system	Premiums approved by Ministerio de Comercio, Oficina Regulación de Precios

(Table continues on the following page.)

Table 4-4 (continued)

Country and company	Number of members, years in operation	Coverage	Rates
Paraguay			
Santa Clara S.A. de Servicios Asistenciales	Since 1979, 15,000 members, own hospital	10 plans, up to full coverage; two systems: centralized (provides own service), and decentralized (reimbursement scheme)	Family plan, 5,000 guaranies a month; premium checked by Ministry of Health
Peru			
Compania de Seguros Sud America	65 years, thousands of policies	Three plans (maximum coverage: 8 million, 5 million, or 4 million sales); includes maternity and Xray, excludes pharmaceuticals, no deductibles or coinsurance	Premium: 72,000, 60,000, or 48,000 soles (US$21, 17, or 14) a month
Venezuela			
Seguros Sud America	Each firm has at least 20 staff members	Hospital, surgery, maternity up to 30,000 bolivares a year; reimbursement 80 percent of invoice; accident and extraordinary medical expenses	Superintendencia de Seguros fixes standard rates; insurance companies can negotiate that amount.

n.a. Not available.
Source: World Bank

Table 4-5. Employers Providing Health Care in Sub-Saharan Africa

Country and company	Nature of business	Number served	Services supported	Mechanism
Angola				
Cities Service Oil Co.	Oil extraction	n.a.	Comprehensive health care	Direct provision for out-patient care
Gulf Oil Co.	Oil extraction	500 employees and dependents	Comprehensive health care	Contract with providers for inpatient care
Botswana				
Anglo–American Corp.	Mining	n.a.	n.a.	Insurance
Bamangwato Concessions Ltd.	Mining	n.a.	Health care: 25-bed hospital	Direct provision with copayments
Botswana Meat Commission	Meat processing	Employees and dependents	Health care: 2 clinics	Direct provision
De Beers Botswana Mining Co.	Mining	n.a.	Health care: 72-bed hospital, clinics, 50-bed hospital	Direct provision with copayments
Côte d'Ivoire				
Impregilo/Kaiser Foundation International	Construction	9,000 employees and dependents	Comprehensive health care: hospital and satellite dispensaries	Direct provision
Union Carbide	Chemicals	n.a.	Annual medical exam and free meals	Direct provision

(Table continues on the following page.)

TABLE 4-5 (continued)

Country and company	Nature of business	Number served	Services supported	Mechanism
Ghana				
Volta Aluminum Company and Kaiser Aluminum and Chemical Corporation	Mining	15,000 employees and dependents	Comprehensive health care: 40-bed hospital	Direct provision
Kenya				
Unilever	Agroindustry	n.a.	Nutrition and health education	Direct provision of inpatient care
Union Carbide	Chemicals	Employees	Annual medical exam and free meals	n.a.
Liberia				
Firestone	Rubber plantation and processing	44,000 employees, dependents, and local population	Comprehensive health care: 2 hospitals (340 beds), 7 clinics and dispensaries, 46 first aid centers	Direct provision
LAMCO-Bethlehem Steel-Granges	Mining	Local populations of Bassa and Nimba counties	Comprehensive health care: 110-bed hospital, 150-bed hospital	Direct provision

	Sector	Coverage	Type of care	Financing arrangement
Malawi				
Admarc	n.a.	54,000 employees, dependents, and local population	Comprehensive health care	Reimbursements, small copayments for hospitalization, ceiling of 200–1,000 kwacha on annual cost to company of US$275,000 (1982)
Hogg Robinson	Education	600 employees	Comprehensive health care	Reimbursements, some copayments, employee chooses provider
Malawi Railways	Transport		Dispensaries and material units	Direct provision
National Bank	Banking	4,000	Comprehensive	Insurance: employee pays 1–10 percent copayment with 200 kwacha maximum per incidence at cost of 7–8 percent of salaries to the bank
University of Malawi	Education	320 employees and dependents	Comprehensive health care	Reimbursements (self-insurance)
Nigeria				
Gulf Oil Co.	Oil extraction	700 employees and dependents	Comprehensive health care: 5 clinics	Direct provision for outpatients, contact with local hospitals for inpatient care

(Table continues on the following page.)

TABLE 4-5 (continued)

Country and company	Nature of business	Number served	Services supported	Mechanism
Nigeria (continued)				
Phillips Petroleum Co.	Oil extraction	4,000 employees and dependents	Comprehensive health care, including dental and preventive care: 25-bed hospital	Direct provision
Rwanda				
Rwanda Army	Military	Employees, dependents, and local population	n.a.	Direct provision; local population pay a fee for service
Zaire				
Unilever	Agroindustry	n.a.	Comprehensive health care: 9 hospitals, 4 dispensaries, health education, food provisions	n.a.
Zimbabwe				
Union Carbide	Chemicals	1,000 employees and dependents	Comprehensive health care: 60-bed hospital, 36-bed hospital	Direct provision
Railways	Transport	n.a.	n.a.	Contract with providers

n.a. Not available.
Note: The information presented in this table is for illustrative purposes only and may be out of date.
Source: Stinson and others (1985).

152

The Role of the Government

This chapter suggests that governments can play the following important roles in activities pertaining to health:

- Ensure that all reasonable preventive measures are taken to protect the health of the population. For example, governments could be responsible for disease-prevention measures such as inoculations, the destruction of disease-causing organisms such as mosquitoes that transmit malaria, and the isolation of known carriers of contagious disease.

- Implement and promote health education programs for the general public. The target groups for such programs could be mothers of young children, the children themselves, road users (through accident prevention campaigns), and other groups at risk.

- Provide training to health practitioners. Courses for TBAS and other traditional practitioners improve the skills of those who already have some knowledge of medical procedures and who enjoy the confidence of their patients. Such courses should offer diplomas or certificates to those who complete them successfully.

- Encourage health insurance. In addition to being the "insurer of last resort," a government can encourage the formation of private health insurance schemes and, if necessary, inspect them to ensure that they can deliver what they promise. A government can reasonably require that all its citizens be insured, so that they do not become a charge on public funds in the event of accident or illness.

All of these acivities can of course be financed by a government without being implemented by government personnel. Training activities, in particular, can be carried out by professional trainers under contract, but so can the other activities.

One question that remains difficult to answer is whether governments should outlaw "unqualified" medical practitioners, recognize and certify them, or merely tolerate them. In view of the shortage of medical personnel in many developing countries, it would seem counter-productive to outlaw the traditional practitioners. Toleration seems to be the most promising approach in most countries, with voluntary certification a valuable adjunct. Certificates that recognize skills not only raise professional levels but also help the consumers—those seeking medical help—to make intelligent choices in the selection of practitioners.

Conclusion

The question posed at the beginning of this chapter was, What roles, if any, can private health services play in reducing the incidence of disease among the world's poorest populations? This brief review of the confused health scene in developing countries points to several answers.

People everywhere dislike, even fear, disease and are prepared to go to considerable lengths to stay healthy or to be cured when ill. People are also prepared to pay substantial amounts for health care, and as a result medical practitioners have come forward to meet these needs. Medical practitioners tend to have a high status in their societies and succeed in earning their livings through voluntary transactions while in competition with one another and with providers of other goods and services.

Cultural beliefs and scientific attitudes vary widely, as do incomes. Some patients may not feel at ease with practitioners from another culture, and cross-cultural misunderstandings can occur. Statistical evidence shows, however, that Western methods are more effective than traditional ones in curing and eradicating certain diseases and in prolonging life. Thus, the road ahead for health care would seem to lie in the direction of maintaining existing relationships, but improving the skills of the traditional practitioners by teaching them to apply appropriate Western medicines and procedures.

The private sector can be used to provide the necessary goods (medicines) and services (practitioners at all levels) within the means of the communities concerned. The private sector can also provide, under contract if necessary, the requisite training needs, physical facilities, and sanitary services; it can also organize health maintenance organizations and health insurance schemes.

How private resources are mobilized to do more for health will vary from society to society. The task appears to be particularly complex in Africa, because of the lack of the written, comprehensive systems that are to be found in the other continents. More work needs to be done to inform government officials of the possible benefits of private sector health services, especially in Africa, and to spread the stories of success—and failure.

The question was also asked under what circumstances public policy should encourage private sector activities in the health sector, with regard to efficiency and equity. It is impossible to answer this question in a way what will satisfy everyone, if only because not everyone can agree on what is meant by "efficiency" and "equity." The problem may be illustrated by a hypothetical example: suppose that a scientist claimed to have discovered a cure for cancer, and suppose that the treatment could save some of those affected, but not all. Would "equity" require that the treatment be withheld to avoid the inequitable result of some being cured and some not?

People who are concerned (as is this volume) with making the best use of scarce resources must reject the option of destroying the chance that some may survive. But how would available supplies of the curative substance be allocated? Would they be sold in the market to the highest bidders? Would they be distributed by the medical profession to the patients most likely to recover? Or should the government seize the supplies and determine the priorities in their use? Different people, all of them reasonable, may have different views on this subject. Medical practitioners and researchers, who determine such priorities in many situations, may claim the right to the last word. So may government officials claiming to speak on behalf of society. In the face of such strong opinions, held by so many experts, can there be a case for allocating scarce medical resources by price by bidding in the marketplace?

The case for the market would not be based on the proposition that the rich in some way "deserve" better health care than the poor, but on the need to stimulate the supply of health services and to reduce their cost. There are numerous examples of remedies (for example, penicillin) that were scarce and expensive soon after their discovery but that came down in price and became widely available as a result of competitive pressures to supply more goods more cheaply to meet growing demands. Furthermore, there would be nothing to prevent a government from entering the market as a buyer and securing as much of the scarce remedy as it deemed appropriate; in other words, the government always has the option of contracting with the private sector to produce what it requires.

It might also be argued that government laboratories could develop and produce the remedies without the stimuli and signals of the marketplace. This may be true in some societies; certainly, the purpose of this book is not to argue that private markets are to be preferred in all circumstances. But in view of the thousands of remedies that might have to be produced, even if government laboratories were to produce what people want, they would be unlikely to do so more successfully than private firms responding to market demands.

Some experts have suggested that the private sector should not be allowed to operate in the health field because the resources that society can devote to health are fixed and public policy requires that these available resources be devoted to meeting the needs of all, not merely those of the rich. But the essence of economic development is that resources are not "fixed." Even if they are, in the short run, constrained in total (as is unlikely, in view of the prevalence of underemployed resources), resources can always be shifted from one sector to another. More can be spent on health if less is spent on other things—personnel can be trained, materials can be obtained, literature can be distributed. Except in emergencies such as floods and earthquakes, when special short-term measures are needed, the health sector is not served by the view that resources cannot be expanded.

It may therefore be concluded that, with regards to both equity and efficiency (in the sense that these terms are generally understood), public policy in developing countries should encourage private activities in the health sector, either in the provision of goods and services responsive to market forces or in the production of goods and services under government contracts.

References

Bannerman, Robert H., John Burton, and Ch'en Wen-Chieh. 1983. *Traditional Medicine and Health Care Coverage: A Reader for Health Administrators and Practitioners*. Geneva: World Health Organization.

Basham, A. L. 1976. "The Practice of Medicine in Ancient and Medieval India." In *Asian Medical Systems: A Comparative Study*, ed. Charles Leslie. Berkeley: University of California Press.

Burgel, J. Christoph. 1976. "Medieval Arabic Medicine." In *Asian Medical Systems: A Comparative Study*, ed. Charles Leslie. Berkeley: University of California Press.

Claquin, Pierre. 1981. "Private Health Care Providers in Rural Bangladesh." *Social Science and Medicine* 15B:153–57.

de Ferranti, David. 1985. *Paying for Health Services in Developing Countries*. World Bank Staff Working Paper 721. Washington, D.C.

Donaldson, Dayl Susan. 1982. "An Analysis of Health Insurance Schemes in the Lalitpur District of Nepal." Master's thesis, University of Washington.

Farnsworth, N. R. 1980. "The Development of Pharmacological and Chemical Research for Application to Traditional Medicine in Developing Countries." *Journal of Ethnopharmacology* 2, no. 2 (June):173–81.

Ferguson, Anne E. 1981. "Commercial Pharmaceutical Medicine and Medicalization: A Case Study from El Salvador." *Culture, Medicine and Psychiatry* 5: 105–34.

Golladay, Frederick, and Bernhard Liese. 1980. *Health Issues and Policies in Developing Countries*. World Bank Staff Working Paper 412. Washington, D.C.

Hu, Teh-wei. 1976. "The Financing and the Economic Efficiency of Rural Health Services in the People's Republic of China." *International Journal of Health Sciences* 6 (2).

ILO (International Labour Organisation). 1985. "Provision of Medical Care through Employer-Based Systems in LDCs." Geneva.

Merrill, Henry, and others. 1980. *Thailand Health, Population and Nutrition Needs Assessment.* Compiled by Henry Merrill, David Oot, Surindra Satchakul, Karoon Rugvanichje, Charunee Bejvakashem, and Kanda Suraskulwat. Washington, D.C.: U.S. Agency for International Development.

Micou, Ann McKinstry. 1985. "The Invisible Hand at Work in Developing Countries." *Across the Board* (March):8–9.

NCIH. 1984. "Alternative Health Delivery Systems: Can They Serve the Public Interest in Third World Settings?" Washington, D.C.: National Council for International Health, Cooperative League of the U.S.A., and Group Health Association of America, Inc. Processed. See especially papers by Carl Taylor and Michael Halse.

Neumann, A. K., and P. Lauro. 1982. "Ethnomedicine and Biomedicine Linking." *Social Science and Medicine* 16:1817–24.

Pei, Wang. 1983. "Traditional Chinese Medicine." In *Traditional Medicine and Health Care Coverage,* ed. Robert H. Bannerman and others. Geneva: World Health Organization.

Raymond, Susan Ueber, and Anne F. Glauber. 1983. *Beyond the Public Prescription: Private and Public Roles in Near East Health.* New York: Center for Public Resources.

Roemer, M. I. 1971. "Social Security for Medical Care: Is It Justified in Developing Countries." *International Journal of Health Services* 1 (4): 354–61.

Said, H. M. 1983. "The Unani System of Health and Medicine." *Traditional Medicine and Health Care Coverage.* Geneva: World Health Organization.

Slikkerveer, Leendert Jan. 1982. "Rural Health Development in Ethiopia." *Social Science and Medicine* 16:1859–72.

Stinson, W., M. Favin, D. Prevoo, and M. Reinhold. 1985. "Employer Supported Health Care in Developing Countries." American Public Health Association, Washington, D.C. Draft manuscript.

Taylor, Carl E. 1976. "Indigenous Medical Practitioners." In *Asian Medical Systems: A Comparative Study,* ed. Charles Leslie. Berkeley: University of California Press.

Telesphore, Abbe Kayinamura. 1982. "The Bare Traditional Medicine Center, Rwanda." *Contact.* 70:13–15.

UNDP (United Nations Development Programme). 1983. *Human Resource Development for Primary Health Care.* Los Angeles: University of California Press.

World Bank. 1980. *Health. Sector Policy Paper.* Washington, D.C.

World Bank. 1984. *World Development Report 1984.* New York: Oxford University Press.

5

Telecommunications

*That there is a real danger of the valuable public property—
the telegraph system—being injured by the extension of this
telephone system is proved by the fact that, wherever the
telephone system has been principally developed, there the
growth of the telegraph revenue has been checked. . . . If the
telephone companies were in communication with all the large
towns and sent messages all over the country, undoubtedly the
system would to a large extent supersede the telegraphs and
consequently largely diminish the telegraph revenue. Therefore, it is an essential feature of the scheme, if carried out, that
the Government should have possession of the trunk wires.*

—SIR JAMES FERGUSSON, POSTMASTER
GENERAL, UNITED KINGDOM, 1892

IN THE SPRING OF 1984, Suzanne Lascot spent five frustrating
weeks trying to get two telephones installed in her new office in
New York. The New York Telephone Company installed one
phone instead of two, and it didn't work properly. Complaints to
the telephone company went unanswered. Finally, in desperation,
Miss Lascot and her partner placed a desk next to two public
phone booths on the sidewalk of a busy Manhattan street corner.
They told their customers to call them on those numbers, and the
system worked just fine. Suddenly, the New York Telephone
Company sprang into action. "Within a half hour, I had a crew of
three telephone men at the phone booth," said Miss Lascot. Four
hours later, the crew installed her second telephone and repaired

Stephen C. Littlechild made a substantial contribution to this chapter. Thanks
are also due to staff of the World Bank's Telecommunications Division, particularly Bjorn Wellenius and Timothy Nulty, for their assistance. Much of the
material was obtained from Saunders, Warford, and Wellenius (1983) and Samuel
(1985).

the first. Business then proceeded as usual, and the episode was soon forgotten (Ricci 1984).

To a non-American, the interesting point about this story is not the way in which an aggrieved customer drew attention to the lack of telephone service, but rather the way in which it is taken for granted in New York that five weeks is an absurdly long time to wait for the provision of new telephone service. In developing countries, the waiting time for new service ranges from three weeks in Cyprus to three months in Costa Rica to four years in Peru. (These data, which are reported by the telephone administrations in the countries concerned, are set out in table 5-1.)

The shortage of telephones is often reflected in high prices payable in "black" or "grey" markets. For example, in prime

Table 5–1. Number of Telephones and Average Time for New Service

Region	Number of telephones		Average waiting time (weeks)	
	Total	Per 100 population	Business	Residential
North America				
Bermuda	51,374	92.3	4	3
Dominican Republic	175,054	3.0	n.a.	13
Jamaica	132,517	6.6	6	156
Central and South America				
Chile	608,200	5.3	22	30
Costa Rica	281,040	11.7	13	13
Peru	519,703	2.9	208	260
Venezuela	1,021,136	6.4	4–13	55
Europe				
Cyprus	164,000	25.0	2–3	2–3
Denmark	3,633,784	69.7	2	2
Finland	2,643,574	54.6	2	2
France	29,373,663	54.1	4	4
Germany, Fed. Rep.	31,370,099	50.9	4	4
Iceland	116,856	49.1	2–4	2–4
Italy	21,670,001	38.2	13	33
Netherlands	8,023,000	56.0	3–5	3–5
Spain	1,566,942	16.0	39	39
Sweden	7,132,000	85.6	n.a.	2

(Table continues on the following page.)

Table 5–1   (continued)

	Number of telephones		Average waiting time (weeks)	
Region	Total	Per 100 population	Business	Residential
East Asia				
Taiwan	4,356,765	23.5	2	2
Hong Kong	1,947,476	36.4	1	1
Korea, Rep. of	5,158,357	13.8	9	26
South Pacific				
New Zealand	1,939,488	60.0	1	1
Philippines	658,415	1.4	13–21	18–26
Singapore	870,804	35.0	2	2

n.a. Not available.

Sources: Waiting times from *Telephony* (1985). All other data from AT&T (n.d.). All the AT&T data were obtained from the countries concerned and are subject to the qualifications given in footnotes in the original source.

business areas in Bangkok, those in a hurry to own a telephone frequently have to pay the equivalent of US$2,500–3,000 to obtain a line from an existing subscriber (Habir 1984), while in Rangoon in 1977 and in Lima in 1985 the going rate was equivalent to US$1,000–2,000. In Jakarta, officials who retire from the telephone administration have been known to receive not a gold watch as a retirement gift, but a telephone line (Gray 1984).

The data in table 5-1 do not reveal the full extent of the demand for telephones in the developing countries because waiting times for the least developed systems—for example, those in China, South Asia, and Sub-Saharan Africa—are not reported to the Telephony Publishing Corporation. Furthermore, the figures that are available are country averages. In the rural areas of developing countries, where the delays are greater, whole sections of the population have no prospects of obtaining telephone service for many years to come.

Long waiting times for telephone lines are associated with low levels of penetration. The differences in the numbers of telephones per 100 people in different parts of the world are illustrated in figure 5-1 (AT&T n.d.). Most countries in Western Europe have more than 40 telephones per 100 population; a few have nearly twice that many. In contrast, in most developing countries the density is less than 10 per 100, and often less than 1 per 100. These figures, too, are countrywide averages and do not reflect dis-

Figure 5–1. Countries Reporting More than 1 Million Telephones

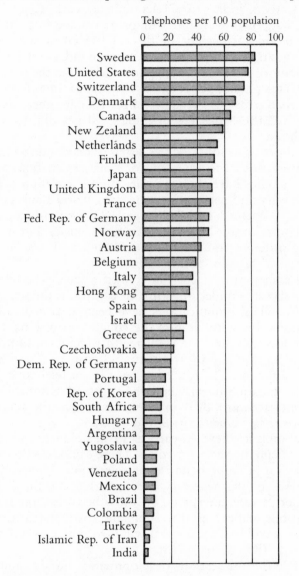

Telephones per 100 population

Note: Only five African countries reported more than two telephones per 100 population, and fourteen reported less than two per 100 population.

Source: AT&T (n.d.). Reprinted with permission.

parities between different areas—which may be considerable. For example, a study of India's rural telephone network (*Capital* 1983) has shown that, of India's 2.01 million telephone lines in 1980, only 140,000, or 6.9 percent of the total, were located in the 580,000 villages that account for 80 percent of India's total population. Furthermore, the average telephone density in the rural areas of India (0.03 telephones per 100) was fifty-seven times lower than that in the urban areas (1.71 telephones per 100). In other words, in 1980 more than three-quarters of India's villages did not have a single telephone.

What are the reasons for these low levels of telephone ownership and use? Low national income is one obvious explanation. Several econometric studies have shown a very high correlation between telephone density and national income. In a World Bank publication (Saunders, Warford, and Wellenius 1983) for example, strong correlations were found between telephone density and income, both among different countries at a given point of time and in a given country at different points of time.

A second contributory factor, in countries where the telecommunications sector is under government control, is the scarcity of public funds. Telecommunications have been accorded low priority in national budgets, despite the congestion of circuits, the waiting lists for lines, and the evidence that some consumers are more than willing to pay up front the full costs of installing the additional equipment. The result has been lower telephone densities per 100 population (even where the effects of national income are taken into account) than in countries where the telephone system is privately owned (Littlechild 1983).

This situation is not new. As early as 1915, a pioneer and scholar of the early telephone service wrote: "There can be no doubt that the low position of some countries in telephonic development is due to the lack of the necessary appropriations by the Governments. Under private enterprise, on the other hand, the internal communications will extend if the demand exists, for the demand indicates that it will pay, and capital will flow where its remuneration is assured" (Kingsbury 1915).

Thirdly, telecommunications development is highly capital-intensive. In all but a few developing countries that have domestic telecommunications manufacturing, this implies heavy demands on the countries' scarce foreign exchange resources. Typically, about half of the expansion cost—or about $1,000 per telephone line added—is for imported equipment. Irrespective of who owns the telecommunications company, this places telecommunications development in direct competition with other sectors often given higher priority by those who allocate foreign exchange.

The Importance of Telecommunications

Telephone service in virtually all developing countries is provided by government agencies. These governments would like to expand telephone coverage throughout their countries, but most have judged that food, transport, power, health, and other needs are more pressing and should receive greater emphasis. Telephones used to be viewed as inessential and largely luxury items. But this view is changing. A few examples recorded by World Bank staff (Saunders, Warford, and Wellenius 1983, pp. 19–21) illustrate the importance of telecommunications technology to economic development, and hence to the lives and welfare of ordinary people:

- Dairy enterprises in West Bengal depend on telecommunication services for the collection, processing, and marketing of milk products.
- The introduction of telephone services into several rural towns and villages in Sri Lanka has allowed small farmers to obtain, among other things, current and direct information on wholesale and retail prices of fruits and other produce in Colombo, the capital city. As a result, the farmers have begun to demand and receive higher prices for their products.
- A grocer in Rosario, Uruguay, who sells and delivers groceries to homes, is now able to serve a large clientele beyond his immediate neighborhood primarily because the local residential telephone system has made it possible for customers to order his goods by telephone for home delivery.
- The Paraguayan National Development Bank found that, without telecommunications links to its rural branches, its effectiveness was much curtailed. In addition, without access to a telephone, local farmers were unable to relate effectively with markets and obtain information about current market prices (many farmers sold their products to truck owners at prices substantially below prevailing market field prices) and had difficulty procuring fertilizers and other supplies in a timely manner.
- In Korea, a Ministry of Communications survey has shown that public telephone offices in rural areas average 85 local and 160 long-distance calls a month and that the calls help to remove feelings of isolation. The local government administration is able to disseminate information to the villagers more quickly and to save time and funds by reducing personal visits to the villages by government staff.

- After disturbances in Ogaden blocked the road between the port of Assab and Addis Ababa, the Ethiopians established a series of checkpoints linked by radio along the road to speed the flow of supplies and to improve security. The progress of individual trucks was monitored, and, in case of a breakdown, spare parts were ordered and brought on the next truck. The radio-linked system cut the average journey time in half, and in a matter of weeks the port of Assab was cleared of the goods that had accumulated there.

- A Ministry of Agriculture official in Tanzania responsible for project implementation required daily information from parastatals and ministry departments. Inadequate telecommunications links necessitated frequent visits, which averaged three hours of travel by car each day. Without adequate long-distance telephone connections, several other officials needed to make between eight and twelve costly and time-consuming safaris by automobile each year.

More important, the use of the telephone in emergencies can make the difference between life and death. For example, during a hurricane in Fiji, one of the smaller islands suffered severe damage, some loss of life, and many injuries. The only telecommunications link with the main island was an old radio, which was destroyed during the hurricane. It was one week before assistance was sent to the distressed island because the authorities on the main island were unaware of the severity of the problem. A long-distance telecommunications system strong enough to withstand hurricanes could have been used to summon immediate assistance.

In urban areas, the demand for telephone service is often intense, even among the nonrich. For example, a street trader in Lagos without adequate telecommunication service is unable to find out quickly the most suitable supplier to replenish his inventory. He cannot save valuable time by "letting his fingers do the shopping" with the aid of a telephone trade directory. A reliable telephone system would enable suppliers to arrange for sales and delivery on a regular basis.

Criteria for Public Sector Provision

If government ownership has contributed to the backward state of telecommunications systems in developing countries and if an expansion of this sector is now considered important as a means of promoting economic growth, the question that needs to be asked is how and where an increased role can be found for the private sector. The next section considers, first, the arguments for and against transferring the entire telecommunications sector to private ownership and, second, the various possibilities for allowing competition and private ownership at the margins of the system.

The Case for Private Ownership

In many countries, perhaps even in most, the telephone system was developed by one or more private companies (Kingsbury 1915). Nowadays, only a dozen or so countries have privately owned systems: these include the United States, Puerto Rico, Hong Kong, and Barbados. The United Kingdom recently privatized its telephone system, selling half the shares to private investors. Other countries—for example, Singapore—are reported to be considering a similar policy. Italy and Spain have jointly owned systems. Still other countries—for example, Canada, Denmark, and Norway—have a mixed private and public network. Further examples from developing countries are discussed later in the chapter.

The arguments put forward for the private ownership of telecommunications systems include the following:

- Private owners who will seek a profit and will be subject to competition (including in the capital market) will have greater incentive to be efficient, to introduce new lower-cost technology, and to seek out and provide what customers want.

- In a competitive economy, prices will accurately reflect costs of production so that resources will be channeled toward the production of the goods and services that consumers most prefer.

- Private investors will be able and willing to supply more funds for telecommunications than a government will be able to allocate since there are many other competing claims on funds raised by taxation.

- Private ownership will be able to draw on more skilled entrepreneurial and managerial talent than is available in government, thereby allowing government officials to concentrate on other duties for which no private sector replacements are appropriate or available.

- A substantial private sector reduces the threat of excessive government power, helps to preserve individual freedom, and reduces the scope for corruption (since more transactions are made on the open market instead of on the black market).

The Case for Government Ownership

The arguments put forward in favor of government ownership include the following:

- Telecommunications systems are characterized by such great economies of scale ("decreasing costs") that the industry is a natural monopoly; hence public ownership is required to achieve the lowest possible costs and to protect consumers against serious "market failure."
- Competitive private enterprise would lead to the emergence of several local systems that need not be technically compatible; this situation would increase costs, cause inconvenience to users, and hold back technological development.
- By means of cross-subsidization, public ownership makes it possible to extend telephone ownership to more people— especially in rural areas where costs are higher—and thereby increases the value of the entire system (which depends on the number of subscribers that can be reached) and supports broad development policies (for example, countrywide extension of physical infrastructure).
- Public ownership of telecommunications is a valuable source of government revenue.
- Public ownership prevents domination by wealthy foreign countries and limits the influence of multinational corporations.

An Evaluation of the Arguments

Studies that have compared the performance of public and private enterprise in several industries and several countries, notably electric power industry in the United States (see De Alessi 1974, 1980), by and large confirm the claims made for private ownership. Some, however, would argue that the influence of competition is as great as that of ownership (see Millward 1982).

Management would also be attracted to the sector if it were under private ownership. The developing world is full of under-utilized human resources, of potential managers and entrepreneurs seeking outlets for their energies. What was achieved in the past by large and small entrepreneurs in the United States could surely be achieved today under favorable investment climates in, say, India, Nigeria, or Peru. These entrepreneurs might require finance, equipment, and technical training, but these factors could be supplied by private companies, for example, by telecommunications multinationals eager to expand their markets.

How far the government ought to require technical compatibility of different systems or to enforce cross-subsidies in pricing is a matter of debate; the issue is touched on below. Suffice it to note here that government regulation of private systems is an alternative means of achieving the same end. Certainly the privately owned U.S. telecommunications system has been characterized both by technical compatibility and extensive cross-subsidy.

Apart from occasional nuisance calls, it is difficult to believe that telecommunications generate significant negative externalities. Some would argue that there are positive externalities (because benefits increase more than in proportion to the number of connections), but this does not in itself make the case for public ownership, because a private company can take this factor into account in its pricing policy and subsidize connection charges. Telecommunications are not pure public goods (such as radio services) for which users cannot be made to pay; nor have they the characteristics of merit goods, since the users of these services do not underestimate their value. On the contrary, there are large unsatisfied demands for service.

Nor is government ownership the only way of collecting revenue or of preventing foreign takeover. In many countries taxes could alternatively be imposed on company profits or on turnover. Undesired takeovers in the United Kindgom are prevented by government minority shareholdings, by judgments of the Monopolies and Merger Commission, or by a special "golden share."

Perhaps the most important issue is that of economies of scale (decreasing costs) and the need to protect against monopoly power. This deserves to be examined in more detail.

Decreasing Costs

Many people believe that the telecommunications sector is characterized by decreasing costs that are so great that the sector has the elements of a natural monopoly; that is, it is "an industry in which economies of scale are so great, compared with the size of the market, that it is inefficient to have more than one firm producing the industry's output, and in fact, only one firm would be able to survive in such an industry" (Littlechild 1979). This point has been used in both the United States and the United Kingdom to argue that entry into the telecommunication service should be restricted and that existing providers should be allowed to retain their monopoly. It is also used to justify government ownership rather than private ownership. Can this view be sustained?

The argument is stronger for some parts of the system than for others. The main elements of a telecommunications network are shown diagramatically in figure 5-2. Messages consisting of voice or data signals start at the callers' homes (or at a factory, shop, or office); are routed to local exchanges on lines and cables; then are routed to other exchanges via cable, microwave radio, satellite, or other transmission media; and from local exchanges are routed to the final destination.

The typical cost of telephone plant per subscriber today (that is, total investment cost divided by number of local lines) is about US$2,000, about half of which is the cost of local line plant per subscriber (Skey 1979). Those parts of the telephone plant that cannot be allocated to individual subscribers (exchange equipment, long-distance cables, and so on) comprise indivisible units that can be used by few or many subscribers. As the number of subscribers increases, unit costs fall; that is, decreasing costs become evident. For example, in local transmission, costs can decline dramatically up to about 200 circuits and then level off. In main network transmission systems, costs decline until 2,000 circuits are provided.

An empirical study of 141 private microwave systems in the United States confirms the existence of scale economies up to a capacity of 1,000 circuits (Waverman 1975). Whether there are significant economies beyond that level is a matter of debate. The willingness of new competitors to provide long-distance service in the United States and the United Kingdom reflects their belief that their unit costs will not be significantly higher than those of the

Figure 5–2. Elements of a Telecommunication System

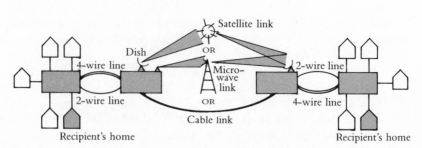

Source: Center for the Study of Services, *The Complete Guide to Lower Phone Costs* (Washington, D.C., August 1984).

large incumbent systems, in part because they can offer more advanced technology to the user. In developing countries, where there is less traffic, economies of scale are more important in relation to the size of the market. For example, very few interurban links have as many as 1,000 circuits, and duplication of long-distance plants would often result in considerably higher system costs.

Significant economies of scale cannot usually be achieved in the switching of calls; that is, it is roughly twice as expensive to switch 100,000 calls as 50,000 calls. There are economies of scale in the manufacture of subscribers' terminal equipment, but the economies relate to the scales of production and distribution, not to the size of the telephone networks that use the equipment, so they have no bearing on the case for ownership or competition in telephone networks.

Wherever a system is subject to many demands coming at random (as is typical with telephones or electricity), a large system requires proportionately less reserve capacity to provide a specified standard of service than does a small system. However, this additional cost is proportionately smaller as the size of the system increases; thus the "price" of duplication tends to become less important and may be completely offset by the advantages of competition. Similar qualifications apply to the argument that large systems require smaller proportions of spare parts and can make better use of scarce technical skills.

Do these examples of decreasing costs imply that the telecommunication service is a natural monopoly, in the sense that production by one firm alone is less costly than production by a number of firms? This is a matter on which there is no universal agreement, but such authorities as Baumol (1977) and Beesley (1981) state plainly that "the existence of scale economies is neither necessary nor sufficient to prove natural monopoly." Furthermore, even if a natural monopoly can be proved to exist in the case of existing technology, telecommunications technology is changing rapidly with microelectronics and the intertwining of telephone and computer services. "Communications networks today are bursting with productivity-raising possibilities that any number of profit-seekers would be glad to try to realise. These possibilities are more obvious now in the developed world but not confined to it. Californian software companies are on-line to employee-programmers at terminals in Mexico and Chile" (Rohwer 1985, p. 40).

Many technical developments in telecommunications that have made it possible to reduce costs or introduce new services pose a threat to the established monopolies. Large telecommunications users can reduce their costs by bypassing local exchanges and connecting directly to long-distance services. For example, Merrill Lynch's New York offices and IBM's North Carolina offices are directly connected to AT&T long-distance networks by fiber optic cables. Conventional local exchanges can also be bypassed via cellular telephone systems (which require no cables) or possibly even via cables being installed for cable television (Samuel 1985).

Thus the case for treating the sector as a natural monopoly is not obvious even where there are scale economies in the supply of telecommunication services, and it is being continually weakened by technological progress.

Regulation of Private Ownership

Regardless of one's views on the importance of scale economies in telecommunications, there is no doubt that transferring existing networks from public to private ownership would provide great scope and incentive for the exercise of monopoly power. The extent to which competition might reduce this power is discussed shortly. But some form of government regulation would certainly be called for, at least with respect to the main network, although not necessarily with respect to subscriber equipment or to services largely resulting from attaching additional facilities at the ends.

This then raises the question: Would government regulation reduce the benefits of private enterprise to the extent that private ownership would no longer be more advantageous than government ownership? Experience in the United States is of direct relevance in answering this question.

Before it was broken up in 1983, the Bell telephone system consisted of interconnected monopolies, all of which were regulated by public bodies to ensure that stipulated services were provided at "reasonable" prices. The pricing system was based on costs, and permitted profits were calculated as "reasonable" rates of return on assets. This system is applied in the United States not only to telephones, but also to privately provided electricity, water supply, urban transport, and many other services. It has the disadvantage that since any reductions in costs require the companies to reduce their prices, the incentives to reduce costs are limited. The regulating authorities are in practice not so much concerned with reducing costs as with ensuring that no "excessive" profits are made.

The Bell service was indeed excellent—especially when compared with what was available in most other countries—but it was expensive. In the early 1980s local calls in the United States were priced at about 10 cents, whereas in the Dominican Republic the equivalent service provided by a local company managed by GTE cost less than 4 cents. The Bell system products were solid and durable. Its home telephone instruments (which it rented out and did not sell) were built to last. Its microwave towers are solid pyramids, whereas those of its rival, MCI, are light, guy-wired structures. As Samuel (1985, p. 179) pointed out, "Since it was not allowed by regulators to benefit in its profits from taking a prudent risk, it naturally tended to invest its way out of risk taking. It overbuilt everything."

Partly under pressure of regulatory authorities, the Bell system made extensive use of cross-subsidies. It could load on some customers costs directly incurred by services to others. For example, according to Samuel (1985, pp. 179–80):

> For years, the Bell system made a virtue out of its free services like directory assistance that save consumers from using the telephone book or maintaining a list of numbers. These services have been free of direct charge to the subscriber but cost somewhere in the region of 40 cents to $1 per call serviced to the telephone company. The cost of these services was loaded onto telephone bills somewhere else. That lack of a direct charge meant the service was used wastefully. People made little attempt to record numbers. There was no scope for anyone to try to run a competitive and more efficient directory assistance service. And the telephone company had no measure of the real economic demand for these services. Now that there is competition in long-distance telephony, AT&T cannot afford to load the directory assistance costs onto its calling tariffs. It is proposing a 75 cent charge for long-distance directory assistance calls, and the local companies are starting to charge for local directory assistance calls, as they should. People will have an incentive to record numbers and will use the service only when it is worth 75 cents to them, approximately its cost. Also, companies now have an incentive to find a more efficient way than AT&T's for giving people numbers.

More important, the Bell system also subsidized local services by the revenues from long-distance calls, thus providing more of the former and less of the latter than consumers would otherwise have purchased. For example, the average cost of providing residential service in California was about $29, and the Bell system charged $8.25. As is shown in this volume, cross-subsidies of this kind are endemic throughout the developing world, not only in telecommunications, but also in electricity supply, water supply, and urban transport. Cross-subsidies, which force consumers of profitable services to subsidize consumers of unprofitable ones, are not necessarily an efficient way of helping those in need, since they are received by rich and poor alike. They also prevent the fullest development of the services that earn the surpluses. Cross-subsidies cannot be sustained under competitive conditions, and this is indeed an important advantage of competition.

These considerations suggest that government regulation can have severe disincentive and distortionary effects. Other countries besides the United States provide further evidence of this (De Alessi 1974), although some would challenge its magnitude. However, it may happen that other forms of regulation will be designed to minimize these disadvantageous consequences. An alternative arrangement, just implemented in the United Kingdom, requires British Telecom to reduce the average price of a representative "basket" of telecom services by 3 percent a year in real terms for five years, but it can keep whatever profits it generates through reductions in costs beyond the 3 percent level (Littlechild 1983).

Thus suitably designed regulation can protect customers from the disadvantages of private natural monopoly without losing all the benefits of greater efficiency associated with private ownership. The problems of regulation need not be a bar to private ownership.

Sector Composition and the Role of Competition

Should telephone systems be *monolithic,* in the sense that their operations and finances are controlled from one central point, or should they be *fragmented* and have independent entities in charge of administrative and financial affairs? In either case, it is obviously advantageous if each element of the system is *connectable* to others so that all the users of the system can communicate with one another. Before such communication can take place, common specifications must be adopted with respect to frequencies, signaling levels, codes, and the like. Although government direction may be required to establish such specifications, this does not mean that telephone systems should be monolithic. Some of the most successful—those in the United States, Finland, and Western Europe—are in fact fragmented.

What role should competition play? The fragmented systems of Europe and the United States are, in fact, associations of regulated monopolies, not subject to competition. The competitive model was tried in the Philippines but is not considered to have been successful, for reasons that merit further study. Some areas reportedly receive more than one service, whereas others receive none. Telephone users in the United States and the United Kingdom, however, now benefit from extensive competition in subscriber equipment and in long-distance service.

U.S. subscribers also appear to have benefited in the past from competition in local service. Alexander Graham Bell obtained his patents for telephone service in 1876. After trying to sell the patents to the Western Union Company (which turned them down because it was more interested in its telegraph system), Bell and his associates developed the telephone system themselves, under patents protected until 1893. Between 1876 and 1893, the system grew at an average rate of 16 percent a year, from nothing to 266,000 telephones. But the maximum growth in the United States occurred after 1893, when Bell's patents expired. Thousands of entrepreneurs rushed in to wire up farms and small stores and began to make telephones available in the homes of the middle classes. Between 1894 and 1907, open competition promoted an annual growth rate of telephones in the United States of 27 percent. By the end of that period, there were 6.1 million telephones in the United States, or one telephone for every 14 Americans compared with one for every 250 thirteen years earlier. During these years there was considerable service duplication. About 15 percent of Bell-AT&T's (Bell became the American Telephone and Telegraph Company in 1900) subscribers in 1909 had lines and telephones from another telephone company. Although its market share dropped from 100 percent in 1893 to 51 percent in 1907, the company reacted vigorously to its competition; between 1893 and 1907 it cuts its charges and added more than ten times as many phones as it had put into service during the period of its monopoly (1876–93).

As a result of this competition, AT&T's telephone revenues per station dropped from $76.41 in 1894 to $35.71 in 1909. It had been making profits of 40 percent on capital in its patent monopoly period. After 1900, the hectic competition from the independent companies reduced its rate of return to around 8 percent. It saw an easier and more profitable life through a restoration of monopoly. Government regulation was to be the means. Under the influence of financier J. P. Morgan, AT&T brought in a new chairman, Theodore Vail, who began to buy up independent telephone companies and launched a propaganda drive against the supposed wastefulness of competition. That campaign bore fruit in 1910 with a law that brought telephones under the regulatory control of the Interstate Commerce Commission (ICC) and thus put an end to competition for more than half a century. Under Vail (1908–13), the growth in the number of telephones dropped from 27 percent a year to 8 percent. From 1914 onwards (under ICC control, and from 1934 under FCC control) annual growth was between 4 and 5 percent. Although the competition to Bell-AT&T had resulted in substantial duplication, it also pushed prices down and helped spread the service, whereas monopoly ushered in higher prices, slower growth, and higher profits for the monopolist.

Private ownership and unrestricted competition (freedom of entry) are not necessarily appropriate for every situation and may often be ruled out by political or other considerations. Nevertheless, recent experience in the United States and the United Kingdom, in both long-distance and local service, and the rapid technological changes and business pressures that are now occurring suggest that moves in this direction deserve careful consideration by governments in developing countries.

Would private enterprise provide the necessary funds? Private enterprise has rarely been given a chance to compete in the telecommunications sector, since governments have generally disallowed such investment by the private sector. Where it has been allowed (for example, in Latin America at the turn of the century), governments have often imposed conditions that essentially made private investment unprofitable. But it is likely that, if permission were granted, funds would be attracted for the development of telecommunications where investors did not fear expropriation or other noncommercial risks.

Five Levels of Private Sector Involvement

Although Saunders, Warford, and Wellenius (1983) do not advocate wholesale privatization of telecommunications, they concluded that private entrepreneurs could play a greater role in the sector and thereby facilitate innovation, promote lower costs (through competition), mobilize new financing, and relieve public enterprises of some of the burden of sector development. They identified four levels at which private enterprise could help provide telecommunications services, and a fifth level (private local services) is added here. They are discussed in the following order:

> Subcontracting
> Equipment supply
> Network access and use
> Private local services
> Purchase or lease of franchises.

Subcontracting

Many telecommunications entities subcontract some of their requirements. Equipment and civil works are frequently purchased on the basis of competitive bidding. However, it is also possible to subcontract some of the routine activities, such as system management (as in Botswana), the preparation and printing of telephone directories (as in Argentina, Bahrain, and Brazil), the operation of call boxes (as in Malaysia), and the collection of payments (as in Ethiopia).

An example of how the management of the entire telecommunications sector can be subcontracted comes from Botswana, where the government is employing Cable and Wireless PLC to modernize the country's telecommunication system. The country is about the size of France but has a population of less than one million, so that financial viability is difficult to achieve. Cable and Wireless recommended the use of solar-powered radio links to minimize capital costs and meet the initial requirements of 20,000 lines in an economical manner. As part of the management contract, Botswanese staff are being trained in all the required techniques, including the most complex, with a view to reducing the proportion of expatriate staff from 22 percent in 1980 to less than 2 percent in 1992. The subcontracting of management services brings fresh expertise to the sector but, in the absence of competition, leaves the government to judge the costs and benefits of the policies and techniques proposed.

The preparation of telephone directories requires considerable technical skills, and thus is subcontracted in a number of countries, among them Argentina and Brazil. The profitability of these directories arises not only from advertising in the yellow pages, but also from boldface entries in the white pages and from less obvious sources such as fees for ex-directory listings and the disposal of used directories. Typically, the advertising revenues are shared by the contractors and the telephone companies. The production of telephone directories is particularly well developed in Brazil where three directories are routinely produced: white pages, yellow pages, and street directories that list telephone numbers by the addresses of subscribers.

Another difficult task that is often subcontracted is the maintenance and operation of public telephone booths, with or without automatic coin boxes. In Latin America agents "retail" the use of telephones in booths, shops, and other public areas and receive a percentage of the users' payments. This is of course common

practice in hotels, where guests are charged extra for calls connected to their rooms. In Malaysia the supply and operation of
public coin boxes is contracted out to a private company, Sapura
Holdings Sdn. Bhd.

Billing and the collection of accounts are not often subcontracted since telephone authorities have relatively little difficulty in collecting money owed to them: they generally have the
option of stopping service to defaulters. (Government departments are the main exception; it is difficult to cut them off,
however poor their payment records.) For many years, however,
the Ethiopian Telecommunications Authority subcontracted the
collection of accounts to bonded private entrepreneurs. They
worked on an incentive system, which gave them an increasing
percentage of all revenue collected above 85 percent of the amount
billed (Saunders, Warford, and Wellenius 1983).

Equipment Supply

Even where economies of scale in providing telephone service
may be significant enough to create monopoly conditions, and
thus to justify government ownership or the regulation of the
transmission and distribution networks, these decreasing costs do
not justify monopoly in the supply of telecommunications equipment to final consumers. There is therefore considerable scope for
allowing final consumers to shop around for the items that suit
them best. The equipment that can be bought in this way ranges
from telephones for home use to private branch exchanges, telex
machines, on-line computers, and so forth. Telephones for home
use can be bought in department stores throughout Latin America,
and private branch exchanges are sold competitively by the multinationals. To ensure overall technical compatibility and to maintain the quality of the network for other subscribers, telecommunications entities often specify standards for equipment
compatibility and maintenance. One advantage of such arrangements is that, to the extent that the final consumers buy their
equipment directly from the private sector, the telecommunications entity's financial needs are reduced.

The equipment needed by the telecommunications entities
themselves is generally supplied by the private sector. Some typical contracts executed recently are shown in table 5-2. To an
increasing extent, such equipment is being assembled or manufactured in developing countries. Brazil alone has at least six manufacturers of telephone equipment.

Table 5–2. Examples of Telephone Equipment Contracts for Developing Countries

Purchaser	Supplier and delivery date	Contract and equipment
Indian PTT (India)	Philips, first half of 1984	$16 million for containerized processor controlled telephone exchanges
Republic of Korea	Lynch Communication Systems Inc., June 30, 1983	$5 million for electronic subscriber carrier systems
Government agencies (Lebanon and Syria)	Broxming Communications Inc. (United States)	$1.4 million for Eagle rural radio and mobile telephone system
Sultanate of Oman exchange (private network) bought by Royal Dutch Shell subsidiary)	Philips Telecommunications Industrie BV (Netherlands)	1,000-line branch exchange
R&D center of Telebras (Brazil)	ITALTEL (Italy)	$800 million for plant and technology for thick film hybrid circuit production
Data Communications Corp. (DACOM, Korea)	ITT World Communications Inc.	Data transfer between United States, Korea, and seventeen other countries
High Gain Antenna Co. (Korea)	GTE Corp.	Upgrading the earth station for dual polarization operations
Telecommunications administration (Algeria)	Ericsson	$36 million for crossbar exchange equipment for 70,000 subscriber lines
Korea Telecommunications Authority (KTA)	Ericsson, 1984–86	$50 million for digital telephone system; 750,000-line expansion of Korean telephone network

(Table continues on the following page.)

Table 5-2 (continued)

Purchaser	Supplier and delivery date	Contract and equipment
Nepal Telecommunication Corp.	Plessey controls	$1.2 million for telex exchange. U.K. aid program to provide Nepal with international telecommunications satellite earth station as well as telex
New Zealand, Korea, Israel	Western Union International Inc.	Expansion of international facsimile bureau service
Huaying Nanhal Oil Telecommunication Service Co. Ltd. (China)	Cable and Wireless Plc. 49 percent China Nanhal Oil Joint Service Telecommunications Co., 51 percent (joint venture)	$22 million for oilfield telecommunications network providing services to the oil and support companies offshore and their control and supply bases in Guangdong province
Philippine Long-Distance Telephone Company	Syndicate loan with Asian Bank as lead manager, August 10, 1979	$307 million package loan for telephone equipment and phone investment
Iranian Telecommunication Manufacturing Co. (ITMC)	60 percent Iranian owned, local manufacturing company since 1968, still working in 1975	50,000 line units a year, with ultimate capacity for 120,000 line units
PTT (Turkey)	Northern Electric Co., 1968	Local factory to manufacture automatic telephone exchanges in Istanbul
Malaysia	Nippon Electric (NEC), 1981	$952 million for digital electronic switching systems
China, Singapore, Dominica, Colombia	Fujitsu, 1981–84	Digital electronic switching systems
Mozambique PTT (national telecommunications administration)	ITALCOM (joint venture ITALTEL, GTE Telecomunicazioni, Telettra, 1984	$50 million supply of digital exchanges, five-year contract, 40,000 lines

Table 5–2   (continued)

Purchaser	Supplier and delivery date	Contract and equipment
Mauritania PTT (national telecommunications administration)	Thompson–CSF Telephone (France)	$2.7 million international transit exchange
Colombia	Philips–AT&T Telecommunications (Netherlands), early 1986	Three telephone exchanges totaling 50,000 lines
Jabatan Telekom Malaysia (JTM)	Perwira Ericsson Sdn. Bhd. (Ericsson jointly owned subsidiary, in Malaysia)	15,000 lines of digital exchange capacity
PTT (national telecommunication administration, Thailand)	FATME (Ericsson subsidiary, Italy)	$58 million for digital exchanges in 28 cities
Haute Autorité du Développement Intégré de la Région Liptako-Gourma (multinational integrated development authority set up by Burkina Faso, Mali, and Niger)	Alcatel Thomson Faisceaux Hertziens (France)	Ten microwave stations (five powered by solar energy) Société de Télécommunication Africaine (Abidjan) main contractor; local subcontractor
Teléfonos de México, S.A.	LM Ericsson, June 1985 deadline for service	$30 million for 130,000 lines, local and transit digital telephone exchanges in Mexico City and the provinces
Telephone administration (DGT, Taiwan)	Bell Telephone Manufacturing Co. (ITT subsidiary, Belgium), in cooperation with Taiwan International Standard Electronics (ITT subsidiary, Taiwan)	Two digital toll exchanges, each providing 30,000 trunk lines
Compania de Teléfonos de Chile	Thomson–CSF Communications (France), ready for 1985	Two digital exchanges bringing to 186,000 the total number of lines ordered by Chile

(Table continues on the following page.)

Table 5–2   (continued)

Purchaser	Supplier and delivery date	Contract and equipment
Petroleum Pipelines Co. (Egypt)	Microware Division of Thomson-CSF (France), by the end of 1985	Telecommunications network connecting Cairo to Suez-Alexandria and Asyut, $16 million contract

Note: Dollar amounts are U.S. dollars.
Source: Telephony, various issues, 1983, 1984.

Network Access and Use

There are many examples of privately provided services that are linked by contractual arrangements to national networks. These services include the transmission of data, provision of international services, information retrieval, and the linking of privately organized and financed local systems to long-distance networks. Such services (which also flourish in Europe and North America) are illustrated by examples from Chile, Indonesia, Jamaica, and the Philippines.

Transradio Chilena Cia. de Telecomunicaciones S.A. Transradio Chilena has been providing telegraph and telex services in Santiago, Valparaíso, and several other cities since 1928. Although most of its shares are owned by foreign telecommunications companies, the profits have been steadily reinvested in Chile. There are no government subsidies to Transradio and prices are largely determined by market forces. The company has more than 900 subscribers and is undergoing a significant expansion in other areas, for example, Concepción and Antofagasta. It competes directly with the state-owned Telex Chile Comunicaciones Telegráficas S.A., which, incidentally, also became a profitable undertaking once established as a corporation separate from the posts and telegraph administration.

International Telephone Service for Indonesia. In 1967, International Telephone and Telegraph (ITT) entered into an agreement with the government of Indonesia to construct and manage an earth station in Indonesia to handle international traffic. A company entitled PT Indostat was established in which ITT and the government each shared 50 percent of the profit and ITT invested the equivalent of US$10 million. Indonesian nationals were trained to run the service, and this approach produced considerable economic and financial benefits. For example, the local services networks in Indonesia were stimulated to increase the market for the more profitable international traffic. PT Indostat proved to be so successful that after ten years of operation the government of Indonesia asked ITT to sell its interest, although the original contract allowed for a twenty-year term. The sale to the government was concluded in 1980, and ITT still maintains good relations with both PT Indostat and the government of Indonesia.

Competitive Message and Information Services in the Philippines. Private "record business" (telegrams, telexes, and data) has been provided in the Philippines by the Mackay Radio and Telegraph Company, which began operations there in 1952. In 1960, ITT acquired Globe Wireless Ltd., which had been in the Philippines since 1935, and in 1965 changed its name to Globe-Mackay Cable and Radio Corporation. Complying with the wishes of the Philippine government, ITT in 1974–75 sold 60 percent of its holdings in Globe-Mackay to a variety of local Philippine owners, including employees, veterans' associations, and local business interests.

The company continues to be independent and is still managed by ITT under agreements with Globe-Mackay and its principal Philippine shareholders. Virtually all of the 320 employees are Filipinos. The total annual revenues of Globe-Mackay are approximately $15 million, and the company continues to be profitable in competition with several other international firms, both locally owned and foreign owned.

Private Teleport in Jamaica. An example of a commercial initiative to access a private satellite telecommunications network is the teleport that is being established in Jamaica's Montego Bay Export Free Zone. Management and finances are provided by a U.S.-Japanese joint venture.

The purpose of a teleport (which consists of a satellite earth station linked to a local telephone network) is to provide high-speed, high-quality voice and data lines for companies engaged in telecommunications. The emergence of such companies has been stimulated by the development of automatic collect-call systems. To reserve a hotel room in the United States or to contact a credit card company, for example, one can use a number on the 800 exchange that makes the connection at no charge to the caller and

automatically bills the subscriber of the number called. This innovation, which may seem of minor consequence, is having a significant effect on the location of jobs in the United States in that
factories in remote areas can now sell directly to customers
through national advertising; orders are taken by long-distance
telephone calls that cost callers nothing. The same technique has
also made it possible for companies that depend on large volumes
of telephone orders to set up order departments in low-wage areas.
Nationwide orders for Hertz rental cars, for example, are taken in
Oklahoma.

The search for higher profits via lower costs has led several U.S.
companies to move some of their data-handling operations outside
the country. For example, American Airlines airfreights its used
tickets to the Caribbean to have the data processed for input into
computers; the data are returned to the United States via satellite
and the INTELSAT system. Savings of 40 percent over U.S. costs
are claimed.

The Jamaica teleport is designed to provide lower-cost satellite
facilities for operations of this kind. The Montego Bay Export
Free Zone is being developed in large measure as an office park
with special facilities—such as sales points, reservation centers,
and data entry—to attract companies engaged in information service activities. The information will flow between the United
States and the teleport on voice and data lines via an American
Satellite Company satellite and a specially constructed ground
station in Jamaica. The price of private leased voice and data
circuits will be comparable to U.S. domestic operations that are
competitively determined and therefore will be much lower than
the charges for international voice and data services via INTELSAT.
These low rates are expected to make the free zone's facilities
especially attractive to U.S. firms and to generate 10,000 new jobs
in Jamaica. And many of the users accessing the operators at the
teleport will not realize that their phone calls, placed through the
800 network, will be earning valuable foreign exchange for Jamaica (*Journal of Commerce,* May 19, 1986).

Private Local Services

Examples of cooperatives or private companies that provide
telephone service in towns or villages can be found mainly in Latin
America, but also in the Philippines. Typically, members of the
group subscribe money to the cooperative, and then purchase a
small exchange, cables, telephone sets, and other necessary equip-

ment and establish a local telephone network. If the quality of the local installation is considered adequate and if financial terms are agreed, connection to the national service is allowed. Bolivia, Brazil, and the Philippines provide some interesting examples of private local services.

Santa Cruz, Bolivia. In 1963, in a restaurant in Santa Cruz, a handful of influential businessmen conceived the idea of a local private telephone company, financed and operated as a cooperative. They formed a commission (Consejo de Administración) to represent all the shareholders, of whom there were initially 2,000. Most subscribers received shares on the basis of one share per telephone line, but some of the founders held twenty to thirty shares each. At that time there were no automatic telephones in Santa Cruz, and the government, aware of the problems plaguing the Bolivian telecommunications sector, was more than willing to let enthusiastic entrepreneurs improve the telephone service in the area. They founded the Cooperativa de Teléfonos Automaticos de Santa Cruz de la Sierra Ltda. (COTAS). The commission made the necessary arrangements to obtain government approval and to finance the equipment. From the beginning, government intervention has been minimal and its attitude supportive, not only to COTAS but to eleven other telephone cooperatives that have been formed in Bolivia.

Until 1980, COTAS was advised on technical matters by Oki Electric Company of Japan. In 1980 COTAS established its own planning department and since has been advised by the Intel España Company. During the period 1967–70, COTAS was the first telephone company in Bolivia to install a microwave system—it did so even ahead of the national entity, ENTEL. In 1973, the four largest companies involved in the main microwave system (COTAS among them) signed a contract of interconnection with ENTEL for long-distance operation. The long-distance calls provide the cooperatives with an additional source of funds, since they receive an agreed proportion of revenues for calls handled on ENTEL's long-distance networks at the national and international level.

COTAS serves Santa Cruz district with a staff of 300, including technicians, workers, and management. The organization is not allowed to make a profit and keeps any surplus as reserves. It receives no subsidy. Tariffs have to be approved by the government. COTAS has variable tariffs, unique in Bolivia, that are based on the numbers of calls and electronic impulses (the first sixty impulses free; thereafter the charge is 50 pesos each). In 1984 COTAS had 35,000 telephone lines in use and a further 30,000 planned for the 450,000 inhabitants of Santa Cruz. COTAS also operates about 550 public telephone call boxes (400 in the city of Santa Cruz, 150 in the rest of the region), in which it is introducing a token system.

The cooperative is fully integrated and self-reliant and by itself provides all the telephone and ancillary services in Santa Cruz de la Sierra. For example, the phone directory is produced and distributed by COTAS, which not only recovers costs, but makes a profit on the advertising.

The twelve Bolivian telephone cooperatives are fully autonomous. However, they interact closely under the formal umbrella of the Asociación Boliviana de Empresas Telefonicas (ABET) in La Paz, which defends their interests from undue government regulations and encourages cooperatives among all the telephone companies outside ENTEL. The cooperatives also enjoy excellent relations with the government officials who are concerned with telecommunications.

However, long-term financing has not been available, and expansion is limited to what subscribers can finance fully up front. Because of this and other problems, large parts of the country have no service at all, and Bolivia's telecommunications system remains the least developed in Latin America relative to population size.

Brazil. A limited number of rural telephone cooperatives have been operating in Brazil for some years. Rural cooperatives buy and operate their own telephone subsystems and interconnect them with Telecommunicações Brasileiras S.A. (TELEBRAS), the state monopoly, subject to technical standards and usage charges. Provided national technical standards are established promptly and the regional advisory capacity is strengthened to help the cooperatives plan, develop (with private contractors and suppliers), and operate their systems, this may help to speed up the development or rural services. On the basis of experience in the São Paulo region, it is claimed that the rural telephone cooperative system is particularly effective in mobilizing local participation and private funds for investment. In addition, initial and recurrent costs are said to be lower than those of TELEBRAS, owing to the lower cost of local labor, some self-construction (for example, digging trenches and installing poles), low overhead, and the use of simple techniques (for example, direct buried cables). These claims are disputed by TELEBRAS, which believes that the quality of service may be compromised.

The Philippines. Telephone communication was introduced to the Philippines in 1890 when the Spanish government established a system in Manila. In 1903, another system was established in Cebu City by an American lawyer residing and practicing there. Further companies were formed, and some were dissolved. In 1928 J. B. Stevenot was granted a franchise by the Philippine legislature to organize the Philippine Long-Distance Telephone Company (PLDT), which purchased many of the existing systems and established new ones. Meanwhile, a number of provincial governments started their own telephone systems to serve government offices, and some private concerns—such as mining companies and large plantations—also set up local exchanges for their own use. By 1933, a wire and radio telephone long-distance network had been installed to interconnect the various PLDT exchanges with those of the government and all the private companies. By 1940, PLDT was operating fifteen exchanges connecting 34,000 telephones and an interisland and overseas long-distance radio telephone network.

During World War II, 90 percent of the facilities of PLDT were destroyed, and it was not until 1953 that PLDT was able to restore its telephone service to the level of December 1941. However, the demand for telephone service in the Philippines after the war was greater than could be met by PLDT, and private enterprises established other telephone systems in areas that were not franchised to PLDT. By 1970, there were seventy-eight private telephone systems and eleven government operations in the Philippines, all interconnected with the PLDT domestic network. Many of these systems had fewer than 2,000 subscribers (AT&T 1975).

Despite the large number of telephone companies in the Philippines today, many areas still have poor service and some have duplicate facilities. Opinions differ as to whether the telephone problems in the Philippines are due to an excessive number of operators or to other reasons. Whatever the reason, there seems little doubt that many of the privately owned telephone systems in the Philippines—including PLDT—are viable entities and that interconnection via the PLDT network is practicable.

Purchase or Lease of Franchises

Even though the market may be able to support only one supplier at any given time, an element of competition can still be introduced into that monopoly. Government agencies can sell or lease to private companies the right to provide telecommunication services in agreed areas. For example, GTE is franchised to provide service in the Dominican Republic, Ericsson Communications operates in parts of Argentina, and Cable and Wireless PLC provides service in parts of the West Indies. It has not been possible to obtain the cost–of–service data needed to show whether franchised operations are more or less costly than those carried out directly by government departments. However, even if there are no explicit cost savings, the awarding of such franchises relieves government administrators of tasks that franchised operators may be expected to carry out with at least equal efficiency. But the process of awarding franchises, monitoring performance, and approving tariffs raises difficult problems for the authorities, particularly during periods of currency inflation.

Telephone franchises are not identical to fully competitive markets for several reasons: the operators do not have freedom to fix tariffs, the terms of the franchise are set by the government rather than by consumers, the concessionaires are themselves protected from competition (except at the time that they bid for the right to provide the service), and incumbent concessionaires may have an unavoidable advantage at the rebidding stage. Nonetheless, uncertainties about renewal of contracts may deter investment. Despite these difficulties, which extinguished many franchise operations in Latin America in the 1960s, franchises may be beneficial in some circumstances. The following examples illustrate apparently successful franchising operations.

CODETEL in the Dominican Republic. The first telephone system in the Dominican Republic is reported to have been installed in 1884 by Preston C. Nasson. The network in the capital city that he established gave unlimited local service to subscribers at a rate equivalent to US$3 a month, which compares well with the 1984 monthly rate, equivalent to US$3.42—possibly the lowest in the world. The first long–distance lines were built in 1887 (AT&T 1975). The present company, Compania Dominicana de Telefonos C. por A. (CODETEL), has been operating since 1930 and has expanded steadily since—in the quality and variety of services offered, in technical sophistication, and in the number of subscribers, which was expected to reach 200,000 by 1984. In 1955 CODETEL was purchased by GTE and remains part of that multinational to this day. Its concession, approved by the National Congress, is for a period up to the year 2010. It also provides long–distance connections for eight small local systems in the republic.

In addition to providing a service that is considered to be one of the best and cheapest in the world (the charge for a local call–box call is the equivalent of 4 cents), CODETEL pays the government 10 percent of gross receipts in tax. The company employs 1,900 people and is considered a desirable employer (it receives ten or more employment applications for each vacancy). But two problems tend to slow down its progress.

- Its tariff structure is fixed by the government in a form that takes insufficient account of cost differentials; thus, the expansion of capacity in some areas cannot offer an acceptable financial return.
- Although the investment by GTE is in U.S. dollars, the earnings are in Dominican pesos and are therefore subject to an exchange rate risk; the government does not protect the investors against losses resulting from fluctuations in its currency.

As a result of these problems, CODETEL's investments are limited to internally generated surpluses, and the telephone network is not being developed as rapidly as it might be if the company were allowed to charge more for high-cost investments and if earning were protected from inflation.

Commercial Telegraphy in China. The first telegraph cable in China was laid in 1866 and connected the Shanghai office of Russell & Company, an American firm, with its warehouses. Telegraphy on a commercial scale was introduced into China by two companies, one British and the other Danish, that were the predecessors respectively of the Eastern Extension Australasia and China Telegraph Company Ltd. (now Cable and Wireless Ltd.) and the Great Northern Telegraph Company Ltd. (of Denmark). The British company approached China from the south, laying a cable between Singapore and Hong Kong in 1871. In the same year the Danish concern, which had a line across Siberia, extended it to Nagasaki, and then to Shanghai and (via Amoy) to Hong Kong. In 1883 the Great Northern duplicated its cables between Vladivostok and Nagasaki and Shanghai, while the Eastern Extension laid a line from Hong Kong to Foochow and Shanghai. From the outset, the two companies worked closely together. In 1900, for example, they laid a cable from Shanghai, via Chefoo, to Taku, near Tientsin; this opened direct telegraphic communication between Peking and Shanghai. The companies made these lines for the Chinese government and lent it the funds needed to install it. By agreement, the two companies were to work the cables on behalf of the government until the loans were repaid. Repayment was completed in 1933. In 1906 an American concern, the Commercial Pacific Cable Company, laid a cable between Manila and Shanghai.

The Eastern Extension and the Great Northern had a large part in training Chinese telegraph operators. In 1876 the Chinese authorities established a school of telegraphy at Foochow and staffed it with some of the Great Northern's officers. Operators were also trained by the companies directly. Most of these remained in the employment of the companies but some entered the Chinese Telegraphic Administration. The Great Northern Telegraph Company compiled a Chinese dictionary that organized Chinese characters into four-figure groups that could be sent by cable; the addressee reconverted these groups into the corresponding characters.

With the growth of nationalism in China, the companies relinquished to the government their telegraphic functions. Their concessions expired in 1944 and were not renewed (Allen and Donnithorne 1954). However, the franchising concept itself does not seem to have been found inadequate.

The Role of the Government

When the private sector plays a significant part in the provision of telecommunication services, governments may need to play three important roles:

> Award and regulate franchises
> Specify appropriate technical standards
> Ensure access to all systems.

Award and Regulation of Franchises

If a telecommunication service is to be provided by a private company on a monopoly basis, the government will have to ensure that the monopoly supplier's tasks are clearly defined and that prices (or profits) are acceptable. Selecting a suitable person or firm is not easy. Some governments find it helpful to use a process of bidding for this purpose: they specify the tasks in detail and invite bids from qualified contractors. First, however, they must decide what tasks ought to be specified (for example, they must determine what levels of service consumers should receive and how far consumers are willing to trade off quality against price).

The profits allowed to the successful bidder are often expressed as a percentage return on the capital invested in the enterprise. As mentioned earlier, this arrangement gives the contractor an incentive to broaden the capital base of the enterprise unnecessarily and no incentive to reduce costs. An alternative method of price control adopted in the United Kingdom has already been described.

The structure of relative prices in the permitted tariff is also important. If prices are allowed to cover incremental costs, contractors can charge more for high-cost than for low-cost services. If charges are uniform, however—as they are in the Dominican Republic—service to potential high-cost customers may have to be denied, even though many of them would prefer to pay a higher rate than go without the service. Governments will also need to monitor and prevent various anticompetitive practices on the part of franchised and other suppliers to ensure that competition and customers are protected by the force of law.

Specification of Technical Standards

The examples from Bolivia, Brazil, and the Philippines along with the U.S. experience early in this century show that local telephone systems covering large towns or small villages can be technically and financially viable. But how can one ensure that the local systems will be able to communicate with one another? Telecommunication authorities would certainly wish to avoid the experience of Manila, where two competing suppliers reportedly refused to interconnect their systems, with the result that subscribers needing complete coverage had to have two telephone instruments. Nevertheless, when technology is developing rapidly, a period of unrestricted experimentation allows time to see which type of equipment is most suitable in practice.

Successful communication depends on the technical compatibility of signaling levels, transmission characteristics, and other aspects of the communication system. Uniform specifications may therefore have to be established at a national level. Recent experience in the United Kingdom suggests that government bodies may take time to develop appropriate standards and thus may restrict both competition and technical progress. Since manufacturers have an incentive to provide system-compatible equipment (to increase its usefulness, and hence their reputation, sales, and profits) an unrestricted market may not be as chaotic as some believe. In the United States, for example, technical specifications for telephones are not laid down by government; the industry voluntarily uses Bell system standards. Even the interconnection problems that have arisen during the hectic development of microcomputers are being overcome by the industry, and there is no consensus that governmental standards should be imposed.

At the same time, it can be argued that standardization should be not only national, but international, and that an organization such as the International Telecommunications Union (ITU) should issue specifications that could be supported by individual governments. ITU engineers are in fact working to produce worldwide telecommunications standards. The experience in other industries is worth examining. In air travel, for example, safety standards for aircraft maintenance and air traffic control are specified by the International Civil Aviation Organization and are followed by most civil aviation authorities, in both developing and developed countries. The system seems to work well, possibly because all the decisionmakers concerned have a strong personal interest in travel safety. Similarly, ITU members have a strong interest in securing international standards that will speed up technical change in international communication. It is probably for this reason that ITU has been successfully setting international standards for more than 100 years.

Thus, the setting of standards can be an appropriate role for government, even though the U.S. experience indicates that it is not an essential role.

The Need to Ensure Access

Because telecommunication services become more useful the more points that they can connect with, the public is interested in ensuring that service providers do not impose arbitrary barriers to such connection. When service is provided by more than one supplier, however, one company may find it advantageous to refuse connections that would help its competitors. For example, until 1977 local U.S. companies belonging to the Bell system refused to allow connection to long-distance Bell competitors, such as MCI. Now that the Bell system has been dismantled, all public local phone systems in the United States have to give equal access to all long-distance carriers.

If telecommunications systems are to be connectable to others, two requirements must be met: first, they must be technically compatible; second, the providers must agree on financial terms, for example, with respect to the sharing of revenues resulting from calls that use both networks. If different operating companies are unable to agree on technical standards or financial terms, the government may have to intervene on behalf of public interest to ensure connectability.

Conclusion

In general, (though not always) telecommunications systems in developing countries are restricted and backward, to the disadvantage of the users. Such systems also hamper the growth of the economy. One reason for this situation may be the restricted role allowed to private enterprise and competition.

Inasmuch as the improvement of communications is generally considered to be in the public interest, the expansion of telecommunications should surely be encouraged. The World Bank has been in the forefront of those who believe that the communications revolution requires developing countries to rethink their telecommunications strategy and make appropriate adjustments to meet escalating needs and pressures. Greater commercial orientation among existing systems and a larger role for the private sector are two important and highly desirable adjustments. But the Bank also recognizes that such changes need careful thought, since the problems involved are extremely complex and the technology is rapidly evolving.

Some would argue that a comprehensive, well-planned telecommunications system based on accurate forecasts of demand can best be provided by the government or by a government-protected monopoly, and that piecemeal development by competing private systems is likely to be less effective. But in real life comprehensive systems are not always well planned, and forecasts of demand are often widely inaccurate. Competing suppliers may also be imperfect, but they have strong incentives to get their forecasts right, to react quickly to changes in demand, to discover and provide the kinds of new services that customers want, and to keep their costs down through efficient management and astute purchasing policies.

Each case has to be examined on its merits and due consideration given to the actual operation of government systems and to the advantages and disadvantages of competition and private ownership. Broadly speaking, it seems that there is now greater scope for private sector involvement in long-distance transmission, value-added services, and terminal equipment, but the scope for private provision is not confined to these areas.

The private sector, which pioneered the development of telecommunication services at the end of the nineteenth century, can now play a major role in meeting the demands of those who are still without services. Experience in the Caribbean region shows how a multinational firm can provide service that combines low cost with financial viability. For societies that prefer other solutions, there are subscriber cooperatives, along the lines developed in Bolivia and Brazil, or the private companies developed in the Philippines.

The telecommunications sector provides scope for private sector involvement at the local, national, and international levels. At the local level, small entrepreneurs or cooperatives have the opportunity to raise capital, establish a service, and operate it, possibly using self-help and part-time labor. At national levels, there are opportunities to provide long-distance services, not only for voice transmission but also for the communication of data. The private sector in some developing countries can assemble or manufacture telecommunications equipment.

At the international level, the demand for long-distance communication is growing rapidly. Here there is also scope for suppliers to manufacture equipment that will meet the needs of many localities and be compatible with national standards. It is possible to envisage the equipment being bought in bulk—possibly with the aid of an international financing agency—so that even small operators will be able to reap economies of scale in the purchase of equipment.

Where a shortage of funds precludes rapid expansion of a single national system, the development of large national networks from small systems would be more satisfactory for the people concerned than no service at all. As is well known, the United States telecommunications system was developed from a large number of smaller systems. Some of these were operated by single families in which the women ran the switchboards while the men installed telephones and repaired lines (USTA 1972). Even in 1986, the U.S. system comprised more than 1,500 separate companies, many of which covered small areas and employed only a handful of people.

Because of the growing range of telecommunications activities and the variety of available equipment, compatibility will always be a concern, but it can be achieved even where different kinds of equipment have to be interconnected. Obtaining financial support and technical skills may also be a problem, but the private sector is able to provide these at terms commensurate with the risks and rewards involved. Security needs must also be taken into account, but they do not preclude private provision in a variety of contexts.

Thus there do not appear to be any insuperable financial or technical constraints that prevent the private sector from satisfying the intense unmet demands for telecommunication services in developing countries. The constraints in many countries are political, and their removal is likely to promote economic growth.

References

Allen, G. C., and Audrey G. Donnithorne. 1954. *Western Enterprise in Far Eastern Economic Development*. London: Allen and Unwin.

AT&T (American Telephone and Telegraph). 1975. *Calling the World 1975*. New York: AT&T Long Lines.

———. n.d. *The World's Telephones as of January 1983*. Morris Plains, N.J.

Baumol, W. J. 1977. "On the Proper Tests for Natural Monopoly in a Multiproduct Industry." *American Economic Review* 67(5):809–22.

Beesley, Michael E. 1981. *Liberalisation of the Use of British Telecommunications Network*. Report to the Secretary of State. London: Her Majesty's Stationery Office, January.

Capital (incorporating *Indian Financial Review*). 1983. "Comeback at Delhi." No. 139, February.

De Alessi, L. 1974. "An Economic Analysis of Government Ownership and Regulation: Theory and the Evidence from the Electric Power Industry." *Public Choice* 19 (Autumn).

———. 1980. "The Economics of Property Rights: A Review of the Evidence." *Research in Law and Economics* 2 (September 6):1–47.

Gray, Clive S. 1984. "The Jakarta Telephone Connection Charge and Financing Indonesian Telecommunication Development." *Bulletin of Indonesian Economic Studies* 20(2).

Habir, Manggi. 1984. "Progress in Communications Should Benefit Other Sectors." *Far Eastern Economic Review*. September 6.

Kingsbury, John E. 1915. *The Telephone and Telegraph Exchanges: Their Invention and Development*. London: Longman Green.

Littlechild, S. C. 1979. *Elements of Telecommunication Economics*. London: Peregrinus for the Institution of Electrical Engineers.

———. 1983. "The Effect of Ownership on Telephone Penetration." *Telecommunications Policy* (September):246–47.

Millward, Robert. 1982. "The Comparative Performance of Public and Private Ownership." In *The Mixed Economy*, ed. Eric Roll. New York: Holmes and Meier.

Ricci, Claudia. 1984. "Phone Company Got You on Hold? Here's a Way to Make Connections." *Wall Street Journal*, May 11, p. 33.

Rohwer, Jim. 1985. "The World on the Line." *Economist* (November 23).

Samuel, Peter. 1985. "Telecommunications: After the Bell Break-up." In *Unnatural Monopolies*, ed. Robert W. Poole, Jr. Lexington, Mass.: D. C. Heath.

Saunders, Robert, Jeremy J. Warford, and Bjorn Wellenius. 1983. *Telecommunications and Economic Development*. Baltimore, Md.: Johns Hopkins University Press.

Skey, P. L. 1979. "Digital Techniques—How Do They Affect Telephone Network Development?" *Telephony,* July 30.

Telephony. 1985. *World Telecommunications Plans: Business Communications Capability.* Chicago, Ill.: Telephony Publishing Corp.

USTA (United States Telephone Association). 1972. *The Ring of Success.* Washington, D.C.

Waverman, L. 1975. "The Regulation of Intercity Telecommunications." In *Promoting Competition in Regulated Markets,* ed. Almarin Phillips. Washington, D.C.: Brookings Institution.

6

Urban Transport

A few billion people cannot all be wrong, and there is really no need for us to painfully invent a new urban transportation mode when there are literally thousands of jitney systems in flourishing operation. . . . At first glance they all appear to be different, but this is primarily because of variations in hardware—from bicycle rickshaws to sleek European minibuses. The institutional structure and basic operations are quite similar: private individuals acquire the highest technology vehicle that they can afford, and respond to the mobility demands of their neighbors at a tariff that most of them can pay.

—SIGURD GRAVA, "LOCALLY GENERATED
TRANSPORTATION MODES OF
THE DEVELOPING WORLD"

URBAN TRANSPORT is intimately linked with the growth of cities, which in its turn reflects the development of specialization and trade. Because of the limitations of land transport, most large cities grew up beside rivers or lakes. For those unable or unwilling to walk, public transport was by boat and was generally provided to the public by private entrepreneurs. This is still the case in Bangkok, Venice, and other cities. In some cities private enterprise also provided public transport by means of porterage, when laborers were hired to pull or carry their patrons. To this day, the rickshaw is the most common form of public transport for the elderly and handicapped in many cities in China.

One of the earliest examples of a land-based public conveyance for passengers in an urban area was the horse-drawn bus introduced in Paris in 1662, although the business failed. The first horse omnibus was introduced in London in 1829 by the private entrepreneur, coach builder George Shillibeer. It operated along a

Thanks are due to Alan Armstrong-Wright and other World Bank transportation specialists for information unstintingly given over many years.

fixed route from Paddington Green to the Bank of England. This vehicle held up to twenty passengers, who entered from the rear and sat facing each other along the sides. Similar vehicles powered by internal combustion engines are to be seen in Manila and Bangkok today. The first horse omnibus in New York was operated by Abraham Brower along Broadway in 1831. Horse omnibuses spread rapidly throughout the world and were operated in many cities until the early 1900s.

Because it was difficult to pull wagons on the rough streets common during the nineteenth century, the idea was conceived of pulling vehicles on rails laid on the streets. The first cars on rails (which became known as streetcars) were reportedly organized by the Harlem Railroad in New York in 1832. They were drawn by horses. The horse-drawn streetcar had a number of advantages over the horse-drawn omnibus. Metal wheels operating on metal rails were much easier to pull, the streetcars could be made larger than the omnibuses, and they could maintain a speed of up to four miles an hour, whereas the omnibus reached only three miles an hour. By the middle of the nineteenth century, "almost all American cities and towns of any size, or those with even a modest delusion of metropolitan grandeur, had horse- or mule-powered street railway companies" (Smerk 1979, p. 6). But, as with the omnibuses, there were typically many competitors in the business, which is now thought of as a natural monopoly. Philadelphia at one time had thirty-nine streetcar companies operating at the same time.

But horses had their disadvantages. As a mode of transport they were slow, and they polluted the environment. Many attempts were made to replace the horse with some form of mechanical power. One solution was to use steam trains and to run them on separate rights of way (because of the growing congestion in the streets). In 1863, underground steam trains were introduced in London by the (private) Metropolitan Railway Company. In 1868, similar equipment was put into service in New York, but at an elevated level, not underground. The cable car was another solution. It was invented in 1869 by Andrew Hallidie and was first used in San Francisco in 1873. The cable system employed giant engines to keep endless cables moving continuously just under street level. Streetcars were put into motion by a device that grasped the moving cable, and they stopped when the cable was released. Cable systems had low operating costs but required very heavy investments and were not profitable unless they moved large masses of people.

In the 1880s, however, urban transport was revolutionized with the introduction of the electric streetcars, or trams. The first electric line was operated in 1883 by Charles Van Depoele. The state of the art greatly improved in 1888, when Frank J. Sprague electrified a portion of the horse car lines in Richmond, Virginia. Within two years of the completion of the project in Richmond, electric railways were rapidly taking over the horse car and cable operations in the United States. Similar systems were being established all over the world. Unlike the rickshaws and horse-drawn buses that preceded them and the buses and jitneys that followed, the cable cars and streetcars exhibited substantial decreasing costs. Once the motive power needed to pull the cables or to power the streetcars was in place, additional vehicles could be added to the systems at little additional cost. Thus, with increases in system size, costs per unit of output were lower. In 1916 urban electric railways peaked both in the United States and in other parts of the world. The decline of urban railways—and interurban railways— was associated with the development of new motorized forms of public transport: the bus and the jitney, which, thanks to the development of gasoline and diesel engines, were able to operate independently of rail lines and electric cables.

Buses were first used by an existing transit firm in the United States in New York in 1905, when they were allowed to run along Fifth Avenue. In 1912 Cleveland Railways began to use buses as feeders for its streetcars. Development in Europe proceeded in parallel, but in the United States the automobile developed another mode for public transport, which was not paralleled in Europe: on July 1, 1914, L. P. Draper ascertained that he could legally use his Model T Ford touring car as a common carrier if he secured a chauffeur's license. Draper picked up his first passenger at a streetcar stop on Broadway and charged him 5 cents, which in slang was known as a "jitney."

This episode sparked a movement for the use of private automobiles as common carriers; by 1915 some 62,000 vehicles were being used in this way. Jitneys did not run on fixed routes or at fixed schedules, nor did they have fixed fares (their fares tended to rise when the street railways were not running or during storms or at night). Because of the threat they posed to the established companies, municipal governments were unanimously hostile to jitneys and outlawed them so quickly that by the 1920s they were operating on only three streets in the United States: Mission Street in San Francisco, what is now Martin Luther King Drive in Chicago, and Pacific Avenue in Atlantic City. According to George Hilton,[1] the suppression of the jitneys amounted to a nationwide prohibition of competition in urban transport in the

1. Much of the material in this chapter is based on Hilton (1985).

United States. Because automobiles could not be used as common carriers, they seldom carried more than one person to and from work. To this day, the empty seats in cars during rush hours have constituted a serious waste of resources.

In the 1920s and 1930s, competition in urban transport was also prohibited in Europe, although the consequences there were not as severe as in the United States, where more people owned automobiles. In England, for example, following considerable competition in bus services in the 1920s, a law was passed in 1930 that controlled entry into the urban transport industry and thereby eliminated competition in public transport in Britain.

But what, the impatient reader is bound to ask, has all this to do with developing countries? Many of these countries at one time had political ties with the countries of Europe and the United States, and they tend to follow the same legalistic patterns. The consequences of the British 1930 Road Traffic Act and the 1933 London Passenger Transport Act (which created a transport monopoly in London), for example, are still to be found all over the world in countries that were once subject to British influence. Similarly, the rules and practices of France are followed in West Africa, and the regulatory systems of the United States are very much in evidence in Latin America. The influence of these laws has been pervasive and long lasting. For example, to this day there is a strange contradiction in taxi regulation in Papua New Guinea: small vehicles may be used as taxis in Lae, but only large vehicles (which are more expensive) may be used in the capital city, Port Moresby. It is possible that the regulations in Port Moresby derive from those in Australia, which derived from those in Britain, while those in Lae (which had a German colonial administration) do not. If this is the case, taxi users in Port Moresby have to pay high fares because the authorities in nineteenth-century London decreed that taxicabs had to be tall enough to accommodate gentlemen in top hats!

Criteria for Public Provision

To what extent do urban transport services possess the characteristics (see chapter 1) that justify provision by the public sector? Public provision cannot be justified on the grounds that urban transport cannot be charged for or that urban transport is a merit good insufficiently appreciated by users. Indeed, urban transport has substantial externalities, both positive and negative. The positive ones, which result from improved accessibility, are wide-ranging and include changes in land values. The negative externalities are those associated with noise, pollution, and congestion. As in the case of water, many of these externalities are associated with uneconomic pricing of transport and of roads: underpricing of commuter services produces substantial benefits for long-distance commuters, whereas underpricing of roads imposes heavy congestion costs on those who place a high value on their time. But there is no reason to believe that transferring services to the public sector is an efficient way of dealing with these externalities. For example, even if publicly owned buses could be shown to cause less pollution than privately owned ones, the appropriate remedy would seem to be better enforcement of antipollution laws.

There remains the point that public transport exhibits decreasing costs, even to the extent that it can be considered a natural monopoly. As noted earlier, this was the case for the early systems that depended on cable power or electric power provided by large power stations. These systems showed decreasing costs in the sense that an additional cable car or streetcar could be added to the system at an insignificant additional cost. In all but a few cities, however, these systems have been superseded by buses, minibuses, and taxis powered by internal combustion engines. Systems using these vehicles do not exhibit scale economies and, indeed, there is evidence that costs increase with the size of the companies providing the service. A recent World Bank publication (1986, pp. 20–21) summarized the point as follows:

> The economies-of-scale argument . . . has been discredited by both empirical evidence and experience. The management and labor problems of large bus undertakings that have often dominated the agendas of cities in both the developing and the industrial worlds have revealed the diseconomies of large-scale operations. Small, competitive, and highly variegated transport enterprises usually find it efficient to operate small vehicles rather than the large costly buses characteristically chosen by large organizations.

One other important factor must be kept in mind here: at least for some journeys, all travelers have the option of using private transport—such as automobiles, motorcycles, bicycles, or their feet. Therefore a monopoly on urban transport cannot be envisaged under any circumstances. That is to say, urban transport is not inherently suitable for provision by the public sector. Thus it comes as no surprise that hundreds of privately provided transport systems are operating successfully and efficiently throughout the world, despite the difficulties often put in their way by well-meaning but short-sighted officials. A few of these systems are described in the next section.

Examples of Private Provision

The Gbakas of Abidjan

Until 1974 Abidjan was served by a very active informal system of common carriers known as gbakas, which held fourteen to twenty-two people (see Lehuen 1983). Originally, they brought goods from outlying areas to city markets but evolved into "illegal" common carriers for the low-income areas of the city. In 1974, Abidjan's bus system, Société de Transport d'Abidjan (SOTRA, then controlled by Renault but now owned mainly by the government), urged the authorities to ban the gbakas in the city limits because they represented unfair competition. The government agreed to do so. The consequences were unfortunate—for the people of Abidjan, for the municipal and national budgets, and even for SOTRA. Before 1974, SOTRA had operated a profitable system, despite competition from the informal carriers. It had a well-managed fleet of 300 buses. With the banning of gbakas, SOTRA launched a massive fleet expansion and capital construction program. By 1981 the fleet had 900 buses and was expected to expand to 1,600 in 1985, but SOTRA has had deficits since 1975.

According to studies carried out for the Bureau de Circulation of the Côte d'Ivoire, informal services provided by gbakas in 1983 had a daily traffic of 15,000 vehicle trips that carried about 200,000 passengers on two main routes adjacent to the city center, while the public bus company carried 160,000 passengers on the same two routes. Since 1980 the service provided by the informal sector on these routes has jumped by 75 percent on one and 21 percent on the other.

Surveys conducted on board the gbakas showed that the costs per seat-kilometer are roughly similar to the costs for the public standard buses. However, the public service operates with a heavy deficit, whereas the privately owned gbakas seem to be making comfortable profits. By and large, this difference in performance can be attributed to more strenuous working conditions for gbaka employees, who run three times as many vehicle-kilometers as do the public bus employees, and to higher loading factors, which average 73–85 percent a day, compared with 45 percent for the public bus company. Consequently, the revenue per kilometer is far higher for the private gbakas.

These studies recommend that similar privately operated systems be introduced in the medium-sized cities of Côte d'Ivoire, instead of the centrally controlled fleets of large buses that are currently being proposed.

Private Buses in Buenos Aires

Buenos Aires, the capital of Argentina, has a population of 9 million living in an area exceeding 1,500 square miles. It has a variety of transport modes, the most important being the microbus, or *collectivo,* which accounts for 54 percent of all trips and 75 percent of public transport trips (see Ogueta 1977). The collectivos were developed in the 1920s when, as a result of a general economic crisis, many people could not afford to take taxis on their own. These vehicles were therefore used by groups of passengers, who paid their fares individually. The collectivos ran on fixed routes that were chosen by the drivers themselves. The shared taxi showed certain virtues of its own and was favorably received by the general public because it offered more flexibility, was faster, and ran more often than the underground and electric tramways. The collectivo evolved from a seven seater to the twenty-three seater that is the typical unit providing service today.

These microbuses offered stiff competition to the tramways and underground systems. As a result the government in 1936 established a Corporate Enterprise that was to have a total monopoly on the city's public transport services. Nevertheless, several microbus lines remained in existence until 1951, when a national enterprise known as Transportes de Buenos Aires took charge of all the services, including those of the Corporate Enterprise.

Both the quality and financial condition of the service operated by the Transportes de Buenos Aires deteriorated rapidly. By 1959, it was losing the equivalent of US$40 million a year. In 1962, the situation became intolerable and Transportes de Buenos Aires was dissolved. All the transport services, except the underground railway, were turned over to private companies. The trams and trolleybuses dropped out of service and were replaced by regular full-size buses. It is significant, however, that many of these were subsequently replaced by the microbuses.

The microbuses still operate profitably and provide a level of service that is praised by all visitors to Buenos Aires. The organizational unit of the service is the route association (*empresa*), which is an association of owner-drivers empowered to serve just one route. The owners joining an empresa have to abide by its rules, which govern such matters as schedules and fares.

The empresa is the formal employer of the drivers and assumes all the responsibility arising from the labor laws. The vehicle owners choose and replace the drivers and pay the operating expenditures of the vehicle. The income goes to the vehicle owners, who either turn it over to a common fund for distribution among members of the empresa, prorate it according to the mileage run by each vehicle, or divide it through any other method that the empresa may choose.

The empresa charges each of its member a monthly fee for a share of the administrative expenditures corresponding to each vehicle, the salaries paid, goods and services supplied for maintenance, and, in the event that the company is financing the purchase of a vehicle, an installment payment. The investments in vehicles and in repair facilities are part of the company's capital. The shares of successful operation will increase in value, but they cannot be sold in the free market. Any disputes within an empresa are settled at a meeting of members. Each vehicle owner is generally entitled to one vote. Empresas have a great many members: although a member can own several vehicles, and several people can own a single vehicle jointly, on the average, there is one partner per vehicle. About one-third of the members drive their own vehicles. The microbuses in Buenos Aires are regulated by the Ministry of Public Works and Services (MOSP), which fixes fares and minimum frequencies for individual routes and governs the formation of new empresas.

The empresas offer several advantages: each member is directly responsible for the operation of his unit and, with the aid of his family, does much of the work required to run and maintain the vehicle. The public benefits from the competition between empresas. Labor productivity is high: on the average, three persons are employed to drive, maintain, and repair each microbus. Since each vehicle produces 1.3 million to 1.6 million passenger-miles a year, average labor productivity is around 480,000 passenger-miles a year per person employed. The total fleet consists of 13,000 microbuses; on the average, 60 microbuses are used on each route, or about 4 per route-mile.

Taxis and Jitneys in Cairo

Cairo, the largest urban center in the Middle East, has a population of 8.5 million spread over an area of 800 square miles. It suffers from severe traffic congestion and a heavily overloaded network of bus and tram services. In recent years the transport system was substantially improved by the development of privately owned shared taxis and jitney services.[2]

Metered taxis in Cairo provide two kinds of service: exclusive service, which means one or more passengers are carried from the point of origin directly to their destination, and (illegal) shared service, which means the driver may stop along the route to pick up or drop off passengers without obtaining the permission of other passengers in the taxi. In general, the price for the exclusive service is negotiated at a rate that is substantially higher than the metered rate (at least for tourists), whereas the price for shared trips is based on the meter. These services appear to work quite well, although the fare levels are not clearly specified. Cairo also has a substantial number of unmetered taxis, some of which operate illegally between cities. The existence of these taxis—which suggests that the number officially licensed for public service is insufficient—is difficult to explain as there are no restrictions on the number of taxis that may be licensed.

Fixed-route jitney services were allowed to operate in the late 1970s. As is usual in the Middle East, vehicles normally wait until they have a full load and then leave the terminal, rather than leaving at fixed intervals and keeping a few seats for passengers along the route. Passengers are able to join the jitneys at midroute only when the vehicles stop to drop passengers off. About 800 vehicles running at intervals of three to five minutes were in operation in 1979. The system expanded rapidly that year and the maximum legal seating capacity was increased from twelve to fifteen seats.

A union of taxi drivers and minibus operators runs the system. It organizes new routes, determines the fares to be charged, and employs and pays dispatchers from a 5 percent ticket tax collected by the dispatchers at the terminals. The dispatchers receive a fixed salary plus a bonus if they collect more than a certain amount of money per day. The ticket tax is also used to finance the construction of signs and waiting facilities at jitney terminals. The union representatives claim that a demand exists for at least 2,000 vehicles and that the service can be substantially expanded.

The most sought-after vehicle is the locally assembled Ramses minibus. It owes its popularity not only to its comparatively low cost (US$7,000 compared with US$12,000 for a Volkswagen or Mazda vehicle of the same capacity), but also to its powerful engine and its durability under Cairo driving conditions. Eighty

---

2. Ron Kirby provided much of the information in this section.

percent of new vehicles are said to be owned by persons outside the taxicab industry who lease vehicles to drivers for 25 percent of their fare collections. Many investors own four or more vehicles. About 20 percent of the vehicles are driven by owners. Minibus fares are three to four times the regular Cairo bus fare, which is equivalent to 5 U.S. cents. Much of the repair and maintenance is done by the drivers themselves in small workshops.

Cairo's conventional bus and tram services do not cover their costs and are subsidized to the equivalent of more than US$50 million a year. The rapid growth of high-quality informal systems provides yet another illustration of the willingness of travelers to pay for improved service and of the ability of the private sector to provide, at a profit, services that the public sector finds unprofitable.

Special express (limousine) taxi services are also provided to and from the airport. The charges are fixed according to destination. One company alone operates about 500 of these vehicles.

Private Buses in Calcutta

Calcutta is one of the largest, most densely populated, and poorest cities in the world. It supports a population of some 10 million in an area that covers less than 600 square miles. Private buses first appeared in the city toward the end of the nineteenth century but were banned in 1960 when all bus services were vested in the Calcutta State Transport Corporation (CSTC). The CSTC suffered from managerial and financial problems and in 1966 was paralyzed by strikes. In response to public demand before the 1966 elections and to its need for ready cash, the government of West Bengal sold permits that allowed 300 private buses to be put into operation. These vehicles made a profit, even though they charged the same fare (equivalent to about 5 U.S. cents per mile) as the money-losing CSTC and had inferior routes. By the late 1970s, some 1,500 full-sized private buses were operating in Calcutta in addition to about 500 private minibuses. Today, unsubsidized private buses account for about two-thirds of all bus trips in Calcutta. Meanwhile, the CSTC, which operates similar routes at the same fares, has to be subsidized to the equivalent of US$1 million a month by a government that is desperately short of funds for other purposes.

The success of the private bus operators has been attributed to three factors:

- *Keeping vehicles on the road.* As soon as a private bus breaks down, it is repaired, often on the road, and the parts, if necessary, are bought on the black market. The CSTC, in contrast, has to go through formal channels to obtain spare parts, and only half of its buses are generally on the road.

- *Fare collection.* The private bus crews (who are paid a percentage of the revenues) make greater efforts to collect the fares than do CSTC employees. Fare evasion is estimated to be 25 percent on CSTC buses, whereas it is negligible on private buses.
- *Higher labor productivity.* The private buses use fewer staff than the CSTC, which employs fifty employees per bus (1980) and thus has among the highest staffing levels in the world.

Another factor in the success of the private buses in Calcutta is the route association. These associations—in general there is one for each route—were formed voluntarily and spontaneously by the private owners. Each owner retains control over the operation and maintenance of his own vehicle and receives the fares collected on it. The associations have rules to govern relationships between the members; for example, vehicles have to run on time. This is important because a bus running late tends to pick up more than its fair share of passengers, at the expense of the following bus. Owners of buses that do not run on time are fined. The fine money is distributed among the other members. It has been reported that the fines are, in some instances, proportional to the delay (at a specified rate per minute) and are paid directly to the owner of the following bus.

Deregulation in Colombo

Colombo, the capital of Sri Lanka, is a city where private bus services are subject to relatively little government regulation. Bus operators select their own routes, set their own fares, and determine when they will begin daily operations and when they will stop. The government does, however, impose stringent requirements with regard to safety, insurance, and vehicle inspection.

The private provision of public transport in Colombo has benefited greatly from the liberalization of national economic policies in the late 1970s. First, the easing of import restrictions stimulated the purchase of new vehicles. Then in 1979 the government put an end to the monopoly on public transport services held by the Central Transport Board (CTB). These actions by the government evoked a strong response from private bus operators, who imported more than 6,000 buses between 1979 and 1981. There are now some 7,000 private buses in operation throughout Sri Lanka. Of these, about 3,500 operate in the Colombo metropolitan region. These private buses hold 30 to 60 passengers. Meanwhile, CTB operates 5,800 buses in the region, each one able to carry between 100 and 120 passengers. Thus far, private bus services have managed to capture more than 25 percent of the market, despite having to compete with the heavily subsidized and well-established CTB bus services.

Although the private bus operators are permitted to set their own fares, these are greatly influenced by CTB fares, which are held artificially low (approximately 1.5 U.S. cents per kilometer). As a result, some private operators have found it difficult to compete, while others have resorted to overloading and other malpractices. A few routes that proved to be unprofitable have been shunned by private operators and are now served by CTB buses, which have become chronically overloaded. Special arrangements to overcome this problem are being formulated by the government.

The overall effect of deregulation has been a substantial increase in capacity, particularly at peak periods. It has also led to more frequent and less crowded bus service. CTB's operations and large subsidy are likely to be reduced as the private sector increases its share of the market (World Bank 1986).

The Minibuses of Hong Kong

The 5 million people of Hong Kong occupy an area of about 400 square miles on the south China coast. Although the main populated parts of Hong Kong were once served by bus companies enjoying exclusive franchises, after 1933 the existence throughout the colony of illegal taxis (known as *pak pais*) caused concern to the authorities. These vehicles were used as small buses hired either by a group at an agreed rate for a specific journey or separately by a number of individuals who paid by the seat. In February 1960, the government allowed these vehicles to be licensed for the transport of workers, schoolchildren, airline staff, and hotel patrons. In 1961, it licensed dual-purpose vans to provide transport for both freight and passengers. In addition to these legally registered vehicles, a considerable number of minibuses registered as private cars operated illegally for hire.

Although the government's policy favored the franchised services, on many routes their level and standard of service were so far below requirements that the traveling public was induced to use the nonfranchised services. The number of vehicles offering such services is estimated to have more than tripled between 1961 and 1968.

During the political disturbances of 1967 when the franchised public transport services were seriously disrupted by strikes, the illegal services filled the void and for a time became an essential element of the colony's transportation system. Their operations, which had previously been located in the comparatively remote areas near the Chinese border, were extended to the main centers of population. After the disturbances were over, the franchised services slowly recovered their predisturbance patronage, and police action against illegal operators became more severe. Nevertheless, the popularity of the illegal services, particularly the minibuses that had played a major role in coping with travel demand during the disturbances, increased. It was clear that a considerable proportion of the public preferred this mode of travel and was prepared to pay for the higher level of comfort and convenience that it offered.

After considerable deliberation, the government decided to legalize the minibus as a form of public transport, and in 1969 the public light bus (PLB) was introduced as a legal form of public transport. It proved so popular that by 1972 it was carrying one-quarter of all public transport trips and by 1976 one-third. By then the number of PLBs had reached 4,350, and the government, concerned about their effects on the franchised services, froze the number of licenses at that level.

The success of the PLBs was reflected in their profitability to their owners. A 1972 government study (Barden and Seneviratne 1972) estimated that owners would recoup their outlay within one year, but revised calculations made in 1980 estimated that two-thirds of the purchase price of a vehicle would be recovered in one year—not an unacceptable rate of return, even for Hong Kong.

The PLBs were criticized, however, for congregating on major routes and causing congestion there. Some transport planners argued that they should be banned from major corridors and relegated to the provision of feeder service to the franchised bus companies. These criticisms posed a dilemma for the Hong Kong government, which, in essence, had to choose between consumer sovereignty and planner sovereignty. By their patronage, the consumers demonstrated their preference for the faster and more comfortable PLBs on which all passengers had seats. The government attempted to resolve the problem by introducing "maxicabs," which can be described as franchised PLBs. The differences between these services are summarized in table 6-1.

Table 6–1. Characteristics of Maxicabs and Public Light Buses, Hong Kong

Characteristics	Maxicab	Public light buses (PLBs)
Route structure	Routes fixed by authority as feeder services; major bus corridors avoided	No fixed routes; busy streets where customers can be picked up easily
Fare	Fares fixed by authority according to a mileage scale; no difference between peak and off-peak periods	No fixed fares; often a high price is charged in the peak hours and a low fare (sometimes lower than buses) during slack periods
Timetable	Timetable detailing hours of operation and frequency of service laid down by the authority	No fixed timetable; driver may cease service at any time; sometimes operate late at night for much higher fares
Form of ownership	Fleet under central control and staffed by regular drivers	Varied: owner-drivers, vehicles on rent to drivers, and salaried drivers
Maintenance facilities	Garage maintenance and depot facilities provided	Maintenance by contract with garages; no depot (usually park overnight at PLB stands)
Restriction	Fixed routes authorized by authority; maxicabs allowed to let off passengers in some busy main streets	Most main streets have some form of PLB restriction

Source: World Bank.

By the end of 1985 there were about 1,050 maxicabs operating in Hong Kong on a total of thirty-six routes, in comparison with 4,350 PLBs. The government endeavored to expand the maxicab network further and to encourage ordinary PLBs to join the scheme.

The Dolmus-Minibus System in Istanbul

Massive migration from rural areas to major urban centers in Turkey has created complex problems of urban living that have strained the capacity of the local authorities to provide even the most essential public services. One feature of this general problem has been the failure of the municipal bus and other government-operated public transport systems to meet the routine travel needs of people. As a result of this situation, the *dolmus*-minibus system has emerged as an indigenous form of public transport in Istanbul. Today, more than one-half of the daily travel needs of the public is served by the dolmus (which are four- to five-seat passenger cars that can operate either as sole-use taxis or as shared taxis), and twelve-seater minibuses. In Istanbul there are currently about 16,000 dolmus ("dolmus," which means "stuffed," is used both in the singular and in the plural) and about 4,000 minibuses (these and the following details are based on Sanli 1977).

Istanbul traffic options are not as simple as they might appear on the surface, and the dolmus-minibuses can provide a panoply of services:

- *Dolmus only.* Service along fixed routes is provided by some seven-seater station wagons, but primarily by five-seater vehicles distinguished by a continuous yellow band around the vehicle or the "dolmus" sign placed or written on the vehicle.
- *Dolmus-taxi.* The operator may switch from dolmus to sole-use taxi either instantly (when congestion and demand levels are high) or on days that he prefers to operate his vehicle as a taxi. This kind of operation is conducted mainly in five-passenger vehicles.
- *Taxi-dolmus.* Another mixed operation uses five-passenger vehicles mainly as taxis and occasionally as dolmus.
- *Taxi and dolmus on the way back.* A taxi may operate as a dolmus on the return trip to the driver's home or to his usual taxi queue. (London taxi drivers and users recently asked for this kind of service, but the licensing authorities turned down the request.)
- *Taxi.* A conventional taxi service is generally provided in four- or five-passenger vehicles.
- *Minibus.* An operation along a fixed route is generally carried out in minibuses seating nine or ten passengers.
- *Midibus.* The vehicle is used as a minibus but has a capacity of thirteen or more passengers.

There are also variations on these categories, such as the express dolmus, a service provided at twice the regular fare when demand is high (a practice resented by the traveling public); the shared taxi, whereby a number of passengers in the waiting line share a taxi to the same destination; and the unlicensed dolmus service provided by private passenger cars. Some private cars also operate illegally as taxicabs, a practice not unknown in New York. In peak periods the minibuses and midibuses tend to be severely overloaded; this overloading adds significantly to the profits of the operators and to the discomfort of the passengers. It seems to be associated with a restriction on the number of minibus licenses and the consequent power of the operators to obtain "abnormal" profits.

The public transport situation in Istanbul cannot be described as a happy one. The buses operated by the franchised company are overcrowded and run at a large financial loss. The dolmus and minibuses provide profitable services, but some members of the public resent being "taken for a ride." Finally, private car users also object to the dolmus on the ground that they take up valuable road space—although dolmus use much less space per passenger than do the private cars. Nevertheless, there can be no doubt that the dolmus and minibuses of Istanbul are successful business enterprises.

The Bakassi of Khartoum

The single bright spot in the public transportation scene of Khartoum (population 1.6 million) is provided by the *bakassi* (the Sudan's version of Kenya's *matatu,* discussed below), which carry tens of thousands of passengers daily.[3] Nonexistent in 1973, their number grew to 3,300 in mid-1979 when a ban on further licenses was imposed by the local authorities because of the part the vehicles play in the bustling capital's perennial traffic jam—the bakassi have been adding to the chaos in the streets because they take on and discharge passengers anywhere. The fact that they have no fixed stops and parking places adds to their appeal from the public's point of view. However, they employ underage boys as fare collectors and hawkers, and accidents involving the children have tarnished the bakassi owners' image with the authorities and the traveling public. Yet they constitute a thriving industry despite numerous strictures, including a daily gas ration totaling a mere five gallons that forces owners to buy fuel on the black market. Bakassi are banned from several squares in the center of the city and they have trouble getting spare parts, which are always in short supply and must be bought under the table at exorbitant prices.

3. This and the other information in this section was provided by George Wynn.

The bakassi—also known as *boks* because of their box-like appearance—sprang up as a free market answer to a steadily deteriorating city bus service. Less than 140 of the public bus company's fleet of about 450 Mercedes and Magirus Deutz buses are in operation because of the difficulty in obtaining spare parts. The remaining buses have to cover a network of forty-six lines. As a result, passengers have to put up with hours of waiting and intolerably crowded conditions unless one of the speedy, privately operated boks can be hailed.

The publicly owned Capital Transport Company currently employs a staff of about 1,400, or about 10 people (including maintenance and management personnel) for each bus now on the road—and it operates at a huge deficit. A consortium of businessmen reportedly is planning to import and operate 200 microbuses to cope with and profit from the mobility needs of the capital's expanding population.

The Minibuses of Kuala Lumpur

Kuala Lumpur, the capital of Malaysia, is a rapidly expanding urban area with a population of about 1 million. Public transport service has been traditionally provided by eight private companies, each franchised to operate over a specific sector in the area (these and the following details are based on Walters 1979). In the early 1970s, the authorities became concerned about the deterioration of the public transport system and the associated rapid rise in private motorization. The problem facing Kuala Lumpur was one with which many city managements are familiar: the private bus companies had obtained their franchises in the 1950s and 1960s, at a time when their service was adequate and the revenues they received were considered fair. However, the spread of private car ownership led to a decline in bus speeds, service standards, ridership, and profitability. The government was reluctant to allow the bus companies to raise fares because of the effect on living costs. It was also concerned that, even if permission was given, the bus companies might not improve their services. The idea of taking the buses into public ownership was considered but was not an attractive alternative; the government suspected that this would create as many problems as it would solve.

Malaysians were familiar with the informal public transport services provided in other cities in southeast Asia and decided to introduce such services in Kuala Lumpur. They invited Anthony Shephard, who had been transport commissioner in Hong Kong when the public light buses were introduced there, to design a scheme for Kuala Lumpur. He recommended that vehicle owners be invited to apply for licenses to run services along specific long-distance routes. To encourage the use of minibuses for long trips, he recommended that they charge a flat fare of 40 Malaysian cents (16 U.S. cents); the conventional bus services charged 5 Malaysian cents (2 U.S. cents) a mile.

The scheme was introduced as part of an urban transport project supported by the World Bank, which favored the introduction of the minibuses, although its funds were not required to finance them. The operators were able to tap other sources for funds. More than 2,000 applications were received in response to the government's invitation. By the end of 1975 there were about 100 minibuses in the city; by October 1976 the number had risen to 320, and by 1978 to 400, the level at which the number was frozen. Subsequently, the minibus service, which was conceived as a luxury service for long-distance commuters, became degraded by overcrowding and standing passengers. The ratios of load to capacity (based on fifty-eight passengers for a conventional bus and sixteen for a minibus) were 68 percent in the morning and 78 percent in the evening peak periods for conventional buses and 114 percent and 125 percent, respectively, for the minibuses (ratios in excess of 100 percent reflect standing passengers).

The scarcity of minibuses also affected their profitability. Transport experts in Malaysia estimated the annual return on investment for an operator who had a license at 37 percent (the return was lower for operators who had to rent their vehicles or their licenses, or both). Another characteristic of the minibus, referred to earlier, is its relatively high occupancy rate compared with that of the conventional bus. Surveys carried out in 1978 indicated that in peak periods the minibus accounted for 35 percent of all bus trips to the central area and 53 percent of the passenger-miles (the percentage of passenger-miles was higher than the percentage of trips because the average trip length by conventional bus was 2.4 miles compared with 5.1 miles by minibus). Thus, a fleet of 400 sixteen-seat minibuses "produced" more passenger-miles than did the 600 conventional buses with fifty-eight seats that were operating at the time. The estimated costs, revenues, and profits of Kuala Lumpur's minibuses are shown in table 6-2.

The Jeepneys of Manila

The predominant public transport carrier in Manila is the *jeepney*, which has become the Filipinos' favorite form of urban transport. Their fondness for this unique vehicle is rooted in the fact that it was invented in the aftermath of World War II when the

**Table 6–2. Estimated Costs, Revenues, and Profits
of Kuala Lumpur Minibuses**

Expenditures and income	Malaysian ringgit[a]
Costs	
Wages[b]	19,800
Depreciation[c]	6,000
Fuel	7,500
Repair	7,500
Office	1,000
Tax	1,440
Insurance	1,800
Total	45,040
Revenue	58,500 (US$27,200)
Profit[d]	13,460 (US$6,300)

a. Average figures derived from interviews by government staff during 1978.
US$1 = 2.15 ringgit.

b. Driver receives 350 ringgit a month and conductor 300 ringgit a month; two shift
operation; no wages for inspectors.

c. A six-year life for a 36,000 ringgit vehicle and a five-year life for a 30,000 ringgit
vehicle give the same annual depreciation of 6,000 ringgit.

d. Annual return on 36,000-ringgit minibus is 37 percent.

Source:. World Bank.

city of Manila was just beginning its recovery from wartime
devastation and neglect. The jeepney was made from—and named
after—the U.S. Army jeep. The chassis was extended and its back
portion opened and adjusted to provide a central entry and exit.
The roof was curved on all sides with prominent overhangs at the
back. Two upholstered benches were attached lengthwise to accommodate the passengers. Thus the jeepney became a symbol of
the Filipinos' indomitability in times of crisis and of their capacity
to survive. The jeepneys, which are locally manufactured, also
nurtured Filipino ingenuity and craftsmanship as they underwent
various renovations and improvements. Their bodies are made of
sheet steel, some painted with various decorations that provide a
wide variety of color and design.

According to figures compiled by the Manila Board of Transportation, there are about 28,000 jeepneys in Manila (unofficial
estimates put the number at 60,000), but only 2,900 buses. Jeepneys are a major form of transportation in Manila, accounting for
about half of total trips, while buses and private cars (including
taxis) account for about 25 percent each.

The enterprising jeepney operators provide living proof that
even the unskilled and poorly educated can succeed through ini-

tiative, hard work, and calculated risk-taking. As an employment medium, the jeepney industry in Manila alone gives direct employment to more than 100,000 people. This includes two to three drivers for each of the 28,000 vehicles, about 10,000 jeepney owners and several thousand more who are involved in servicing the vehicles and building bodies for them. It is estimated that a further 400,000 depend for their livelihoods in one way or the other on the jeepney industry. There are, for instance, manufacturers of jeepney cassette radios, plastic ornaments, and seat upholstery, not to mention trip dispatchers at jeepney terminals.

Since their inception, the jeepneys have provided stiff competition to the regular buses, and the representatives of each mode regularly call for the suppression of the other. Transport experts have long disputed the relative merits of jeepneys and buses in Manila, where their operations almost completely overlap. The fares are also the same, and the services are equally acceptable socially. Buses are perceived by some to be more comfortable for longer journeys, whereas jeepneys are more agile and therefore faster for short runs. Within recent years the conventional buses have had difficulty in maintaining their services, while jeepney operators have been agitating for more licenses and have been operating illegally. This suggests that the jeepneys are the more cost-effective form of transport, and published figures on the two modes (see table 6-3) show that the costs of a fourteen-seat jeepney are about one-quarter of the costs of a bus with fifty-eight seats.

Since 1976, the transport policymakers in the Philippines have been trying to rationalize the urban transport system in favor of conventional buses, which they consider to be more cost-effective and fuel-efficient than the jeepneys. The authorities have no way of replacing the jeepneys, however, without massive public investments in transport, which they are reluctant to undertake; the national leadership is also unwilling to deprive the tens of thousands of Filipino jeepney owners, drivers, and their respective families of their primary source of income. The government therefore decided to "freeze" the size of the jeepney fleet and to discourage jeepney use on main roads. "Instead of loitering over the main city roads," declared a senior government official, "jeepneys will now be concentrated on complementary, secondary or feeder routes where they will virtually act as primary linkages or conveyor belts between residential areas and certain business districts" (Lavares 1980). This is not the place to discuss transport policy in Manila. Suffice it to say that the development of the Filipino jeepney industry provides evidence that public transport can operate profitably and successfully in a large metropolitan area.

Table 6–3. Manila Bus and Jeepney Costs
(1976 U.S. cents)

| | Cost per mile | | Cost per seat-mile | |
Cost	Bus	Jeepney	Bus	Jeepney
Depreciation	7.40[a]	0.75	0.128	0.054[a]
Interest	4.90	0.55	0.084	0.039
Maintenance	6.70[b]	0.85	0.116	0.061
Tires	2.16	0.48	0.037	0.034
Fuel	5.50	4.48	0.095	0.320
Fuel tax	0.55	1.70	0.009	0.120
Factor cost of				
fuel	4.95	2.78	0.086	0.200
Oil	0.38	0.17	0.007	0.012
Wages	9.60[c]	3.40	0.166	0.243
Management	0.44[d]	—	0.008	—
Total	37.08	10.68	0.641	0.763
Total excluding				
wages	27.48	7.27	0.475	0.519
Total excluding				
wages and				
fuel tax	26.93	5.58	0.465	0.400
Total operating				
costs[e]	24.34	9.38	0.421	0.670

— Not applicable.

Note: Bus: fifty-eight seats; jeepney: fourteen seats. Columns may not add because of rounding.

a. Depreciation estimates are based on a capital cost of US$30,666 for a fifty-five seat stage bus with an expected ten-year life. The jeepney costs US$2,972 for a fourteen-seat vehicle lasting on average 7.5 years. Buses average 46,500 miles a year; jeepneys 50,000 miles. The capital cost per seat-mile of a bus is about 2.5 times that of a jeepney; 75 percent of depreciation cost is treated as dependent on the distance traveled, and the remaining 25 percent, on the time in use.

b. Maintenance costs for the two types of vehicle are proportionate: 300 hours of labor time, and parts cost estimated at 10 percent of vehicle cost.

c. Wage costs of jeepneys and buses differ in wage rates paid and size of crew employed. A bus operates with a driver (5 pesos an hour) and conductor (4 pesos an hour). Jeepneys employ only a driver at 2.5 pesos an hour.

d. License and insurance costs are not provided.

e. Total excluding depreciation, interest, and management.

Source: Walters (1979).

The Matatu of Nairobi

Nairobi (population 736,000), the capital of Kenya, is known, among other things, for its heavy traffic congestion in the weekday peak periods. It is also the home of an informal public transport vehicle, the *matatu*. The word "matatu" originates from the Kikuyu phrase for thirty cents, which was a common fare. Like "dolmus," the same form is used in the singular and plural. The matatu appears in several forms: light pickup vehicles seating twelve to fourteen passengers, minibuses seating fifteen (VW Kombis) or eighteen (Nissan E20 with long wheel base), large pickups seating fourteen to twenty-four, and midibuses seating twenty-five (Situma 1977).

A count taken in 1979 showed 1,550 privately operated matatu carrying 66,000 passengers daily. The matatu travel all over Nairobi, along bus routes as well as narrow roads that the buses do not penetrate. They are often overloaded well beyond their payload capacity; the fifteen-passenger VW Kombi has a "crush" passenger capacity of twenty. Some matatu operate only part-time. Some are company cars that reportedly carry passengers in peak periods without the owners' knowledge. Others, primarily the pickups, have foldup seats and are used for carrying goods as well as passengers. Some of the vehicles are in very poor condition and are maintained only to the extent necessary to keep them running.

Most owners have a single vehicle; about 40 percent of the matatu are reported to be owner-driven. Some owners have two vehicles, driving one and employing a driver for the other. When a driver is employed, the driver generally pays the owner a fixed sum each day, and uses the remainder of the collections for gasoline, minor repairs, and compensation for himself and the conductor. (This arrangement is also common between taxi owners and taxi drivers in some U.S. cities.) In some cases, the owner pays the driver a fixed monthly wage.

Because the demand for transport in Kenya is acute, matatu owners seem to have no problem in finding lucrative routes. The profits are high enough to pay off vehicles in two years and can then be reinvested in other vehicles or other ventures. A number of owners are known to have bought farms on the proceeds. The most successful operators own fifteen or more midibuses, which they operate both in Nairobi and on several intercity routes.

The franchised bus company in Nairobi has protested against the activities of the matatu, but it does not protest too strongly as it does not have the capacity to meet full peak demand for public transport. If it were not for the matatu, the franchised operator would need at least twice as many buses as at present, and many would be "peak-hour only" vehicles that tend to operate at a loss (Clymo 1986).

The authorities in Kenya recognize the importance of matatu

operations—both to travelers and to operators—but are concerned about their safety. The matatu have a reputation for being dangerous (the light pickups in particular cause deadly injury when they roll over), although there is no firm evidence that they are more dangerous than other vehicles in Kenya. The authorities are trying to improve the matatu service by enforcing safety and insurance requirements, providing convenient maintenance facilities, and guaranteeing a loan fund to help low-income people buy matatu.

The Publicos of Puerto Rico

For the past twenty-five years the Commonwealth of Puerto Rico has had a dual system of public transport: conventional buses operating along fixed routes and *publicos,* which are defined as "public automobile enterprises which includes any person other than taxi and tour enterprises, who as a public carrier, owns, controls, operates or manages in Puerto Rico any motor vehicle of a capacity not over 14 passengers . . . over any public overland highway, regardless of whether or not such transportation is carried out between fixed or irregular terminals" (Puerto Rico Department of Transportation and Public Works 1981).

Most of the publicos are owned by individuals and families and are driven by their owners. Fares are about 50 U.S. cents (the regular buses charge 25 U.S. cents) and speeds are good. The vehicles are difficult to enter and exit, especially for elderly people, but ridership is encouraged by the "cleanliness and reliability" of the publicos. The publicos are licensed and supervised by the Publico Service Commission of the Commonwealth of Puerto Rico.

Following the decision of the federal government to phase out operating subsidies for public transport, the Puerto Rico Department of Transportation considered the possibility of replacing some of its publicly owned bus services by publico services. A detailed study of publicos in the city of Caguas (population 150,000) carried out in 1980 showed that about five-sixths of public transport trips were made by publicos and one-sixth by regular buses. Of the thirty-nine publico routes studied, twenty-nine were financially viable in 1978, eight were not, and two had ceased operation. The average daily costs per publico vehicle in 1980, including interest and depreciation, were about US$60–65, while daily revenues averaged US$74.

In comparison, bus operating costs in 1980 were estimated to be US$154 per day, *exclusive* of depreciation. Revenues approximated US$173, which meant that the bus system was financially viable only if the vehicles were obtained free or at very low cost. Cagua's public buses operate at a lower cost than those of San Juan because drivers are not unionized and maintenance costs and standards are lower, while fares are higher than those prevailing in the capital city. Certainly the new buses (seating forty-five) that Puerto Rico had obtained for US$140,000 each were not financially viable. It is noteworthy that publico load factors (76–103 percent) were almost double those of the buses (33–50 percent).

The Department of Transportation report concluded that the publico car system was financially and economically viable and deserved to be supported fully. The bus system was not considered viable if conventional buses were used, and the acquisition of vehicles with twenty-two seats was recommended on the grounds that these vehicles would require little or no subsidy.

The authors of the report also recommended improving the public transport system by constructing terminals and improving roads; strengthening the Public Service Commission; organizing an association of operators to provide service during non-rush hours, Sundays, and holidays; and providing repair and mainte-nance shops. In addition, they recommended increasing the autho-rized capacity of the publicos from fourteen to seventeen pas-sengers.

Supplementary Bus Services of Singapore

Singapore is a city-state with a population of 2.2 million people in an area of 227 square miles. In November 1973, as a result of the increase in automobile ownership and traffic congestion, the gov-ernment took a number of radical measures to improve public transport, one of which was to unify the main bus companies into the Singapore Bus Service (SBS), Ltd. Nevertheless, public trans-port services were still considered to be so inadequate that the supplementary Public Transport Service (SPTS) Schemes A and B were introduced in March 1974.[4]

Scheme A. Scheme A was introduced to cater to adult office and factory workers. Under this scheme, trucks, delivery vehicles, and

---

4. The following details are based on the government of Singapore's *Annual Report of the Registry of Vehicles,* various years.

school buses are permitted to transport workers between their homes and places of work. By June 1981, a total of 2,169 vehicles had been issued with Scheme A permits; this group comprised 191 trucks, 379 private hire buses, and 1,599 school buses. Under Scheme A there is no restriction on the operating hours, but individual travelers cannot be picked up on public roads. Payment can only be made by monthly contract, at rates freely negotiated between the operators and their passengers. To appreciate the effectiveness of this scheme, readers should be aware that schools in Singapore operate on a double-shift system; some children go to school in the morning and others in the afternoon. Furthermore, school hours do not coincide with business hours, so that the school bus operator with a Scheme A permit is able to make six trips a day: two round-trips for schoolchildren and one round-trip for adult workers. Similar arrangements are found in New Delhi, where about 2,000 private buses have monthly contracts to carry schoolchildren and office workers.

Scheme B. Scheme B was introduced to cater to peak-hour demand for public bus transport. By June 1981, twenty-seven designated routes were operating between housing centers and the central business district (CBD) and nineteen routes between housing centers and industrial areas. As of June 30, 1981, a total of 610 vehicles were licensed under Scheme B; 395 were school buses. Under Scheme B, vehicles are allowed to pick up and drop off passengers at authorized stopping points, but only during the morning and evening peak periods, which are typically 6:00–9:45 A.M. and 4:15–7:30 P.M.

Scheme A proved to be more popular with operators than Scheme B; in February 1980, more than 80 percent of the vehicles licensed under Scheme A were still operating, compared with only 66 percent of those under Scheme B. Scheme B is thought to be less popular because it is less profitable, as a result of the shorter operating hours and longer waiting periods at starting points.

Although these supplementary services carry a significant number of Singapore's passengers—vehicles make about 144,000 trips a day on these runs—their contribution is small compared with that of the SBS fleet, which carries more than 2.2 million. Supplementary bus services in Singapore other than those already described are the City Shuttle Service, the Singapore Airport Bus Service, and the Air-Conditioned Coach Services (which operate only in peak hours on working days and provide a high-quality bus service to attract the car commuter). All the supplementary services operate at a profit.

Characteristics of Successful Systems

From the preceding examples it appears that viable urban transport systems have at least the following characteristics: ownership is private, vehicles are small, and operating units are small. In addition, route associations are part of many successful operations. Although these characteristics tend to be interrelated (that is, private operators run small fleets of small vehicles), there is evidence to illustrate the effects of each.

Private Ownership

It must not be assumed that the people who operate publicly owned transport systems are less capable or less devoted to their jobs than those who operate privately owned systems. But the availability of public funds to cover losses handicaps publicly operated systems in two ways: it makes them unable to hold down costs and unable to resist political pressures to provide unremunerative services. This point may be illustrated by the case of Bangkok.

In the early 1970s, Bangkok had twenty-four franchised bus companies, all of which provided service for a basic fare of about 4 U.S. cents. The largest company, the Nai Lert, managed by Khunying Loesak (later minister of transport), was consistently profitable. One of its distinguishing characteristics was that most of its 2,000 buses, all single deckers, carried a crew of three—one driver and two fare collectors. In 1976, following recommendations by European consultants, the government decided to amalgamate the twenty-four companies and to create the Bangkok Metropolitan Transport Authority (BMTA). The plan was carried through despite the protests of Khunying Loesak and many of the other operators. Shortly after the buses were taken over by the city, the fares were raised by 20 percent, yet the system started to operate at a deficit. By 1979, the BMTA was losing the equivalent of US$25 million or more a year, while an estimated 7,000 privately owned minibuses were running at a profit. The main reasons for the switch from profit to loss seem to have been the improved wages to bus crews and reduced utilization of vehicles. By 1984, the bus fare had risen to double its 1976 level, and the BMTA had accumulated debts equivalent to about US$185 million.

Evidence from Australia, the United Kingdom, and the United States confirms that publicly owned transport operators have higher costs than privately owned ones, even when they provide similar services, because they have less flexibility in making the best use of their resources and they pay their employees more. In

transport, as in other fields (education, medical services, and housing), the discipline of having to live within one's budget applies a
constant downward pressure on costs, a pressure that is all too
easily relieved by the availability of subsidies from public funds.

A study undertaken by the World Bank (Feibel and Walters
1980) has shown that in a number of cities (for example, Calcutta,
Bangkok, and Istanbul), the cost of private bus services is 50–60
percent of the costs of publicly owned concerns. Although private
bus employees earn less, on the average, than their public counter-
parts, private bus company employees in the three cities earn
average or above-average wages. Wage costs per bus-hour under
private ownership are likely to be much lower than costs in the
public sector because labor contracts are less restrictive and absen-
teeism and redundancy are lower.

Feibel and Walters found little concrete evidence to support the
conventional allegation that private services are less safe than
public ones. In addition, the charge that private operators "skim
the cream" by serving only the most profitable routes does not
seem to be supportable. In Istanbul, the public system has first
choice of routes; in Bangkok, the private minibuses serve the
narrow and sometimes unpaved side roads where regular buses
cannot operate.

It is often argued as well that levels of service deteriorate on
routes taken over by private operators. This contention is not
supported by the evidence. In Calcutta, passengers using routes
taken over by private operators enjoy bus services that are more
evenly scheduled, marginally more comfortable, less subject to
breakdown, and considered to have a better general appearance
and performance. In Istanbul it was found that private minibuses
are faster than public buses. In general, private operators are more
readily inclined to adjust to changing demands than are public
enterprises.

Size of Vehicle

One of the established (but questionable) principles of public
transport is that large vehicles are more economical to operate than
small ones. The reason given is that, since two-thirds of bus
operating costs are due to labor, it pays a bus company to have
large vehicles, even if they are full for only a fraction of their
working lives, so as to avoid the additional labor costs that would
be required to meet peak demand with small vehicles. This reasoning, though logical, may be questioned on two grounds.

The first is that the capital cost *per seat* seems to increase with the
size of the vehicle. Operators in San Juan, Puerto Rico, for exam-

ple, can expect to pay US$17,000 for a minibus seating seventeen, but $140,000 for a full-size bus seating fifty. Thus a full-size bus can cost almost three times as much per unit of passenger capacity as a minibus. (Incidentally, the same pattern is evident for a rail car: a vehicle seating, say, 150 passengers, can easily cost US$1 million.) The main reason for this is that small vehicles (for example, minibuses) can be mass-produced and bought "off the shelf," whereas large ones tend to be made to special order and assembled as separate units.

But there is a second reason favoring the small bus, which, while more subtle, may be more important. For a given route capacity, small buses provide more frequent service than large ones, and therefore the waiting time per passenger is shorter. This factor might not matter to a franchised operator who has to bear the costs of his crew but not the waiting time of his customers; hence the preference of monopoly operators for large vehicles. Where competition is allowed, however, those who provide public transport have to respond to the needs of the passengers, most of whom dislike waiting for buses. One way to reduce waiting time is to use smaller vehicles and provide more frequent service. It is significant that when the private bus operators took over the municipal service in Buenos Aires in 1962 one of their first actions was to replace the large municipal buses by smaller ones. The small bus has other advantages: because it holds fewer passengers, it is easier to fill with people starting at one point and wishing to travel to another. Thus it tends to stop less frequently and for shorter periods than large buses. Furthermore, being more maneuverable, it can often make its way more quickly along congested roads.

But small buses are not suited to all circumstances. Where the demand for travel is heavy enough to sustain large buses at high frequency, as in Calcutta and Hong Kong, they may well provide the most economical solution. The choice of vehicle size is a decision that, under competitive conditions, might best be left to the operators. Where conditions are not competitive, planners have to select a combination of bus size and frequency that best balances the conflicting interests of operators (who prefer fewer, bigger buses) and travelers (who prefer high frequencies). A. A. Walters (1979) discusses this point in detail.

Size of Operating Unit

There is much evidence that large bus fleets incur financial losses under the same conditions that small operators—owner-drivers—

make profits. Although operators the world over are reluctant to admit to making profits, the pressures to obtain permits to provide service and the prices at which permits in some cities change hands (or are hired out) are sure indications of profitability.

The reasons for the financial viability of the small transport firm—be it a mover, a taxi driver, or a bus operator—are well known and typical of other types of small business in the service sector. The owner will be willing to work longer and less regular hours than would a paid bus driver in a large fleet. He will clean his own vehicle or enlist the help of family members. He will recognize the need for regular vehicle maintenance. He will not have his own depot but will service his vehicle on the street or at a local garage. His recordkeeping will be minimal. He will make a greater effort than a paid driver to collect fares from passengers and to ensure that the amounts collected are not lost on the way. He can employ an extra driver if he has to run two shifts a day. The owner can also use certain facilities, such as two-way radio service, to add to his earnings without relinquishing control of his vehicle.

In passenger transport, the basic operating unit is the vehicle and, as the taxi business proves, it is possible for the owner of even one vehicle to operate at a profit. Indeed, evidence from cities in Asia and Latin America suggests that a group of people can own and operate a small bus at a profit.

The Route Association

In order to make the maximum contribution to the provision of transport, however, the individual unit has to work within an appropriate organizational framework. For example, a taxi looking for business must have some way of indicating that it is available for hire. If a vehicle is to carry more than one person, its final destination has to be clearly indicated. Passengers should know the fare being charged and the places at which vehicles can be readily found. Some of these features are provided by route associations, which are to be found in many cities of Latin America, Africa, and Asia.

The essence of the route association is that each vehicle remains under the control if its owner or owners, with regard to both operation and maintenance. Only the route is shared. Members of the association agree to follow a specific route, in conjunction with others, and thus are able to offer travelers frequent service. Fares are generally fixed by the association, but not invariably. In Hong Kong and Istanbul, for example, higher fares are charged in peak periods, when demand is higher and traffic congestion more acute (a similar system obtains in Washington, D.C.). The revenues in some associations are retained by the individual members, whereas in others they are pooled.

The precise organization of a route association varies from city to city. Any group operating a route has an interest in limiting its numbers and also in ensuring that its members work harmoniously with one another. This means that conditions must be imposed on entry (possibly an entrance fee) and that rules must be laid down to prevent members from traveling behind schedules and thus "stealing" passengers from later vehicles. In many cities (such as Buenos Aires, Manila, Calcutta, and Hong Kong) route associations compete with one another so that no group has a monopoly over an entire route. There are also reports of infighting between competing groups of operators. In general, however, the route associations appear to be successful in serving both the public and their members.

Disadvantages of Competition

Competitive urban transport has disadvantages as well as advantages. The following are the most frequently mentioned.

- Service is provided only if it is profitable. Any commodity provided by private enterprise will be affected by profitability. In general, only a monopoly or franchised operation can subsidize unprofitable routes out of the earnings of profitable ones. But cross-subsidization of this kind is an inefficient way to help people who cannot afford to pay the full costs of public transport, as discussed in the next section.

- Low-density or poor neighborhoods remain unserviced. Although this criticism is often made, there are many places in which it is not valid. For example, in Nairobi and in many cities of Latin America, it is only the informal sector that serves the poor neighborhoods.

- The high competitiveness of the activity can keep the income of drivers at the bottom level. Competitiveness can affect incomes, but that is part of the price of keeping fares down. Although many of the drivers work at relatively low wages, they earn more than they could in other occupations. And many earn substantial wages—enough to enable them to buy their own vehicles.

- There are opportunities for illegal operations, even for gangsterism. It is true that in some cities the methods used by route associations to protect their territory can become criminal, unlawful, perhaps even homicidal. But the institution of "protection" is not practiced only by unregulated transport systems. It behooves society at large to guard against illegal practices through its law enforcement agencies.

- The scramble for fares necessitates an undisciplined attitude and behavior toward traffic regulations. This seems to be a fair criticism, but one that applies to the taxi business in many cities. And private motorists are often no better. Here, too, the strict enforcement of traffic rules can prevent antisocial behavior.

- Maintenance of equipment can be deficient, at a cost to safety. Although some operators may not pay enough attention to maintenance, it is fair to point out that operators of transport systems have strong incentives to avoid accidents. Local government inspection systems and regulations can help overcome this problem.

- The regularity and reliability of service can be affected by the whims of owners and drivers. This, too, is a valid criticism, but this problem is usually negligible when there are large numbers of operators.

These, then, are some of the reported characteristics of urban transport provided by free enterprise in developing countries. Why, then, are private systems not welcomed in all cities?

Obstacles to the Introduction of Competitive Urban Public Transport

In view of the many advantages of the systems described above, one can only speculate as to why such systems have not gained wider acceptance. Opposition from the operators and employees of public systems is to be expected—and is very strong in Europe and the United States—but two other reasons may also be suggested: in some countries, public transport has traditionally been provided as a duty, to standards set by government, rather than as a commercial service; and cross-subsidization has been used to finance "weak" routes out of the surpluses earned on "strong" ones.

All societies entrust some activities to the provision of commercial interests, which operate for profit, and entrust others to elected or appointed officials. The provision of passenger transport is often regarded as an activity that is too important to be left to the free play of economic markets, an activity that must be provided either directly by government or else by the private holder of a government franchise. The public—which does not usually share the faith of economists in the virtues of economic markets—often prefers the certainty of a government-provided service (such as a train running on time) to the uncertainty of privately provided services (such as taxis, which are less predictable, especially when urgently needed). A service that is certain and predictable, however, must by its nature be less responsive to the vagaries and nuances of public needs, especially in high-income societies. Furthermore, when some of the required services are more profitable than others, the officials who regulate the franchised operators often rely on cross-subsidization as a means of financing the less profitable services.

Any organization that provides a variety of services inevitably earns higher profits from some than from others. A profit-seeking management will strive to expand its high-profit operations and to eliminate the loss-making ones. In some fields, of which urban public transport is a notorious example, loss-making services are subsidized by profitable ones as a matter of deliberate policy. This policy—known in jargon as cross-subsidization—is incompatible with free competition and can only survive under the protection of an areawide monopoly. For, without such protection, competitors will inevitably eliminate the excess profits earned on the profitable operations and leave no surplus with which to subsidize the unprofitable ones.

Cross-subsidization is pervasive in the provision of urban public transport. Not only do busy routes support thin ones, but off-peak services support the peak-hour ones (which are generally the least profitable because of their use of equipment that is idle for most of the time). Furthermore, under the flat-fare system, short-distance (inner city) riders subsidize the long-distance ones from the outer suburbs. This means that in some areas the poor may be subsidizing the long journeys of the rich.

There may be compelling reasons for subsidizing certain classes of travelers or trips, but subsidies can be given directly, by user-side subsidies targeted to specific groups, such as schoolchildren (see Kirby 1981). These subsidies are similar in principle to food stamps; they give the recipients some choice of transport without reducing the efficiency of the service. There seems to be no good reason—other than administrative convenience—for requiring other travelers to pay for subsidies. But cross-subsidization has major disadvantages:

- It is arbitrary, in that it gives powers of taxation and subsidy to bodies that are not appointed for these purposes and are not equipped to decide who should be forced to give how much and to whom.
- Insofar as a cross-subsidy requires surpluses from some operations to be used to maintain others, it prevents the fullest development of the services that earn the surpluses.
- By allowing public transport operators to look only at their *total* expenses and revenues, it discourages them from assessing the expenses and revenues of the components of the system so that fares can be changed when necessary, profitable services can be expanded, and unprofitable lines and schedules dropped.
- Cross-subsidies are an inefficient way of helping those in need, in that many who receive the benefits do not really require them.

Cross-subsidization has done immense damage to the public transport systems in many cities, and it has proved to be as unworkable as would be expected from theory. A principal reason for its failure has been the increasing availability of private transport—a mode that received much stimulation from the poor quality of public transport. The available evidence suggests that the demise of cross-subsidization and its replacement by a competitive system are more likely to do good than harm.

The Role of the Government

A number of transport activities fall within the traditional functions of the government.

- *Maintenance of public safety.* Users of public transport should be entitled to know whether drivers and vehicles measure up to appropriate standards. The government has a role in establishing such standards and in providing inspection services to ensure that they are met.
- *Ensuring that charges are known.* Whether the government should regulate fares is a debatable question but, even if it does not, travelers should be aware of the fares charged before embarking on journeys. The government should ensure that fares are prominently displayed even where they may be varied by the operators themselves, as in the public light buses of Hong Kong and the taxis of Phoenix, Arizona.

- *Provision of rights-of-way.* In all cities the provision of road space is a function of the government. The government therefore has a duty to ensure that good management enables existing roads to be used efficiently and that the road network is expanded when necessary. Good management of the road space can include preferential treatment for public transport, for example, by assigning it special bus lanes and priority at intersections. The government can also help private providers obtain exclusive rights-of-way—surface, underground, or elevated—for public transport systems, but it need not involve itself in the construction or operation of such systems or in financing them.
- *Provision of uneconomic services.* In the event that the government wishes to have (for social or other reasons) transport services that cannot be financially viable, it can contract out such services to private operators, who might be selected by a bidding process. Alternatively, subsidies can be paid to specific classes of people (schoolchildren, soldiers in uniform, and the like) if it is considered that they should not pay market prices for urban travel. Such user-side subsidies can be issued in the form of special tokens or vouchers.

Conclusion

The evidence from a variety of cities in developing countries clearly indicates that urban public transport can be competitively provided by the private sector, that the regulation of fares and entry is likely to do more harm than good, and that there is no reason why progressive developing countries should continue to follow practices that arose in Western countries under entirely different conditions.

The role of the government can be to set and maintain safety standards, to provide appropriate roads (or other rights-of-way), and to contract out uneconomic services that are considered essential for social or other reasons.

References

Barden, S. A., and J. R. V. Seneviratne. 1972. "Public Light Bus Operation Survey—1972." Technical Report 115. Hong Kong: Traffic and Transport Division, Public Works Department.

Clymo, John. 1986. "Setting a Course for Deregulated Bus Operation." *Transport* 7(3), June.

Feibel, Charles, and A. A. Walters. 1980. *Ownership and Efficiency in Urban Buses.* World Bank Staff Working Paper 371. Washington, D.C.

Government of Singapore. Annual Report of the Registry of Vehicles. Various years.

Hilton, George W. 1985. "The Rise and Fall of Monopolized Transit." In *Urban Transit: The Private Challenge to Urban Transportation,* ed. Charles A. Lave. San Francisco: Pacific Institute.

Kirby, Ronald F. 1981. "Targeting Money Effectively: User-Side Transportation Subsidies." *Journal of Contemporary Studies* 4(2).

Lavares, Jose P., Jr. 1980. "Jeepney Transport Policy Formation." Paper presented at World Bank Seminar on Urban Transport, Bangkok.

Lehuen, A. 1983. "Gbakas: Le Secteur des Transports Informels dans la Banlieue d'Abidjan." Abidjan: Bureau Central d'Etudes Techniques, Department Etudes Economiques, Bureau de Circulation.

Ogueta, Ezequiel. 1977. "Bus Transportation in Buenos Aires Metropolitan Area." Paper presented to the World Roads Conference, Japan.

Puerto Rico Department of Transportation and Public Works. 1981. "Level of Service Rendered by Publico Cars and Development of Improvement Plan for the Metropolitan Area of Caguas." April.

Sanli, H. Ibrahim. 1977. "Dolmus-Minibus System in Istanbul—A Case Study in Low Cost Public Transport." Istanbul: Institute of Urbanism, Istanbul Technical University.

Situma, Ian W. 1977. "The 'Matatu' Public Transport of Nairobi." Report to the Mayor and Council of Nairobi. August.

Smerk, George M. 1979. "The Development of Public Transportation and the City." In *Public Transportation, Planning, Operations and Management,* ed. George E. Gray and Lester A. Hoel. Englewood Cliffs, N.J.: Prentice-Hall.

Walters, A. A. 1979. *Costs and Scale of Bus Services.* World Bank Staff Working Paper 325. Washington, D.C.

World Bank. 1986. *Urban Transport.* A World Bank Policy Study. Washington, D.C.

7

Water and Sewerage

Half of the infants that die in the world each year die from water-borne diseases. 80 percent of all diseases in the world are water-related. Half of all the hospital beds in the world are occupied by people with water-borne diseases.

—PETER G. BOURNE, when coordinator
for the U.N. Drinking Water Supply
and Sanitation Decade

Is it not strange that, of all . . . essential services, only water is offered as a free good?

—DANIEL A. OKUN, School of Public
Health, University of North Carolina

OF ALL THE PUBLIC SERVICES, the provision of piped water is the one with which the private sector is the least involved. Nor does history offer many examples. All ancient civilizations had some form of mains water supply, both for agricultural irrigation and for urban communities. But the supply seems to have been invariably a public sector activity, possibly because of the importance of water in times of war. In Buddhist and Muslim societies, the provision of water by a ruler was a traditional form of "merit making." Assyria, Babylon, and Persia had elaborate water facilities, all provided by the public sector. In Roman cities, the state not only built aqueducts for urban water supplies, but was also directly involved in running the public baths.

It may not be a coincidence that water is also the sector that, in

For help in the preparation of this chapter special thanks are due to Richard Anson, Saul Arlosoroff, Joseph Freedman, Fred Golladay, Slaheddine Khenissi, Michel Pommier, and Carlo Rietveld, the World Bank; Terry Anderson, Montana State University; Daniel Okun, University of North Carolina; and Miguel Solanes, the United Nations Development Programme.

230

many countries, seems to have the greatest problems. A regular supply of drinkable water is essential for survival, and yet more than half of all persons in developing countries live without an adequate supply of drinking water; about three-quarters are without any kind of sanitation facility; and, because water in some areas is remote as well as polluted, tens of millions of women and children spend as much as three or more hours daily fetching polluted water. Statistics on the populations served with safe water in eighty-three developing countries are shown in table 7-1.

The cost in human suffering is enormous. Diarrhea, amoebiasis, polio, typhoid, and roundworm are but a few of the infections introduced or spread by insufficient and polluted water supplies and poor sanitation. Unsafe water brings high infant and child mortality, and, for those who survive into adulthood, poor health, loss of productivity, and shortened life. On an average day in the developing world, more than 25,000 people die owing to inadequate water supply and sanitation, while millions more suffer the consequent debilitating effects.

Despite significant efforts by the governments of developing countries to improve water supplies, the situation deteriorated during the 1970s. As a consequence of poor maintenance of water facilities and rapid population growth, about 100 million more people drank unsafe water in 1980 than in 1975 and about 400 million more people relied on unsafe sanitation facilities in 1984 than in 1977. The incidence of water-related morbidity and mortality is expected to rise rapidly unless strenuous efforts are made to combat this deterioration in water and sewerage facilities.

How much water do people require? Individual country data show a minimum use of about 5 liters per person per day (lcd) for seven countries, 20 lcd or less for twenty-four countries, and 40 lcd or less for forty-five countries. Consumption in a developed country—England—is in the range 200–300 lcd. Consumption of 5 lcd is about the minimum necessary to sustain life.

Criteria for Public Sector Provision

How do water and sewerage relate to the criteria for assessing the appropriateness of the public or private provision of a good or a service, as outlined in chapter 1?

Natural Monopolies

Before water can be utilized by consumers, it has to be removed from a natural source, purified, and transported to the point of

Table 7-1. Populations with Access to Safe Water and Targets for Urban and Rural Areas

Country	Percentage of total population with safe water (1970)	(1980)	Percentage of urban population — With house connection (1980)	With standposts	With safe water	Percentage of rural population with safe water	Urban targets — House connection	Standposts	Total	Rural targets	Construction cost (U.S. dollars per person) — House connection	Standpost	Rural
Lao, Peoples' Dem. Rep.	n.a.	47.1	n.a.	n.a.	97	39	n.a.	n.a.	n.a.	n.a.	n.a.	n.a.	n.a.
Bhutan	n.a.	6.8	n.a.	n.a.	50	5	n.a.	n.a.	100	60	n.a.	n.a.	n.a.
Chad	27	26.6	n.a.	n.a.	43	23	n.a.	n.a.	58	77	n.a.	n.a.	n.a.
Bangladesh	45	38.5	n.a.	n.a.	26	40	n.a.	n.a.	n.a.	n.a.	70	n.a.	n.a.
Ethiopia	6	14.7	n.a.	n.a.	56	8	n.a.	n.a.	94	67	42	n.a.	28
Nepal	2	10.8	n.a.	n.a.	63	7	n.a.	n.a.	n.a.	n.a.	n.a.	n.a.	n.a.
Somalia	15	31.4	n.a.	n.a.	56	20	n.a.	n.a.	50	50	50	n.a.	15
Burma	18	21.2	n.a.	n.a.	38	15	n.a.	n.a.	50	50	n.a.	n.a.	n.a.
Afghanistan	3	8.2	7	2	9	8	30	50	80	80	n.a.	n.a.	n.a.
Viet Nam	n.a.	n.a.	n.a.	n.a.	n.a.	n.a.	n.a.	n.a.	n.a.	60	130	65	15
Mali	n.a.	9.8	20	17	37	3	n.a.	n.a.	n.a.	90	n.a.	n.a.	n.a.
Burundi	n.a.	21.4	22	68	90	20	59	39	98	90	100	30	25
Rwanda	n.a.	54.7	30	16	48	55	50	50	100	100	100	40	n.a.
Burkina Faso	n.a.	31.5	16	11	37	31	34	37	71	100	100	40	25
Zaire	11	17.9	n.a.	n.a.	43	5	n.a.	n.a.	n.a.	n.a.	n.a.	n.a.	20
Malawi	n.a.	41.0	53	24	77	37	n.a.	n.a.	n.a.	100	75	40	15
India	17	41.1	n.a.	n.a.	77	31	n.a.	n.a.	100	100	50	n.a.	20
Haiti	n.a.	15.7	n.a.	n.a.	38	7	n.a.	n.a.	n.a.	n.a.	n.a.	n.a.	n.a.
Sri Lanka	21	30.7	n.a.	n.a.	65	18	n.a.	n.a.	90	90	125	n.a.	n.a.
Sierra Leone	12	12.6	20	30	50	2	n.a.	n.a.	n.a.	n.a.	n.a.	n.a.	n.a.
Tanzania	13	42.2	n.a.	n.a.	88	36	n.a.	n.a.	n.a.	n.a.	n.a.	n.a.	n.a.

Country													
China	n.a.	32.4	n.a.	n.a.	34	32	n.a.	n.a.	n.a.	n.a.	40	25	20
Guinea	n.a.	14.5	16	52	68	2	27	50	77	22	n.a.	n.a.	n.a.
Central African Rep.	n.a.	19.4	n.a.	n.a.	40	5	n.a.	49	n.a.	65	n.a.	n.a.	n.a.
Pakistan	21	34.6	30	42	72	20	51	48	100	65	40	n.a.	25
Uganda	22	35.4	n.a.	n.a.	100	29	n.a.	n.a.	80	100	100	25	20
Benin	n.a.	20.2	10	42	52	15	32	48	80	100	100	25	20
Niger	20	32.8	26	12	38	32	n.a.	n.a.	90	143	143	52	40
Madagascar	11	20.1	19	61	80	7	n.a.	n.a.	n.a.	90	90	40	35
Sudan	n.a.	46.0	n.a.	n.a.	49	45	n.a.	n.a.	n.a.	n.a.	n.a.	n.a.	n.a.
Togo	n.a.	38.8	14	56	70	31	20	90	100	91	93	n.a.	29
Ghana	n.a.	47.0	26	46	72	33	42	56	100	78	100	n.a.	n.a.
Kenya	15	24.9	59	26	35	15	90	10	100	60	130	65	65
Lesotho	3	14.1	24	13	37	11	89	11	100	26	n.a.	n.a.	58
Yemen, People's Dem. Rep.	n.a.	43.5	70	5	75	25	85	10	95	40	217	174	58
Indonesia	3	22.6	n.a.	n.a.	41	18	40	35	75	60	60	n.a.	30
Yemen Arab Rep.	4	26.2	50	50	100	18	100	n.a.	100	100	300	250	125
Mauritania	61	93.9	20	60	80	95	n.a.	n.a.	n.a.	n.a.	n.a.	n.a.	n.a.
Senegal	12	38.0	33	44	77	25	42	50	92	n.a.	n.a.	n.a.	n.a.
Angola	n.a.	25.8	30	55	85	10	n.a.	n.a.	n.a.	n.a.	n.a.	n.a.	n.a.
Liberia	n.a.	25.1	n.a.	n.a.	64	6	n.a.	n.a.	90	90	n.a.	n.a.	n.a.
Honduras	34	43.6	46	4	50	40	20	70	90	n.a.	n.a.	n.a.	n.a.
Zambia	37	46.1	n.a.	n.a.	86	16	n.a.	n.a.	90	60	n.a.	n.a.	n.a.
Bolivia	33	29.5	24	45	69	10	60	30	90	60	n.a.	n.a.	n.a.
Egypt	n.a.	74.8	69	19	88	64	92	n.a.	92	60	119	90	88
El Salvador	40	51.5	62	6	68	40	85	n.a.	85	90	60	n.a.	40
Cameroon	n.a.	26.6	n.a.	n.a.	35	22	n.a.	n.a.	n.a.	n.a.	n.a.	n.a.	n.a.
Thailand	17	63.3	n.a.	n.a.	65	63	n.a.	n.a.	70	95	n.a.	n.a.	n.a.

(Table continues on the following page.)

Table 7-1 (continued)

Country	Percentage of total population with safe water (1970)	(1980)	Percentage of urban population — With house connection (1980)	With stand-posts	With safe water	Percentage of rural population with safe water	Urban targets — House connection	Stand-posts	Total	Rural targets	Construction cost (U.S. dollars per person) — House connection	Stand-post	Rural
Philippines	n.a.	n.a.	53	12	65	43	96	4	100	100	45	19	8
Nicaragua	n.a.	n.a.	64	24	68	10	91	9	100	50	n.a.	n.a.	n.a.
Papua New Guinea	n.a.	n.a.	48	7	55	10	n.a.	n.a.	n.a.	n.a.	150	n.a.	20
Congo, People's Rep.	27	18.0	n.a.	n.a.	40	0	n.a.	n.a.	n.a.	100	n.a.	n.a.	n.a.
Morocco	51	41.0	44	56	100	n.a.	n.a.	n.a.	100	100	n.a.	n.a.	n.a.
Peru	35	52.5	57	11	68	21	84	11	95	n.a.	143	57	58
Jamaica	62	87.5	n.a.	n.a.	100	79	n.a.	n.a.	n.a.	n.a.	n.a.	n.a.	n.a.
Guatemala	38	45.7	51	36	89	18	76	24	100	50	75	60	n.a.
Côte d'Ivoire	n.a.	23.0	n.a.	n.a.	50	5	n.a.	n.a.	n.a.	n.a.	n.a.	n.a.	n.a.
Dominican Rep.	37	58.6	65	20	88	28	70	16	66	54	50	n.a.	n.a.
Colombia	83	91.6	74	20	97	79	90	10	100	95	108	n.a.	104
Ecuador	11	45.7	47	35	82	16	65	10	95	70	135	65	n.a.
Paraguay	11	21.3	39	0	39	10	69	n.a.	69	18	125	n.a.	n.a.
Tunisia	49	58.6	71	26	97	17	n.a.	n.a.	n.a.	n.a.	250	n.a.	200
Syrian Arab Rep.	71	72.0	90	0	90	54	100	n.a.	100	60	250	n.a.	100
Jordan	n.a.	84.5	78	22	100	65	95	5	100	95	300	n.a.	197
Lebanon	92	n.a.	n.a.	n.a.	n.a.	n.a.	n.a.	n.a.	n.a.	n.a.	n.a.	n.a.	n.a.

Country													
Turkey	n.a.	78.6	69	24	93	62	n.a.	n.a.	n.a.	n.a.	100	n.a.	n.a.
Korea, Rep. of	58	74.8	86	0	86	61	n.a.	n.a.	n.a.	n.a.	70	n.a.	9
Malaysia	n.a.	60.9	n.a.	n.a.	90	49	100	n.a.	100	83	n.a.	n.a.	n.a.
Costa Rica	74	81.8	95	5	100	68	100	n.a.	100	74	n.a.	n.a.	n.a.
Panama	70	80.7	92	2	94	65	100	n.a.	100	85	100	n.a.	55
Algeria	n.a.	48.8	n.a.	n.a.	60	40	n.a.	n.a.	n.a.	n.a.	n.a.	n.a.	n.a.
Brazil	56	70.7	80	0	80	51	90	n.a.	90	n.a.	100	25	54
Mexico	54	57.1	60	2	64	43	83	n.a.	83	58	105	42	53
Chile	n.a.	83.4	93	7	100	17	100	n.a.	100	39	n.a.	n.a.	n.a.
Argentina	56	56.4	61	4	65	17	80	20	100	99	n.a.	n.a.	n.a.
Yugoslavia	92	n.a.	n.a.	n.a.	n.a.	n.a.	n.a.	n.a.	100	n.a.	n.a.	n.a.	n.a.
Uruguay	n.a.	80.1	90	5	95	2	n.a.	n.a.	n.a.	n.a.	n.a.	n.a.	n.a.
Iran, Islamic Rep. of	35	53.0	n.a.	n.a.	76	30	n.a.	n.a.	n.a.	n.a.	n.a.	n.a.	n.a.
Iraq	51	68.7	82	8	90	14	n.a.	n.a.	n.a.	n.a.	n.a.	n.a.	n.a.
Venezuela	75	82.4	96	4	90	45	90	3	93	85	n.a.	n.a.	n.a.
Hong Kong	n.a.	99.5	n.a.	n.a.	100	95	96	4	100	97	n.a.	n.a.	n.a.
Trinidad and Tobago	96	94.5	79	21	100	93	90	9	99	99	n.a.	n.a.	n.a.
Singapore	83	100.0	100	0	100	0	100	n.a.	100	n.a.	n.a.	n.a.	n.a.
Average	36.7	44.9	52.2	22.9	70.3	29.6	73.3	28.6	91.6	74.9	114	65	53

n.a. Not available.

Note: Countries are listed in ascending order of their gross national product per capita as given in the World Bank, *World Development Report 1982* (New York: Oxford University Press). The targets in the table are those established for the United Nations International Drinking Water Supply and Sanitation Decade, 1981–90.

Source: Sud (1984).

consumption. Each of these three stages can involve monopoly supply, but need not necessarily do so.

The supply, be it for a large town or for a small village, can come from a single source or from a number of sources. In Morocco, for example, the parastatal national water supply company (Office National d'Eaux Potable, ONEP) sells water in bulk to urban distribution systems. But many of the local authorities there have developed their own sources of supply, so as not to be entirely dependent on the national company. Cities can be supplied from different rivers (for example, the city of Santiago is supplied from the Maipo and Mapocho rivers, and also from wells); some communities (for example, in Saudi Arabia) are supplied from desalination plants, in which case there is no monopoly on the source of supply. If the source of water is underground and belongs to the owner of the ground above it, there is in practice no monopoly in the water source, even if all the water derives from one aquifer.

The purification process is not a natural monopoly because water can be purified in large or small installations, or even in the home, by boiling and filtering. There might, however, be scale economies that would make it more economical to purify water in large plants. If water is distributed by means of pipes, the economies of scale are so great that this becomes a textbook example of the natural monopoly. But if water is distributed by water vendors or is carried by the consumers from its source, as is common in many developing countries, there is no natural monopoly in the distribution system.

Decreasing Costs

As mentioned in the preceding paragraph, a number of the processes involved in the supply of water are associated with decreasing costs. The distribution network itself is the most striking example: if pipeline capacity is doubled, the total costs of pipeline construction generally increase by only 35–40 percent (Hanke and Wentworth 1980).

The lowering of per capita costs through an increase in the number of consumers serviced can be illustrated in a rural development project in Tanzania: installation costs more than doubled in a system serving 5,000 people instead of 1,750, but per capita costs decreased by 28 percent (see table 7-2).

Sewerage systems—that is, facilities for the collection, treatment, and disposal of waterborne sewage—exhibit scale econo-

**Table 7–2. Specifications and Cost Estimates
for Water Supply Systems in Four Villages of Tanzania, 1973**

Item	Village			
	I	*II*	*III*	*IV*
Basic assumptions				
Village population	1,750	2,500	3,500	5,000
Per capita consumption (liters per day)	30	30	30	30
Average daily consumption (cubic meters)	52.5	75	105	150
Length of raw-water main (meters)	2,000	2,000	2,000	2,000
Elevation difference, source to village (meters)	100	100	100	100
Length distribution mains (meters)	4,000	5,500	8,500	11,300
Public hydrants	12	18	26	36
Persons per hydrant	146	139	135	139
Cost (U.S. dollars)				
Preparatory works	950	950	950	950
Intake	150	220	300	430
Pumphouse	1,280	1,280	1,280	1,280
Pumps	4,160	4,160	5,120	5,370
Rising main	3,310	3,720	4,670	4,700
Storage tank	1,680	2,130	2,910	3,240
Distribution system	8,760	11,970	18,540	24,820
Hydrants	380	570	820	1,140
Construction plant	950	950	950	950
Transportation	2,190	2,920	4,380	5,840
Subtotal	23,810	28,870	39,920	48,720
Overhead and contingencies (30 percent)	7,140	8,660	11,980	14,620
Total	30,950	37,530	51,900	63,340
Total per capita	17.70	15.00	14.80	12.70

Note: Columns may not add to totals because of rounding.

Source: Saunders and Warford (1976), p. 93; project data assembled by Richard Middleton.

mies of such significance that they can be regarded as natural monopolies. But sewerage is not always the most appropriate technology for sewage disposal. Low-cost alternatives exist and can work well in all but the most densely populated cities (Kalbermatten, Julius, and Gunnerson 1980). These systems do not exhibit significant scale economies and can be installed in most environments by local contractors working competitively.

There can also be substantial scale economies in purification, desalination, or fluoridation. As a result of these decreasing costs, it may be less expensive to have a community served by one large distribution network than by a number of overlapping ones. In large cities, however, it is possible for different districts to be supplied from adjacent networks, as is now the case in Guatemala City and Santiago, with no substantial loss of scale economies in distribution. Although this arrangement does not give users a choice of supplier, consumers can benefit from comparisons of costs and service levels.

Substantial economic advantages would be gained if different qualities of water could be used for different purposes, but this is seldom done in any system of piped domestic supply, presumably because the costs of a duplicate piping network would be prohibitive. But there are exceptions. In the Turks and Caicos islands (population 7,000), every building must have the necessary plumbing to flush its toilets with saline water, while a separate piping system provides freshwater. Similar arrangements can be found in Hong Kong and Singapore. Factories are of course often supplied with "industrial quality" water, and passengers on ships have, within living memory, used seawater in the washrooms.

In some Middle Eastern countries (for example, Saudi Arabia), the use of reclaimed sewerage effluents for industry, agriculture, and even toilet flushing is on the rise: about 400,000 cubic meters a day of reclaimed water are used in the Middle East for nondrinking purposes, while in California some 380 projects provide 800,000 cubic meters a day from 240 wastewater reclamation plants (Okun 1984). The economies that can result from dual distribution systems have been demonstrated in the United Kingdom and the United States (Deb 1978).

Thus not all the processes involved in supplying water result in natural monopolies, and, even where these do exist or where there are scale economies, the private sector can still play a substantial role.

Externalities

Water supply is associated with both positive and negative externalities. On the positive side, since safe water is beneficial to health, an improved water supply can benefit people other than those directly involved in providing or receiving the water. For example, fleaborne diseases are less likely to be transmitted if water for washing is readily available. To the extent that these positive externalities exist, it may be said that, in the absence of community action, too little water would be provided. On the negative side, disease is also spread by inadequate sewerage (for example, surface wastewater disposal and poorly constructed cesspools or latrines). These negative externalities can be addressed either by measures to discourage pollution or by additional costs of purification.

There is, however, a further externality peculiar to water supply, which is due directly to its scarcity. Consider a city, such as Bangkok, Mexico City, or Lagos, that is built over an aquifer that can be drawn upon from wells. If the supply of water in the aquifer was unlimited so that it was completely replenished whenever drawn upon, the drilling of wells and subsequent pumping would involve costs for well construction and for pumping, but there would be no loss of water. If, however, the quantity of water in the aquifer was not replenished at a rate equal to that at which it was removed, each individual drawing water would reduce the quantity available to others, and this reduction would be considered a negative externality. Furthermore, the reduction in the water level could bring about earth movements and cause serious foundation problems, as in fact has happened in Mexico City and Bangkok. One way to deal with this externality would be to prohibit the drilling of wells or to license it, as was the practice in London in the middle of the nineteenth century and is the case in Mexico and the Bahamas today. Another approach, which is followed in Israel, would be to levy a charge on water drawn from the aquifer and to fix the price at whatever level is necessary to maintain a desired water level.

It may be noted that this situation arises from the fact that the underground water does not belong to anybody and, since it is treated as a "free good," it tends to be overused. Similar effects have been described with respect to overgrazing on common grazing land, overfishing on the high seas, and traffic congestion in most cities. In the absence of ownership of a scarce resource, as all these cases show, underpricing is inevitable, too much of the resource is therefore used, and a severe shortage eventually arises.

Water can have alternative uses—for industry, irrigation, power generation, transport, and domestic consumption—each of which can affect other uses and other users. Water projects therefore generate more than their "fair share" of external effects. In the case of both urban and rural supplies, the absence of property rights in water precludes private sector intervention and increases the difficulties in allocating this scarce resource. Thus, the existence of externalities in water supply calls for mechanisms (such as the vesting of property rights) that would promote more—rather than less—private sector involvement. The possibilities of trading in water would encourage it to be conserved and moved to priority uses (Anderson 1982).

Inability to Charge

When water is sold in containers by private vendors, as is common in France and throughout the developing world, there is no problem in charging for it: customers pay on delivery, as they do for milk, wine, or fuel oil. But when water is delivered from pipes, the levying of payments creates substantial moral, political, technical, and administrative problems.

The moral and political problems derive from the question of whether water should be charged for at all, since it is a product of nature, and a necessity of life. Many authorities therefore find it difficult to enforce payment for piped water or to deny water to nonpayers. Even when there are no moral or philosophical qualms, governments find it difficult to charge for water. Politically, it can be easier for a government to decline to provide water altogether, on the grounds that its resources are constrained, than to become involved in recriminations about the charges. Islamic law, however, explicitly recognizes the right to own and sell water, subject to the injunction that the thirsty are never to be denied drinking water, even if they are unable to pay (*Encyclopedia of Islam* 1983).

There are also substantial administrative difficulties in collecting payment for water. In a large urban area, the basic tasks of assessing fees, collecting them, and accounting for them are considerable. In some countries no attempt is made to charge for the amount of water actually used, but households are billed at rates proportional to property values (as in Britain) or to the diameter of the supply pipe (as in Chile or in ancient Rome). Where water is supplied for irrigation, the farmers may be taxed in proportion to the value of the additional crops that can be grown (as in Pakistan). Whatever the method used, there can be no doubt that the levying of water charges on a large scale is a formidable task that requires substantial effort.

Economic efficiency requires that water generally be charged for in proportion to the amounts used and at a rate just high enough to cover the costs of replacement. This implies that the costs of operating existing systems have always to be charged for and that renewal or expansion costs have to be charged for when systems are renewed or expanded. Economic efficiency does not require that all users pay the same rate, however, as long as each pays at least the direct costs arising out of connection and use. In some cases higher charges may be levied from the rich than from the poor, or they may be higher in the dry season, when water is scarce, than in the rainy season, when it is plentiful and easily replaceable.

In order to charge in proportion to the amount used, some form of metering is necessary. The provision and use of household water meters involve costs. In Asia, West Africa, and Latin America, where meters are commonly used, their capital cost ranges from US$15 to US$25. After meters are installed, water charges can be billed to individual households or companies. In a village with one standpipe to serve a whole group of people, it is not practicable to charge individual users by the meter and, indeed, it is difficult to charge at all. In such situations it is common for the villagers themselves to be responsible for the maintenance of the system. For example, Van der Laak (1969) describes a water supply system in Tanzania that was constructed and maintained by the local people, who covered maintenance costs through the cultivation of one acre of cotton in a communal system and agreed on a list of scheduled duties for maintenance workers. The system worked. However, another system in Tanzania in which the water supply system was paid for from local taxes, failed. In that system, not all of the taxpayers benefited, while some nontaxpayers were served with water.

Kia (1981) tells of a situation in Kenya that arose when villagers failed to pay a small monthly tax that was to be used to help operate and maintain their local water supply systems. Another problem here was that frequent acts of vandalism on faucets, drainage facilities, protective fences, and so on, made it difficult to maintain many of the public standposts. The solution devised was to convert public standposts in a few areas to water vendor operations; a licensed vendor pays a subsidized rate for the metered standpost water and sells it to users by the container at a slightly higher fee. As a result of the switch to kiosks, vandalism has been greatly reduced, repair and replacement costs have declined, and a small amount of revenue has been generated. Furthermore, the rate at which people apply for house connections has increased; some people presumably felt that if they were going to have to pay for water, it might as well be convenient water.

One of the disadvantages of metering domestic supplies is that some households find it difficult to accumulate the funds required to pay the bills when rendered. In consequence, some households in Abidjan buy water, when needed, from neighbors. The private company SODECI that manages the water supply in Côte d'Ivoire has attempted to deal with this problem by equipping some of its standposts with coin-operated meters. For about 2 U.S. cents villagers may obtain twenty-five liters from the standpost. The coin-operated standposts are supplied and maintained by a separate contracting firm, which buys the water from SODECI at bulk rates and earns a profit by selling the water through the coin-operated faucets, which cost about US$1,600 each. An operator is employed to guard and service each unit, at a salary of about US$50 a month plus 10 percent of the takings.

Meters may also be used by water authorities to bill local government authorities. In Malaysia, for example, a regional water authority provides water for the rural population by means of standposts along main roadways. Each of these standposts is metered, and the local government authority is responsible for paying the water authority for the water supply. To the extent that payments are made, the water authority has the funds to maintain its standpost and to extend service to other rural areas.

Metering has other advantages besides making it possible to levy charges. It helps the supplier keep track of how much water is being used in different parts of the system. Since unexpected increases of use can be due to leakages, either accidental or deliberate (caused by water thieves), the metering can also help the supplier identify and deal with such leaks.

As Hanke (1981) has pointed out, one of the problems with governmental control of water supply, which is evident even in a country as progressive as Côte d'Ivoire, for example, is that water charges are uniform over the whole country and thus low-cost customers are forced to subsidize high-cost customers, irrespective of income. As a consequence, system expansion is beset by constant tension between existing users (whose payments are apt to increase as the system costs increase) and the potential new users who have not only to contend with existing users but also to vie against one another to obtain priority in the allocation of scarce governmental resources. Difficulties of this kind are avoided when each installation is self-financing.

Thus, although it is not easy to charge for water, particularly for piped water, examples abound showing that it is practicable and that the difficulty of charging is no reason to exclude the private sector from providing water. Indeed, even when water is supplied by the public sector, great difficulties are encountered if water is not charged for at rates that cover all the costs.

Merit Goods

Is water a merit good in the sense that people who receive supplies of safe water benefit from it to a greater extent than they themselves believe? There is evidence that this can be the case. In a potable water project in rural Thailand, according to a USAID report, many people served by the system, including those who have potable water piped directly to their homes through private faucets, still prefer to drink water from traditional sources—that is, rainwater collected in cisterns or water from open shallow wells. To most rural Thai, shallow well water tastes "heavy" and good, but the piped water is "too thin" and, because of chlorination, unpleasant. Boiling removes the bad taste, but is considered troublesome and, according to health personnel, is not commonly done except during epidemics. Nevertheless, the increased availability of water appears to have fostered sanitary practices and to have reduced disease (Dworkin and others 1980).

Piped water supply thus appears to have most of the attributes that make it less suitable for private provision: the decreasing costs are such that some elements have the characteristics of natural monopolies; substantial externalities exist, whether the supply is used for drinking or for irrigating crops; difficulties arise in charging for the service and in excluding nonpayers; and water is a merit good in the sense that some users prefer the more tasty untreated water from traditional sources to the piped, safer, chlorinated variety. These factors may help to explain why piped water is relatively neglected by the private sector in developing countries and why water supply and sewerage are considered to be unsatisfactory in many of them.

Private Sector Involvement

There are numerous examples of nonpiped water being distributed by private vendors, but few cases of piped water and sewerage being supplied competitively, since these services have the characteristics of a natural monopoly. In a number of developing countries, however, private firms have been given concessions to supply water and sewerage systems, using their own equipment under conditions and tariffs regulated by municipalities. Examples of management contracts can also be found; these are situations in which public agencies invest in municipal systems but employ private firms to manage them. Elsewhere, especially in the villages of the Middle East, the Philippines, and Latin America, cooperatives have been established to organize the provision of water services. The private sector also has substantial experience in providing wells for agricultural irrigation. Thus the involvement of the private sector in the provision of water and sewerage may be categorized under the following headings:

Vending of nonpiped water
Provision of piped water (or sewerage services) by

- companies that make their own investments
- companies that manage publicly provided investments
- rural cooperatives

Exploitation of groundwater for irrigation.

Vending of Nonpiped Water

Water vending—the sale of water by carriers—is ubiquitous in developing countries and has been since ancient times. In every town in the old world the water carrier was indispensable. Statues made in ancient Greece show water being carried in large earthenware jars on carriers' shoulders. An edict of Diocletian, which attempted to freeze prices and incomes in ancient Rome, decreed that water carriers were to be paid at the same rate as mule and camel drivers. Some 20,000 water carriers earned a living in Paris at the time of the French Revolution; they used two pails, as in China today, balancing them at each end of a pole. And a drawing of Beijing in 1800 shows a large barrel on wheels, with a bung at the back, which resembles the barrels still used in parts of East Africa.

Under the Ottoman rulers, Istanbul's population was supplied with water, carried in waterbags from public fountains, by two corporations in competition with one another: the *arka sakalari,* which employed human water carriers, and the *at sakalari,* which used horses as carriers (*Encyclopedia of Islam* 1983). At that time, the water in Istanbul was considered to be purer than in any other city, possibly as a result of the Muslim requirement to wash frequently under running water. For a small sum, one could also buy snow water in the streets of Istanbul in summer (Braudel 1973).

Vendors obtain water either from public standposts or directly from the source. They sell it door-to-door or through middlemen. The many routes by which water is delivered from the original source to the final consumer are shown in figure 7-1. A survey of water vending in twelve communities (Zaroff and Okun 1984)

Figure 7–1. Possible Distribution System for Water Vending

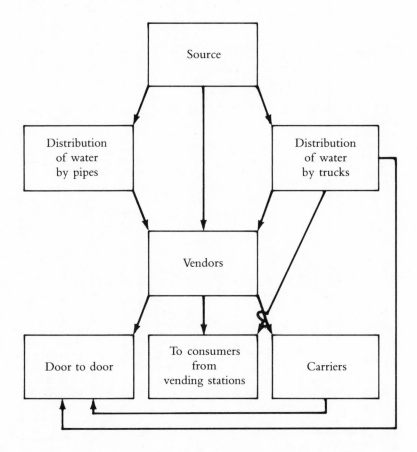

Source: Zaroff and Okun (1984). Copyright © 1984 Pergamon Press, Ltd.; reprinted with permission.

provides examples of consumer use of water vending (see table 7-3) and information on water vendors (table 7-4).

Zaroff and Okun concluded that water vending could be an economic solution for many communities but that the costs to consumers could be high—as much as 30 percent of income in some cases, although not in all seasons. They also found that the quality of vended water was often poor owing to contamination at the source, in the containers, or in handling.

The price paid for vended water is typically ten times as high as the price paid for piped water (see table 7-5), but it can be even

Table 7–3. Consumer Use of Water Vending

Area	Study population	Average household size	Sources other than vendors	Daily per capita liters Consumed	Daily per capita liters Purchased from vendor	Percentage of households served by vendors	Price per liter (U.S. dollars)	Percentage of household monthly income
Cebu, Philippines	1,000	6	Open well, protected spring, rainwater	n.a.	5	60	0.010	16
Ormoc, Philippines	3,520	6	Unprotected spring river, rainwater, public standpost	3	3	10	0.009	19
Diourbel, Senegal	100	10	Open well, piped system	2	1	90	0.008	3
Surabaya, Indonesia	311	6	Piped system, open well	n.a.	30	n.a.	0.003	28
Sawee, Thailand	2,000	5	Protected well, open well, river, rainwater	23	23	10	0.001	6
Ali Matan, Somalia	16,000	5	River, piped system	4	1	10	0.150	>30
Mandera, Kenya	17,000	6	River, irrigation canal, rainwater, piped system	7	7	90	0.040	>30
Gankida, Nigeria	10,000	16	River, open well, rainwater	n.a.	n.a.	15	0.020	n.a.
Ibi, Nigeria	5,000	6	Protected well, open well, rainwater	8	5	40	0.040	>30
Ky Cham, Kampuchea	n.a.	n.a.	Protected well, open well, river, piped system	n.a.	n.a.	50	n.a.	n.a.
Boundiali, Côte d'Ivoire	15,000	10	Open well, rainwater, piped system	11	6	50	0.005	3
Guidan Rouondji, Niger	3,500	9	Open well, river, rainwater	9	8	40	0.007	26

n.a. Not available.
Source: Zaroff and Okun (1984). Copyright © 1984, Pergamon Press, Ltd.; reprinted with permission.

Table 7-4. Information on Water Vendors

Area	Number of vendors	Source	Delivery equipment	Containers	Average annual income (U.S. dollars)			Vendors have other sources of income
					Per capita	Vendor	Carrier	
Cebu, Philippines	1	Springbox	Jeepney	Plastic jerricans	700	>700	n.a.	no
Ormoc, Philippines	2	Public faucet	Push carts	55-gallon drum	700	>700	n.a.	yes
Diourbel, Senegal	1	Open well	Donkey-drawn cart	Kerosene tins, paint cans	700	300	n.a.	yes
Surabaya, Indonesia	52	Piped system	Yoke, wooden cart	Wooden barrels, tins	700	>700	>700	
Sawee, Thailand	8	River	Two-wheeled cart	Kerosene tins	700	200	n.a.	yes
Ali Matan, Somalia	3	Piped system	Donkey cart	Oil drum	300	>300	n.a.	n.a.
Mandera, Kenya	100	River	Donkey cart	Plastic jerricans, buckets	700	>700	n.a.	no
Gankida, Nigeria	24	River, open well	Man	Kerosene tins	700	n.a.	n.a.	yes
Ibi, Nigeria	30	River	Man	Kerosene tins	700	>700	n.a.	yes
Ky Cham, Kampuchea	n.a.	Piped system	Cart	Metal drums	n.a.	n.a.	n.a.	no
Boundiali, Côte d'Ivoire	n.a.	River, piped system	n.a.	Metal buckets, drums	300	n.a.	n.a.	yes
Guidan Rouondji, Niger	n.a.	Open well	Yoke	Kerosene tins, pottery jars	700	n.a.	n.a.	yes

n.a. Not available.

a. With twenty-eight carriers.

Source: Zaroff and Okun (1984). Copyright © 1984, Pergamon Press, Ltd.; reprinted with permission.

Table 7–5. Prices of Vended and Piped Water
(U.S. dollars)

| City | Vended water | | City water system[a] | |
	Per 1,000 U.S. gallons	Per cubic meter	Per 1,000 U.S. gallons	Per cubic meter
Dhaka	4.20–8.40	1.11–2.22	0.35	0.09
Kampala	5.84–14.60	1.55–3.86	0.70	0.18
Istanbul	3.52	0.93	0.35	0.09

a. Metered domestic rate.
Source: 1971 World Bank data.

higher. Mateen Thobani has told me that the price of vended water in Karachi in 1979 was fifty to a hundred times the government subsidized rates for piped water. In some cases, the total amount paid for water by those (generally the poor) who buy from vendors exceeds the amount paid by those who receive piped water. Researchers (Adrianzen and Graham 1974) have shown that sixty-eight families who bought water in cylinders in Lima in the 1960s spent two to six times as much for one-third to one-seventh of the quantity that others obtained from piped sources. When the amounts paid for water are expressed as a percentage of family income or as minutes worked to pay for them, the burden borne by those without access to piped water becomes even more striking. For example, a typical family using water from cylinders would have to work more than seven hours to pay for a month's supply, whereas a family with a private piped supply would have to work just over two hours (see figure 7-2, which also shows, for comparison, the minutes worked to pay for illumination, which show much less variation).

Although vended water in urban areas costs consumers more per unit than piped water, in some circumstances it provides the more economical solution. In Abidjan, Cotonou, and Surabaya, for example, many low-income people buy their drinking water from vendors (or from neighbors with access to piped water) and use the water from shallow wells, which is unsafe for drinking, for other purposes. In this way connection charges are avoided. The vending of special drinking waters is of course a common practice in many developed countries, notably in France. Gordon Tulloch has told me that inhabitants of a high-class suburb of Athens can buy three varieties of water from vendors at different prices.

The operations of water vendors may be illustrated by four of the ten companies serving the people of Santo Domingo, the capital of the Dominican Republic. Santo Domingo does have a supply of piped water (provided by a public sector agency) but it is

Figure 7–2. Monthly Consumption and Cost of Water in Lima

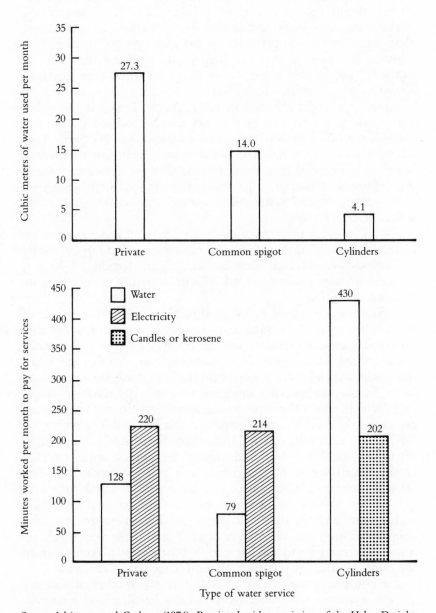

Source: Adrianzen and Graham (1974). Reprinted with permission of the Helen Dwight Reid Educational Foundation. Published by Heldref Publications, 4000 Albemarle St., N.W., Washington, D.C. 20016. Copyright © 1974.

unreliable because electric power is frequently interrupted. As a result, ten private companies have sprung up, all of which are inspected and regulated by the Ministry of Health. All ten companies obtain their water from private sources, all purify and package their products, and all distribute by truck. In addition, all charge the maximum price set by the government, so that competition is based on service. Large-scale trucking of water for domestic use is also common in other countries, for example, Ecuador, El Salvador, and Jordan.

Agua Crystal. Established in 1964, Agua Crystal is the oldest water vending company in the area around Santo Domingo. It owns three other private water companies: Agua Niagara, Agua Montana, and Agua Glacial, which supply different varieties of water to the capital city. Agua Crystal charges the same price as Agua Pureza, although in 1981 the two engaged in a fierce price competition. Agua Crystal sells water in bottles of one gallon with a fleet of thirty trucks.

Agua Pureza. A private company set up in 1981, Agua Pureza is located eleven kilometers from the capital city. Though owned by a religious organization (Iglesia Evangélica Metodista Libre), it pays taxes and is profit-oriented. The profits from the business are devoted to charity.

Purified water is sold in five-gallon glass jugs to the people of Santo Domingo. The water comes from a source in the central mountains that is privately owned by Agua Pureza. The initial capital outlay was US$60,000. The company processes and treats the water, which is then poured into the jugs. Distribution is made by eight trucks, specially designed to carry 104 *botellones* (jugs) each, which deliver the water to the customer's door. The consumers have to make a one-time purchase of a five-gallon glass jug for US$7, and then they pay 75 U.S. cents for a jugful. The trucks distribute the filled jugs and collect the empty ones. Average family consumption is two-thirds of a jug per week. Monthly sales amount to 10,000 jugs. The company also sells water to government institutions, for example, the ministries of Education and Interior and the Police Department. The operation is profitable; operating costs are low except for the botellones, which are imported from Miami and Mexico. Sales are steady, except during the rainy season, when some customers switch to rainwater.

The company employs a total staff of thirty or more: sixteen are drivers (two per truck), ten work in the bottling and purifying operations, and the rest in the office. Truck drivers are motivated to sell water jugs, earning a basic salary plus a commission of 9 U.S. cents per jug delivered.

The Ministry of Health supervises hygiene and water quality by means of weekly inspections. The company subcontracts specialist services to a private laboratory.

Agua San Antonio. A private company owned by a single entrepreneur, Agua San Antonio is a small firm with four tank trucks. It provides water to the capital and the vicinity, including the neighboring district of San Cristóbal, serving families, hotels, restaurants, and firms on a daily basis. It buys the water from a state-supervised source, where the quality is checked. On the average, each customer buys four tankfuls per month at a price of US$20 per tankful. A tank holds about 2,500 gallons of water. With a staff of only ten, the company competes successfully in a market where price is given but the quality and speed of service are all-important.

Servicio de Agua Rosario. A family enterprise established in the capital city in 1964, Servicio de Agua Rosario provides households with drinkable water, which it delivers by tank trucks. The enterprise buys filtered and chlorinated water from government wells, filling the tanks at the source. The price paid to the government is US$3 per tank of 2,500 gallons. The company in its turn sells each tank for US$20 with a margin of US$10. It operates with four trucks in Santo Domingo, and outside on request (for example, for swimming pools) at prices set by competition. It fills the underground cisterns of households once every two weeks (on the average).

Provision of Piped Water

Despite the long history of private vending in all countries, the provision of piped water by the private sector, either for irrigation or for household use, has been comparatively rare. Neither in the Middle East nor in China, India, or Rome does there appear to have been any significant private provision of piped water. The absence of property rights with respect to water, its critical importance in times of war, the difficulty of collecting payments, and the magnitude of the resources required might explain this. There are exceptions, however: in Hawaii, water has been privately owned for many years and is privately provided to this day (Hutchins 1946).

In more modern times, the brothers Perrier, following the example of private provision in London, founded a company in 1782 that was granted a license to supply piped water in the Paris area for fifteen years. The Perriers set up two steam pumps, four tanks, and a supply system. Most of the pipes were made of wood, and they supplied a few standposts and the first private connections. The charge was 50 francs per hogshead, or about 1 U.S. cent per liter. The venture was a success and the company quickly expanded. But it aroused jealousy and the water bearers began to lobby against the Perriers. The French Revolution intervened and the city of Paris took over the firm along with two others that had sprung up. This was the beginning of the Paris Municipal Water Department and was the first reported nationalization of a private water company (Monod 1982). Interestingly, the Chase Manhattan Bank in New York owes its origins to private financing of water in Manhattan.

After 1850 the provision of piped water in urban areas spread rapidly in Europe and America. English private companies were the first to be granted "concessions" in other countries—in Berlin in 1856 and in Cannes in 1866. French companies also turned to foreign markets for water supply concessions and became active all over the world, but especially in Spain and in North and West Africa. In the twentieth century the French private water companies became the most advanced, technically and commercially, both within and outside of the country, so a thumbnail description of the arrangements in France may be in order (see Monod 1982; Coyaud 1985). Their operations are summarized in table 7-6.

Under the French system, water supply companies have a local monopoly, but the tariff is determined by a public authority. The public authority (typically a municipality) often builds and operates the system with its own resources. This is known as the *régie direct* system. It can be managed either by the public authority's own staff (*régie simple*), or by an autonomous board (*régie autonome*) which is a separate local entity owned by the public authority.

When a private sector operator is employed, the three most common arrangements are the management contract (*gérance*), the *concession* system, and the *affermage* system.

In management contracting, a public authority may contract with a private company to provide specific services for the operation and maintenance of a water and sewerage service, or indeed any other municipal function. These services could include loan of staff for technical assistance, metering, billing and collection of bills, maintenance of private connections and meters, maintenance of the distribution networks, and the like. Compensation to the private company would be of the type made under contracts for consulting services (time-based, lump sum, percentage, cost-plus, and so on). The responsibility of the private company would be limited to that part of the system operated on behalf of the public authority. Where the complete operation is contracted out, the system is known as gérance. Under the gérance system customers legally remain clients of the public authority, and bills are collected by the private company only on behalf of the public authority, which compensates the private company in accordance with the terms of the contract. When the management contract includes a productivity bonus to the contractor or a share of the profits, it is called a *régie intéressée*.

In the concession system, the public authority contracts a construction and operation concession to a single private operator. The concessionnaire finances, constructs, or subcontracts the construction of, and operates at its own risk, all the facilities for the supply of drinking water. On termination of the concession, it must return the system to the public authority in perfect condition; that is to say, during the life of the concession it must replace worn-out equipment as well as recover its invested capital. To realize a return on its investment, the concessionnaire sells the water to the consumers in accordance with its concession contract. The price takes into account economic trends during the life of the concession—inflation, economies of scale, taxation, legislation, and so on. It is not a single figure but a set of rules by which the sale price is to be calculated every year. The concession contract also fixes the level of service to be provided by the concessionnaire: for example, water quality and source, quantity of water to be supplied without charge to the public authorities (standposts, sewer flush, fire hydrants, and street cleaning), and the obligations and terms of connecting up consumers. So that the amortization of the concessionnaire's investment can be spread over a long period, concession contracts are generally for a long term, usually thirty years. This arrangement helps to reduce the price to the consumer.

In the affermage system, the public authority handles the construction of the system by itself and contracts out the operation and maintenance work, collection of charges, and relations with the consumers to a single private operator, the fermier. This is an operating concession only. As is the case under the concession system, the fermier discharges its assigned tasks at its risk. This means that it must discharge them according to its contract and is compensated only by means of its sale of water. The contract sets the sales prices. So that the public authority can amortize its initial investments, the water price customarily includes a surcharge collected by the fermier for the authority's account and paid over to it. The authority retains title to the system.

Table 7-6. Comparison of Management Options under the French System

Institutional alternatives	Government-owned (*régie directe*)		Private or mixed government-private company					
	Government department (*régie simple*)	Autonomous board (*régie autonome*)	Services contract	Management contract		Leasing contract (*affermage*)	Concession contract (*concession*)	
				Gérance	Shared profit (*régie intéressée*)			
Legal autonomy	No	Yes	Yes	Yes	Yes	Yes	Yes	
Responsibility for setting tariffs	Public	Public	Public	Public	Public	Public	Public	
Financing of fixed assets	Public	Public	Public	Public	Public	Public	Private	
Ownership of fixed assets	Public	Public	Public	Public	Public	Public	Private until expiration of contracts	
Operation and maintenance of system	Public	Public	Public except specific services	Private without commercial risk	Private with full commercial risk	Private with full commercial risk	Private with full commercial risk	

				Private	Private
Financing of working capital for operation and maintenance	Public	Public	Public	Public	Private	Private
Destination of revenues from tariffs	Public	Public	Public	Public	Part to lessee, part to public authority	Part to concessionnaire, part to public authority
Compensation to private company	—	Similar to contract for consulting services	Proportional to physical parameters (volume sold, number of connections, etc.)	Proportional to physical parameters with productivity bonus or shared profits	Part of tariffs reserved to lessee	Part of tariff reserved to concessionnaire
Contract validity period	—	Less than 5 years	About 5 years	About 5 years	6–10 years (possibility renewing contract)	About 30 years

— Not applicable.
Source: Coyaud (1985).

The French systems of concession and affermage were implemented outside France, particularly in North and West Africa, by French specialist water and sewerage firms such as

Compagnie Général des Eaux in Senegal and, to some extent, in Italy and Spain

Société Lyonnaise des Eaux and its local subsidiaries in Algeria, the People's Republic of the Congo, Guinea, Madagascar, Togo, Tunisia, and Vanuatu

Société d'Aménagement Urbain et Rural (SAUR) in Côte d'Ivoire

Société Balency Eau Assainissement (SOBEA) in Algeria.

Companies That Make Their Own Investments. Most of the French systems in Africa were taken over by local authorities, however, when the countries involved became independent. By 1980, only two former concessions were still operated outside France by French companies; both were in Morocco and operated only in the Casablanca and Tangiers areas. Two former affermage operations were still in existence, in Côte d'Ivoire (see below) and in Vanuatu.

Although the French companies have reduced their work in Africa, they have extended their activities to other parts of the world:

In French overseas territories such as French Guiana, Martinique, New Caledonia, and Réunion (through affermage)

In developed countries, by taking shares in existing operating companies, as in the United States and in Spain

More recently in other developed countries (Canada and Japan) and in developing countries (Thailand and Malaysia), by establishing new operating companies with local partners.

Some other regulated private companies operate in European countries (Great Britain and the Netherlands), and in Latin America (for example, in Santiago and Guatemala City). A brief description of three Latin American companies follows.

Santiago, the capital of Chile, has the distinction of accommodating two separate suppliers of piped water, which, although covering different areas, overlap in one zone. One of these is The Empresa de Agua Potable Lo Castillo Ltda., which provides water and sewerage services in the district of Comuna Los Condes. It has 43,000 connections with 100 percent coverage of the people; 98 percent of the water consumption is residential. The company has had a territorial concession since 1943, when it started operations in the high-income district of Los Condes, where it began with only 2,000 connections.

Lo Castillo holds the water rights of the source. It has a staff of 300 and provides an integrated system that goes from planning and construction to supply and maintenance. Metering services are also fully covered by the firm.

Tariffs are approved by the Ministry of Public Works and are the same as those of Agua Potable Manqueue, another private water enterprise in Santiago. In August 1984 there was a fixed charge of US$30 a month for a 1-inch diameter supply, and US$65 for a 1.5-inch diameter supply. The variable charge was 86 U.S. cents per cubic meter.

The Empresa de Agua Potable Manqueue was established in 1981 to provide drinkable water in Manqueue, which is east of Santiago City and north of the Mapuche River. The company obtained a thirty-year concession to supply water to the people of Manqueue. In one zone, Parque Institucional, Lo Curro district, their services overlap with those of Empresa de Agua Potable Lo Castillo Ltda. Competition is based on quality, since tariffs are the same. The Manqueue Company supplies domestic water to only 310 connections (8 people per connection on the average, or 2,400 users), which constitute a very small fraction of the total Santiago population (3.6 million).

The water is obtained from wells, for which the company has the water rights. It is chlorinated before being piped. The enterprise has complete autonomy and thus is responsible for invoicing and collection. It installs, maintains, and reads all the meters (each connection is metered) in Manqueue.

Quality control for both companies is enforced by three public agencies: Empresa Metropolitana de Obra Sanitaria (EMOS), Servicio Nacional de Obras Sanitarias (SENDOS), and Servicio de Sanidad del Ambiente (Ministry of Health).

In Guatemala City the Compania de Agua Mariscal is a fully private enterprise that has provided water for more than fifty years. Construction works, operation, equipment, and the company's maintenance are all under its control, as is house metering. The charge is equivalent to 20 U.S. cents per cubic meter for an initial supply, and 45 U.S. cents for any excess. Quality control is enforced by the Ministry of Health. The enterprise shares the Guatemala City market with Empagua, an autonomous water entity in the public sector.

Companies That Manage Publicly Provided Investments. The French affermage system of private management of publicly financed facilities is still widely used in France. The operation of an affermage system in developing countries can be illustrated by the case of Abidjan (see Golladay 1983; World Bank 1983).

The private firm responsible for water supply in Abidjan is the Société de Distribution d'Eau de la Côte d'Ivoire (SODECI); a counterpart is responsible for sewage disposal. Until 1967 SODECI was a wholly owned subsidiary of a French firm, Société d'Aménagement Urbain et Rural (SAUR). Since 1967, SAUR has retained only a 47 percent interest in SODECI; the remaining 53 percent is owned in Côte d'Ivoire (49 percent private, 4 percent state). SODECI began operations in Côte d'Ivoire in 1960 under a thirty-year concession contract with the government to supply water to Abidjan. In 1973, the contract was converted to affermage and amended to grant SODECI responsibility for the rest of the country—including 122 towns and several hundred villages.

The water supply systems operated by SODECI range from a large and complex piped distribution system in Abidjan to relatively simple systems based on wells in rural areas. A unit in the Ministry of Public Works is responsible for planning and building all large new investments in water. This unit is also responsible for supervising SODECI. Under its contracts, SODECI is paid a fee related to the volume of water sold. The fee is calculated on the basis of agreed standards for staff, equipment, energy, and other inputs, plus a margin based on agreed overheads and profits, which is indexed against inflation. SODECI therefore makes a reasonable profit, whereas other (usually public) water supply companies in West Africa generally operate at a loss. SODECI's fee is about one-third of the water tariff, which is set to cover not only operation and maintenance costs but also debt service.

Despite the rapid expansion of the systems in Côte d'Ivoire, the standard of water supply there is among the highest in West Africa. The systems are well designed, equipped, maintained, and operated. Water quality and pressure are uniformly good. Consumption is metered and water losses are low. Several factors contribute to these good results:

- The institutional separation of investments from operations makes it easier to evaluate SODECI's performance and ensures government control over the expansion of the system.
- By setting water tariffs to reflect total costs fully, Côte d'Ivoire can finance its existing services. Water rates are among the highest in Africa; thus consumers, rather than taxpayers, pay for the services they receive. The low rates for small quantities help the poor to afford the water.

- During periodic traffic reviews, the government can carefully scrutinize SODECI's costs.

- As a private company, SODECI is free (within the contracted limits) to hire, fire, and compensate its staff. This freedom, plus a strong emphasis on training (SODECI operates its own training center), enables the company to attract, train, and keep qualified people.

These examples show that private companies can construct and manage urban water systems in developing countries, with government agencies responsible for monitoring water quality and approving tariffs.

Water Cooperatives. Water cooperatives are to be found in most developing countries, and although not all have been successful (for reasons that cannot be explored here), many have made significant contributions to the development of water supply and other public services. Water cooperatives are common in Argentina, Bolivia, and Chile, in the Philippines, and in the Middle East. They can be particularly helpful at the village level, where informed consumers, sharing common interests within small communities, can take the place of the professional management that can be afforded only by large systems.

The Deeder Cooperative, which serves two villages (Kashinathpur and Balarampur) in Bangladesh, is a good example of how a cooperative can provide effective financial support, which could be extended for water supply facilities. Conceived in 1960 by one villager from a small peasant family, the cooperative was formed by rickshaw-pullers, who are landless and land-poor people. They contributed one anna (about 1 U.S. cent) weekly toward the initial purchase of old rickshaws for two members. In less than a year, they paid back the cost of the rickshaws and turned over a profit of 50 rupees to the cooperatives.

With these funds, more rickshaws were bought and the process snowballed. By 1963, membership had shot up to 126. By then there was enough money and confidence to invest in larger enterprises—trucking, a brick kiln factory, and tractors for transportation—and even to rent out rickshaws and provide banking and interest-free credit for members. In addition, several contributing funds were initiated on the basis of ability to pay. These included medicare, life insurance, school supplies, technical education, loss funds, a tubewell purchase fund, a charity fund (disaster relief), and a reserve fund.

To promote general village development, the cooperative has widened its activities: all houses are to be electrified; in 1977, twenty-six water-seal latrines were installed and fifty more were ordered; and a preventive health program was introduced (Kia 1981).

Water cooperatives in Latin America, of which there are many, can be illustrated by the Saguapac Cooperative in Santa Cruz, Bolivia. In 1979, the municipal company that had been serving Santa Cruz was converted into a cooperative to overcome inefficiencies that were blamed on government control. Since then, water services have reportedly improved significantly and are currently being provided without interruption. The cooperative provides drinkable water to a population of 350,000 in the District of Santa Cruz. Neighboring areas are served by other, smaller cooperatives. Saguapac has a staff of 250. Some services—for example, pipe installations and meter readings—are subcontracted to private firms in order to minimize overhead costs. Under the cooperative scheme, each household head has one share that provides voting power. There are currently 43,000 connections and the same number of shareholders.

Saguapac provides a comprehensive water service. Water is extracted from subterranean sources with thirteen pumps. The raw water is considered to be safe to drink, but it is chlorinated as a precautionary measure. After extraction, it is transported to large storage tanks, from which it is finally distributed to the urban area through a network of pipes owned by the cooperative. Tariffs are proposed by Saguapac but have to be approved by a government agency. In 1984 the tariff was the equivalent of 3.5 U.S. cents per cubic meter. In 1983 energy costs trebled, but the government did not allow the cooperative to increase its tariff sufficiently to meet this increase. As a result, the cooperative ran a deficit in 1984; it has no public subsidy. It is trying to deal with the situation by negotiating for reduced energy costs and for tariff adjustments.

Exploitation of Groundwater for Irrigation

The private sector in developing countries today does not appear to offer any examples of the exploitation of river water for irrigation, but private water control organizations were common in China in the past. These systems increased in number during the Ming dynasty, and their financing and control moved into the hands of those cultivating the soil. Since irrigation systems often included several villages, coordinating maintenance activities and allocating water were quite complicated tasks. Records had to be kept to schedule the drawing of water, to collect assessments from households to finance the work, and to mobilize labor to repair the dikes and channels. The supervisory and record-keeping duties were rotated among landowning farmers (Rawski 1979). It may be mentioned in passing that these activities required a basic literacy among the Chinese peasantry, which could not have been obtained without private education.

Water has been extracted from private wells since prehistoric times. More recently, World Bank staff have followed with particular care the experience of private and public tubewells in India and Pakistan, of which it has been written: "There can be no doubt that the individually owned private tubewells and pumpsets played a major part in the Green Revolution—more correctly termed the Wheat Revolution—in India and Pakistan" (Carruthers and Stoner 1981, p. 45). Experience has shown that private wells provide a cheaper water supply and are simpler than public ones, are better maintained, and obtain high operating efficiency. In addition, private initiatives have produced a remarkable range of ingenious inventions for the use of cheap local materials. For example, a bamboo tubewell developed in Bangladesh is so inexpensive that several can be inserted in a number of land fragments. With the engine and pump mounted on a bullock cart, an entire farm can be irrigated economically. It is not even necessary for every farmer to own a pump; pump contractors have emerged who will provide the necessary equipment for pumpless tubewells. Another benefit of this technology is that it can be used to power threshing machines and other farm equipment after the irrigation season (Carruthers and Stoner 1981).

Probably the most extensive private sector involvement in irrigation occurred in Pakistan in the 1970s, in the vast Indus Valley, which is about as large as California. The area had serious problems with waterlogging and salinity. In the 1940s, the government of Pakistan installed more than 14,000 tubewells, mainly for drainage, although improved irrigation was expected to be a significant by-product. When the program was being developed, a small number of Pakistani experts, particularly Ghulam Mohammad of the Pakistan Institute of Development Economics, argued that public tubewells should be confined to areas where the groundwater was too salty to be used for irrigation without dilution with river water. He recommended that in areas of good groundwater, development should be left to private users and the government should facilitate development by providing electricity and easy terms for the purchase of pumps and motors. However, the authorities decided to rely on public tubewells, presumably because private tubewell development in the Indus Basin was insignificant at that time. Some also feared that the groundwater aquifer could be damaged through uncontrolled pumpage by private users.

The Indus Basin farmers preferred to have their own wells, however, and the performance of the 14,000 public tubewells was overshadowed by 186,000 tubewells of smaller capacity that were privately installed, 90 percent with no subsidy. Assessments by World Bank staff concluded that the private tubewells had been

- Managed efficiently, particularly in helping to meet peak water requirements
- Imposed a relatively insignificant burden on public resources
- Produced returns that were economically justified and brought significant financial returns to the benefiting farmers
- Did not lead to excessive exploitation of the aquifer
- Provided sufficient drainage to maintain water tables at reasonable levels.

Groundwater pumped by private tubewells now accounts for nearly 80 percent of Pakistan's total "pumpage." The management patterns of private tubewell users are more efficient than those observed for public tubewell users with respect to cropping intensities, yields, and use of inputs. Not surprisingly, suggestions have now been made that public tubewells should either be sold to owners of adjoining lands or transferred to local private enterprises for their day-to-day operations and management.

Although the private tubewells are owned mainly by farmers who have access to capital, the existence of the tubewells has brought about an active water market through which the private tubewell owners can make irrigation supplies available to farmers who do not possess their own wells. Could such markets, operating on a countrywide basis, ease the movement of excess water from areas of surplus to areas of shortage? No examples have been found in the developing countries, but in California an irrigation district that owns the right to take large amounts of water from the Colorado River has hired an engineering company—Parsons Corporation of Pasadena—to undertake a conservation project intended to save millions of gallons a year of this water, now lost through evaporation, seepage, and runoff. The company would then sell to the highest bidder the rights to use the water now wasted.

In another California project, San Diego officials are negotiating to buy large amounts of water from a group of Denver entrepreneurs who are seeking to dam a tributary of the Colorado River more than 1,000 miles from San Diego. The dam, San Diego officials say, would increase the volume of water that flows from the Rocky Mountains into the Colorado River and travels south toward Mexico. For a price, San Diego would be given the right to draw the additional water (Lindsey 1985).

The Role of the Government

The shortcomings in water supply—with respect to both quantity and quality—are generally due not to technical constraints, but to poor management. For example, a study in Manila showed that 48 percent of the water supplied in 1977 was "unaccounted for" (Kirke and Arthur 1984). Management in the public sector can often be improved, but the involvement of the private sector can bring quicker results, and the dimensions of the various problems cry out for quick results.

Because of the universal tendency to politicize and municipalize piped water and sewerage systems, the private sector is unlikely to finance infrastructure in the water sector. It can provide management, however, and the French affermage system described earlier provides a model that can be widely copied and developed. There is indeed scope for public-private cooperation in this sector—the public sector (aided, as appropriate, by international financing agencies) can provide the financing and the private sector the management. The tariffs to be charged would be of critical importance. Possibly they could be determined by a process of bidding; certainly they would have to be high enough to provide, in total, sufficient revenues to cover all capital and operating costs. The government could have an inspection role, to ensure that the water sold for drinking is indeed fit to drink.

In the provision of nonpiped systems, the private sector can—and does—provide both vended water and sanitary systems for human waste disposal (Kalbermatten, Julius, and Gunnerson 1980). Government activities can be confined to safety inspections and to the provision of training in the application of appropriate technologies.

To increase the opportunities for private sector involvement in water supply, laws might be passed making it possible to trade water over long distances. Such an arrangement would provide incentives for the transfer of water from areas of surplus to areas of shortage, even across international boundaries.

Conclusion

This brief review indicates that water supply, especially for drinking, is in a deplorable state in many countries. The private sector plays a relatively minor role in the provision of piped water and a significant (but unquantified) one in water vending. There is enough experience of the private sector throughout the world, however, to confirm that private providers are technically and financially able to supply water through piped systems and that the main obstacles to their participation are political. Governments that prove to be incapable of providing facilities for which there is evident demand sometimes pursue policies that make it difficult for the private sector to provide the required services. The current situation in many countries—in which rich people receive subsidized piped services and the poor pay for expensive water from vendors—is likely to remain until governments encourage economic markets to work for water supply as they already do in many countries for the supply of food, clothing, and other necessities.

The scope for competition in the distribution of piped water may be limited, because of the enormous cost of providing more than one distribution network. But local authorities can use competitive techniques to select monopoly contractors to provide services for a fixed number of years, as in France and West Africa. In rural areas or in small cities, local associations or cooperatives can be formed to provide facilities that users can pay for. In some situations, water vending might offer lower-cost solutions than piped systems; such activity deserves encouragement, as does the large-scale movement of irrigation water from areas in which water is plentiful to areas of shortage.

References

Adrianzen, Blanca T., and George Graham. 1974. "The High Cost of Being Poor." *Archives of Environmental Health* 28(6):312–14.

Anderson, Terry L. 1982. "Institutional Underpinnings of the Water Crisis." Bozeman, Mont.: Political Economy Research Center.

Braudel, F. 1973. *Capitalism and Material Life, 1400–1800*. New York: Harper and Row.

Carruthers, I. D., and R. Stoner. 1981. *Economic Aspects and Policy Issues in Groundwater Development*. World Bank Staff Working Paper 496. Washington, D.C.

Coyaud, Daniel P. 1985. "Private and Public Alternative for Providing Water Supply, Sewerage, and Other Municipal Services." World Bank Water Supply and Urban Development Department, Washington, D.C.

Deb, A. K. 1978. *Multiple Water Supply Approach for Urban Management.* ENV-76-18499. Washington, D.C.: National Science Foundation.

Dworkin, D. M., B. L. K. Pillsbury, T. Thatsanatheb, and S. Satchakul. 1980. *The Potable Water Project in Rural Thailand.* Project Impact Evaluation 3. Washington, D.C.: U.S. Agency for International Development.

Encyclopedia of Islam. 1983 ed. See articles on Ma'a (water).

Golladay, F. L. 1983. "The Role of Private Organizations in Managing and Operating Water Supply and Sanitation Systems in Developing Countries." Research Proposal. World Bank, Washington, D.C.

Hanke, Steve H. 1981. "On Water Tariff Equalization Policies." *Water Engineering and Management* 128, no. 8 (August).

Hanke, Steve H., and Roland W. Wentworth. 1980. "Statistical Cost Function Developed for Sewer Lines." *Water and Sewage Works* (December.)

Hutchins, W. 1946. "The Hawaiian System of Water Rights." City and County of Honolulu.

Kalbermatten, John M., Deanne S. Julius, and Charles G. Gunnerson. 1980. *Appropriate Technology for Water Supply and Sanitation.* Washington, D.C.: World Bank.

Kia, B. 1981. *Internal Financing of Water Supply and Sanitation in Developing Countries.* New York: United Nations Development Programme Division of Information.

Kirke, J., and J. Arthur. 1984. "Water Supply Issues." *Basic Needs and the Urban Poor: The Provision of Communal Service,* ed. P. J. Richards and A. M. Thompson. London: Croom Helm.

Lindsey, Robert. 1985. "Arid West Realizing Water Is a Salable Crop." *New York Times,* June 10.

Monod, J. 1982. "The Private Sector and Management of Public Drinking Water Services." World Bank, Water Supply Seminar, Washington, D.C., January.

Okun, Daniel A. 1984. "An Overview of Water Reuse." Keynote address at the International Symposium on Reuse of Sewage Effluent, Institution of Civil Engineers, London, October 30-31.

Rawski, Evelyn S. 1979. *Education and Popular Literacy in Ch'ing China.* Ann Arbor: University of Michigan Press.

Saunders, Robert J., and Jeremy J. Warford. 1976. *Village Water Supply.* Baltimore, Md.: Johns Hopkins University Press.

Sud, Inder K. 1984. "Is Potable Water Achievable?" Paper presented at 1984 Annual Conference of the American Water Works Association, Dallas, Texas.

Van der Laak, F. 1969. "The Ndoleleji Water Development Scheme." In *Rural Water Supply in East Africa,* ed. D. Warner. BRALUP Research Paper 11. Dar es Salaam: Bureau of Resource Assessment and Land Use Planning, University College.

World Bank, 1983. *World Development Report 1983.* New York: Oxford University Press.

Zaroff, Barbara, and Daniel A. Okun. 1984. "Water Vending in Developing Countries." *Aqua* 5: 289–95.

8

Conclusions

In countries where indigenous private sector performance is weak, we might ask whether this is not perhaps in large part the result of barriers and distortions consciously or unconsciously created by policymakers.

—A. W. CLAUSEN, "PROMOTING THE PRIVATE
SECTOR IN DEVELOPING COUNTRIES"

THIS BOOK has shown that the role of the private sector is pervasive in the provision of services in developing countries. The examples given here are but a small part of the tip of a very large iceberg. This is particularly the case in the education, health, and urban transport sectors, where private services have been provided in all societies from the earliest times. There are fewer examples in the electricity and telecommunications sectors, because these sectors are of comparatively recent origin, but even there volumes could no doubt be written and important lessons learned about private sector roles, both indigenous and foreign. Of all the areas studied, piped water and sewerage systems seem to be the ones in which the private sector is least involved, for reasons to be discussed below.

Relationships among the Sectors

In most societies, there are strong links among the different sectors, and it is difficult to treat any one in isolation. The education and development of children is closely linked to their health and nutrition, which in turn are influenced by the education of the parents. In many parts of Papua New Guinea, for example, people consider it degrading to drink the milk of cows, and children are therefore denied a rich and convenient nutrient that is readily available in many other societies. One way of teaching families the benefits of dairy products would be through educational media such as television, which requires cheap electricity. Students of economic development are aware of a multitude of interrelationships of this kind.

Obstacles to Private Sector Involvement

The examples cited in this volume show that many of the obstacles to the private involvement in public services (as in other activities) are social and political, rather than technical and financial. Although it took a man of extraordinary ability to establish an electricity supply in Caracas at the turn of the century, surely people of equal talent existed in Argentina, Brazil, and other Latin American countries who could have launched similar enterprises if circumstances had permitted. The same can be said about electricity in India: what the Tata Group does in the Bombay area can be replicated in other parts of the country, if not by the Tata organization, then by others. Capital can generally be found to finance activities for which there is evident public demand, and the demand for, say, telephone services exists in all countries, although it is satisfied in only a few.

Thus one is bound to conclude that the obstacles to the development of public services by the private sector are due to institutional weaknesses and governmental policies that make such involvement too risky or unprofitable. These issues are well known: persistent inflation of the currency discourages savings and cuts off potential sources of capital; governmental control of prices and the risk of expropriation magnify investment risks to unacceptable levels; lack of security discourages investments that need time to mature; and bureaucratic requirements can depress the entrepreneurial spirit. If, as in Peru, it takes two years to complete the formalities for registering a business, is it any wonder that enterprises go overseas or underground?

The situation with water is particularly instructive. Why is it that water is privately supplied by vendors almost everywhere, but is seldom privately supplied through pipes? The demand for water is universal, yet there are situations, as in Lima, in which the total monthly payments made by poor people for vended water exceed the total spent by better-off families for piped water. Why do the water vendors or other entrepreneurs not provide piped water? One might hazard a guess that they are discouraged by the riskiness of investing in fixed capital, which would be impossible to recover in a short time. This problem is less acute in water vending, even from trucks, as the capital equipment is mobile and can be used in other places or for other purposes should the business run into trouble. That the mobility of capital is an advantage to investors may be deduced from the fact that road transport is one of the most popular services among indigenous entrepreneurs. Buses, taxis, and trucks are owned privately in all countries in which the operation is permitted (and in some countries in which it is prohibited), presumably because the equipment can be moved to different routes or locations should the need arise.

The Problem of Price Equality

One of the major obstacles to the involvement of the private sector in the provision of public services is the notion that services have to be priced at the same rate for different people even when circumstances differ widely. For example, throughout Côte d'Ivoire, water has to be supplied to everybody at the same price, even though it is cheaper to provide in the capital city, Abidjan, than in rural areas. Price equality is sometimes defended on the grounds of "equity," although it is difficult to see what is "equitable" about charging the same for products that do not cost the same to produce.

Philosophers have long attempted to define the "just price." Although this subject is too complex to discuss here, it can be said that economic efficiency sometimes requires that different prices be charged for apparently similar services (for example, a lower rate might be charged for a telephone call at night than for one by day) or that the same price be charged for different services (for example, postage to different domestic destinations). The important point here is that the politicization of prices can be extremely harmful. When politicians determine prices "in the public interest," they often fix them at a low level, hoping thereby to please many people. But the results can be disastrous to suppliers, as has been seen in connection with electricity pricing in Latin America. Furthermore, when politicians decide that prices have to be the same, irrespective of cost differences, low-cost customers are forced to subsidize high-cost ones. This was seen in the case of water in Côte d'Ivoire and telephones in the Dominican Republic, where expansion of the service was slowed down because of the lack of funds, and attempts to raise funds by raising all charges have resulted in tensions between existing users (whose costs tend to be low) and new users (whose costs tend to be higher). There are many examples of prices being brought down by competition among suppliers and of prices remaining high (or goods disappearing from the market) when price controls discourage supply.

Implications for International Lending Agencies

Many of the international lending agencies, including the World Bank, tend to deal exclusively with governments, and many of them are precluded from lending directly for projects that can be financed on reasonable terms by the private sector. It is therefore not always clear what they can do to support the private delivery of public services. The following courses are open to them:

Improve services that only governments can provide. In every country there are some activities—such as safeguarding security, maintaining sound currency, and providing infrastructure—that the private sector cannot provide, but that it cannot function without. International aid agencies—by providing advice and financing—can help governments carry out such activities.

Assist governments in utilizing their private sectors. It is not easy to induce the private sector to provide services—such as piped water or urban transport—that have a long history of government involvement. International organizations are in a position to offer impartial advice to interested governments and, in particular, to provide information on the experience of other countries. The German aid agency Deutsche Gesellschaft für Technische Zusammenarbeit, for example, is helping the government of Somalia run a private sector promotion unit in the Ministry of National Planning in Mogadishu. The unit, which has a small staff of Somali professionals and a German adviser, serves government departments in an advisory capacity.

Move some operations to the private sector. In some sectors—particularly in telecommunications and electric power generation—the private sector can operate successfully on a commercial basis, without the guarantee of the government. There is a strong case for the agencies that lend directly to governments to wind down their operations in these sectors and to encourage the involvement of commercial organizations such as the International Finance Corporation, private banks, or multilateral investors. If funds are not forthcoming from existing financing houses, new ones can be established, such as a financing organization to specialize in telecommunications or electricity generation.

Guarantee loans made by the private sector. To deal with the risks of political violence, expropriation, and currency situations that the private sector cannot readily handle, the World Bank has already proposed that a Multilateral Investment Guarantee Agency be formed to protect lenders against these special risks. In its own operations, the World Bank is explicitly allowed by its Articles of

Agreement to guarantee "in whole or in part loans made by private investors through the usual investment channels."

Avoid discrimination against the private sector. International agencies should be able to avoid operations that promote government sector activities at the expense of the private sector. Operations coming under this category are, for example, loans enabling government bus companies to obtain advantages that are not available to the private companies competing with them, or loan conditions requiring the establishment of parastatals that inhibit private sector commercial activities.

In the face of current constraints on domestic and external resources, the pursuit of efficiency in domestic resource mobilization is more critical than ever. That is why there is an urgent need to expand and release the energies of the private sector. If the United States, which is not one of the poorest countries in the world, finds it worthwhile to encourage the private provision of public services, might it not be time for countries less rich to look to their own entrepreneurial resources, to ensure that their resources, too, are used to the maximum advantage?

Index

Abidjan (Côte d'Ivoire), 200–01, 242, 248, 258
Addis Ababa, aviation training in, 49–50
Africa: apprenticeship schemes in, 50–51; bus operations in, 200–01, 210–11, 216, 223; education in, 17, 20–22, 29, 31–32, 35–43, 48–50; health care in, 11, 122–23, 124, 127, 133, 134, 135, 136; loan programs in, 59–60; monopoly franchising in, 2–3; water supply in, 241, 256, 258, 264. *See also* Sub-Saharan Africa; *specific African countries*
Aga Khan Foundation, 11
Ahmed, Zulficar, 34
American Telephone and Telegraph Company (AT&T), 171, 173–74
Anderson, J. E., 43
Apprenticeship schemes, 50–51
Arab Pharmaceutical Manufacturing Company, Ltd. (Jordan), 136–37
Argentina, 108, 186, 267; bus system in, 201–02; educational loans in, 55, 57; electrical cooperatives in, 92; private universities in, 44–45; water supply in, 259. *See also* Buenos Aires
Asia: biogas use in, 108; bus operation in, 204–05, 205–06, 206–08, 211–12, 218–19, 221; Chinese education in Southeast, 32–34; education loan programs in, 60–61; health care in, 11, 123, 124; telephone service in South, 160; water

supply in, 241. *See also specific Asian countries*
Asian Institute of Management, 46–48
Asian Institute of Technology, 44
Australia, 123, 198, 220
Automobiles, 197, 198
Aviation Maintenance School (Addis Ababa), 49–50
Ayala Corporation, 47

Bangkok, 160, 195, 220, 221, 239
Bangladesh, 132, 259, 261
Barbados, 165
Baumol, W. J., 169
Beesley, Michael E., 169
Bell, Alexander Graham, 173
Bell telephone system, 170-71, 173-74, 189, 190
Benin, 51. *See also* Cotonou
Bettancour Mejia, Gabriel, 52
Biogas, 107–08
Bolivia, 108; electrical cooperatives in, 93–94; telephone service in, 183–84, 189, 192; water supply in, 259, 260
Bombay: schools in, 19; electricity production in, 82, 87; hospital care in, 131
Botswana, 3, 175
Brazil, 2, 51, 55, 56, 79, 91, 103, 105, 106, 109, 175, 176, 184, 189, 192, 267
Buenos Aires bus system, 201–02, 222, 224
Burton, John, 96

271

The most recent World Bank publications are described in the catalog *New Publications*, which is issued in the spring and fall of each year. The complete backlist of publications is shown in the annual *Index of Publications*, which contains an alphabetical title list and indexes of subjects, authors, and countries and regions; it is of value principally to libraries and institutional purchasers. The continuing research program is described in *The World Bank Research Program: Abstracts of Current Studies*, which is issued annually. The latest edition of each is available free of charge from Publications Sales Unit, The World Bank, 1818 H Street, N.W., Washington, D.C. 20433, U.S.A., or from Publications, The World Bank, 66, avenue d'Iéna, 75116 Paris, France.